The Hassle-Free Walt Disney World® Vacation

Steven M. Barrett

The Hassle-Free
Walt Disney World® Vacation

Published by
The Intrepid Traveler
P.O. Box 531
Branford, CT 06405
http://www.intrepidtraveler.com

Copyright ©2009 by Steven M. Barrett
Eighth Edition
Printed in the U.S.A.
Cover design by Foster & Foster
Maps designed by Evora Taylor

ISBN: 978-1-887140-79-9

International Standard Serial Number: 1543-6225

Publisher's Cataloging-in-Publication Data. Prepared by Sanford Berman.
Barrett, Steven M.

The hassle-free Walt Disney world vacation. Branford, CT: The Intrepid Traveler, copyright 2009.

Includes touring plans for adults and teens, families with young children, and seniors; six maps; and material on "attractions that may frighten children."

PARTIAL CONTENTS: Magic Kingdom. -Epcot. -Disney's Hollywood Studios. -Disney's Animal Kingdom. -Downtown Disney & the water parks.

1. Walt Disney World, Florida--Description and travel--Guidebooks. 2. Walt Disney World, Florida--Description and travel--Tours. 3. Theme parks, Orlando region, Florida--Guidebooks. 4. Epcot, Florida--Description and travel--Guidebooks. 5. Disney's Hollywood Studios Theme Park, Florida--Description and travel--Guidebooks. 6. Travel--Guidebooks (for seniors). 7. Travel--Guidebooks (for parents and children). I. Title. II. Title: Walt Disney World vacation. III. Title: Disney World vacation. IV. The Intrepid Traveler.

Trademarks, Etc.

Photo Credits

Special Thanks

Tim Foster, tgfDesign, for his consultation and suggestions for the redesign of this book's interior.

About the Author

Photo by Vickie Barrett

Author Steven M. Barrett paid his first visit to Walt Disney World in the late 1980s, after attending a medical conference in Orlando. He immediately fell under its spell, visiting it twice yearly with family and friends for the next several years, offering touring advice to the less initiated, and reading almost everything written about the WDW theme parks. When a job in his field of emergency medicine opened up not far from WDW in 1998, Barrett, a Texas native, Air Force veteran, and former Oklahoma City medical professor, relocated to the Orlando area from Houston, Texas. He began visiting the WDW parks every chance he got to enjoy the attractions, sample the restaurants, and escort visiting friends and relatives. Eventually, their feedback made him realize he had better advice on touring the parks than they could get anywhere else; so he decided to write this book. He followed it up with *Hidden Mickeys: A Field Guide to Walt Disney World's Best Kept Secrets*, a guide in scavenger-hunt format to over 700 hidden Mickeys in the WDW theme parks, resorts, and other areas. Barrett continues to visit WDW almost every week, finding the parks and other attractions every bit as magical as they appeared to him on his first visit over 18 years ago.

Dedication

I dedicate this book to my wife Vickie and son Steven, who willingly accompanied me on countless research visits to Walt Disney World and added invaluable insight to the advice in this book.

I am grateful to friends and family who have helped me over the years to field test the touring plans in this book.

Also by Steven M. Barrett

Hidden Mickeys:
A Field Guide to Walt Disney World's Best Kept Secrets

Disneyland's Hidden Mickeys:
A Field Guide to Disneyland Resort's Best Kept Secrets

Table of Contents

Introduction   11
1. Planning Your WDW Vacation   **13**
  When to go   16
  Where to stay   17
  Getting there   24
  Getting around WDW   26
  Admission tickets   27
  Good things to know about   35
    WDW (and related) phone numbers   41
  What to bring   45
  Where to eat   47
    Restaurant recommendations   48
    WDW full-service restaurants rated   51
    Where to dine with your favorite characters   54
      Character meals by character 54
      Character meals by location   56
  Basic rules for touring   57
  Hidden Mickeys   59
  Attraction ratings explained   60
  Using the touring plans   60
  Bringing the magic home (tips for taking great photos)   61
2. Magic Kingdom   **65**
  Attractions   65
    Described and Rated   65
      Main Street, U.S.A.   65
      Adventureland   68
      Frontierland   70
      Liberty Square   72
      Fantasyland   74
      Mickey's Toontown Fair   78
      Tomorrowland   80
      Special attractions   83
    Attractions with minimal waits (usually)   83
    Attractions that may frighten children 84
    Least crowded restrooms   84
    Especially attractive at night   84
    Resting places   85
    Hidden Mickeys   85

Touring the Magic Kingdom   86
    One-day touring plans   93
        Adults and teens   93
        Families with young children   97
        Seniors   102
    Two-day touring plans   105
        Adults and teens   105
        Families with young children   111
        Seniors   119
3. Epcot   **127**
    Attractions   127
        Described and rated   130
            Future World   130
            World Showcase   137
        Attractions with minimal waits (usually)   143
        Attractions that may frighten children   143
        Least crowded restrooms   143
        Resting places   144
        Hidden Mickeys   144
    Touring Epcot   145
        One-day touring plans   149
            Adults, teens and seniors   149
            Families with young children   153
        Two-day touring plans   157
            Adults and teens   157
            Families with young children   164
            Seniors   171
4. Disney's Hollywood Studios   **179**
    Attractions   179
        Described and rated   179
        Attractions with minimal waits (usually)   189
        Attractions that may frighten children   189
        Least crowded restrooms   190
        Resting places   190
        Hidden Mickeys   190
    Touring Disney's Hollywood Studios   191
        One- and two-day touring plans for all   192
            One-day (or day one) plans   192
            Day two plans   197

5. Disney's Animal Kingdom   **201**

Attractions   201

  Described and rated   201

  Attractions with minimal waits (usually)   211

  Attractions that may frighten children   212

  Least crowded restrooms   212

  Resting places   212

  Hidden Mickeys   212

Touring Disney's Animal Kingdom   213

  One-day touring plans for all   214

6. Downtown Disney & The Water Parks   **219**

Downtown Disney   219

  West Side   219

  Pleasure Island   221

  Marketplace   221

WDW Water Parks   221

  Blizzard Beach   222

  Typhoon Lagoon   222

7. Lots More to Do at WDW   **223**

In the theme parks   223

  Magic Kingdom   223

  Epcot   227

  Disney's Hollywood Studios   229

  Disney's Animal Kingdom   229

Fun outside the theme parks   230

  At the Disney resort hotels   230

  Elsewhere in WDW   234

Afterword   240

How well do you know WDW? (photo quiz)   **241**

Index   249

Maps

Orlando/Kissimmee   10

Walt Disney World Resort   14

Magic Kingdom   66

Epcot   128

Disney's Hollywood Studios   180

Disney's Animal Kingdom   202

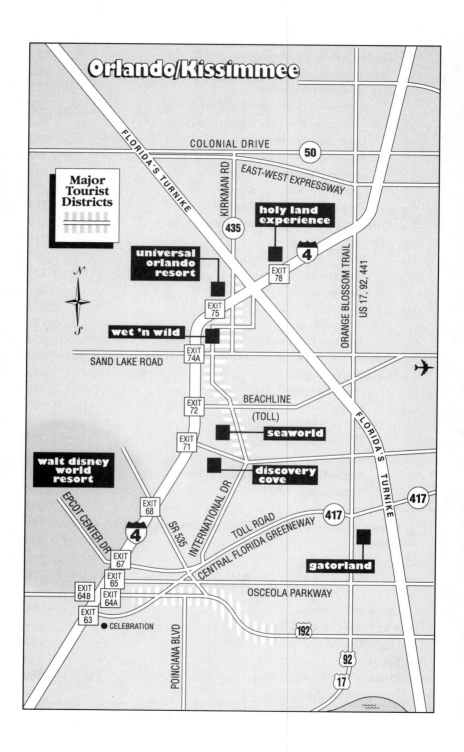

Introduction

No doubt about it, Walt Disney World is one of the most entertaining places anywhere. Yes, I admit it, I'm a rabid WDW aficionado. I have yet to find a ride or attraction at WDW that I didn't enjoy, and I've experienced all of them many times. I began trekking to this mecca of tourism years ago on vacations once or twice yearly. Now I live nearby and can explore the wonders of Walt Disney World® Resort whenever I have the time (that is, as often as I can manage it).

Early on, I noticed an anomaly as I wandered the parks. Despite the worldwide appeal of WDW, some visitors weren't enjoying themselves! Many of these folks had planned their monster vacation months ahead of time and weathered their kids' salivating impatience for weeks, only to arrive at WDW and quickly wither in the crowds, the heat, and the ubiquitous long lines. On a boat ride from the Magic Kingdom to Fort Wilderness, a man uttered a complaint that I've often heard at WDW: "This is supposed to be a vacation? I've been here five days, and I'm more tired than when I left home. I don't feel like I've had a vacation at all!"

I wondered: What could people do to enhance their WDW experience? Some of the answers are obvious and have been mentioned in other guidebooks. Some of the advice is not so obvious and is mentioned only in this book. What I've tried to accomplish in these pages is to give both first-time visitors and seasoned WDW pros the nuts and bolts tips and information for a hassle-free Walt Disney World vacation.

This new 2009 edition contains updated touring plans, descriptions and ratings of new — and established — attractions, and a general update on Walt Disney World Resort that is current as we go to press.

If you follow my recommendations and touring plans, you will be as prepared as possible for a successful voyage to WDW.

Enjoy!

Steven M. Barrett

Chapter 1

Planning Your WDW Vacation

A few miles southwest of Orlando, Florida, lies one of the most popular spots on earth, Walt Disney World® Resort (WDW). This huge complex (twice the size of Manhattan Island) contains four separate theme parks, more than two dozen hotels, scores of restaurants, a campground, water parks, golf courses, miniature golf courses, two evening entertainment complexes, a shopping and daytime entertainment district, and a sports complex.

Whew! WDW is magical and a wonderful place to visit, but it's also complicated and often crowded as well. The unprepared visitor can easily be overwhelmed and left with less than magical memories of long lines, heat and sunburn, exhaustion, expensive food, crying kids, and frazzled nerves.

Don't let that happen to you! With proper planning, any WDW visit can be fun from beginning to end.

This book is dedicated to giving you the insider tips, practical advice, and customized flexible touring plans you need to have one of the best vacations of your life. So take a quick breath and jump right in.

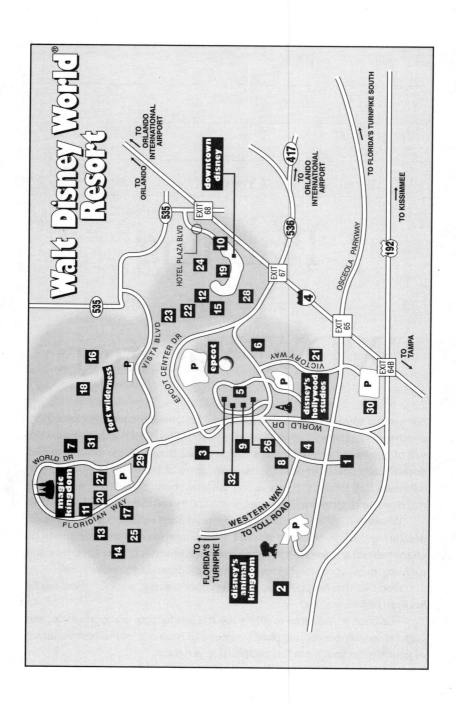

1. All-Star Resorts
2. Animal Kingdom Lodge
3. Beach Club
4. Blizzard Beach
5. BoardWalk
6. Caribbean Beach
7. Contemporary
8. Coronado Springs
9. Dolphin
10. Downtown Disney
11. Grand Floridian
12. Lake Buena Vista Golf Course
13. Magnolia Golf Course
14. Oak Trails Golf Course
15. Old Key West
16. Osprey Ridge Golf Course
17. Palm Golf Course
18. Pioneer Hall
19. Pleasure Island, in Downtown Disney
20. Polynesian
21. Pop Century
22. Port Orleans – French Quarter
23. Port Orleans – Riverside
24. Saratoga Springs
25. Shades of Green
26. Swan
27. Transportation and Ticket Center
28. Typhoon Lagoon
29. WDW Speedway
30. Wide World of Sports
31. Wilderness Lodge
32. Yacht Club
P. Parking

When to Go

You can have fun any time of the year at WDW. In terms of crowds, however, the best time to go is the period from after the Thanksgiving weekend until the week before Christmas (the last days of November and the first two and one-half weeks of December), when the parks are least crowded. The next best times to visit are September through the weekend preceding Thanksgiving, January 4 through the middle of February, and the week after Easter through early June (except for the always-busy Memorial Day weekend).

The most crowded times to come are Christmas Day through New Year's Day, Thanksgiving weekend, the week of Presidents' Day, spring break for colleges, the two weeks around Easter, Memorial Day weekend, and mid June through late August. If you visit during these ultra-busy times of the year, you can expect to pay more for your hotel room and you won't be able to experience as many attractions because long lines build early in the day. However, theme park hours are longer during the busiest seasons and there's more live entertainment on offer.

At slower times of the year, some attractions will probably be closed for maintenance or refurbishment, park hours will be shorter, and you'll have fewer choices of live entertainment. Such drawbacks are outweighed, however, by the pleasant ambiance created by lighter crowds and generally shorter lines. Furthermore, cooler weather tends to prevail during slower times of year.

The slower late November and early December time period offers an additional benefit: Walt Disney World is perhaps at its most beautiful during the slowest time of the year! Christmas decorations abound in the parks and hotels. For example, the five million (and still counting) lights in the "Osborne Family Spectacle of Lights" are draped over the Streets of America in Disney's Hollywood Studios. In addition, special Christmas events, shows, and parades are scheduled in the parks and resorts for your enjoyment. At Epcot, you can make dinner-package reservations for the "Candlelight Procession-al." This program includes a choir, orchestra, and a guest celebrity who reads the Christmas story in America Gardens Theater at The American Adventure Pavilion. Dinner packages cost $30 to $48 per adult, including tax, depending on your choice of restaurant, and about $13 to $15 per child at any of the restaurants (call 407-WDW-DINE for options and reservations). To see the Processional free (without buying the dinner package), line up an hour or so before showtime and you'll usually get in. No guarantees of course.

At Magic Kingdom, tickets go fast for "Mickey's Very Merry Christmas

Party," scheduled for 18 or more November and December nights, usually from 7:00 p.m. to 12:00 a.m. or later. This party includes special holiday shows, a Christmas parade, caroling, discounted photos from Disney PhotoPass (see page 63), free hot chocolate and cookies, and fireworks. Since many attractions remain open for party guests, it's a great excuse for Disney to keep the Magic Kingdom open late.

Please note that some "Christmas Party" nights can be quite crowded, especially those near Christmas Day. Call 407-WDISNEY for information and tickets (up to $51 for adults and $44 for children 3 to 9 including tax). You'll save over $7 per ticket on certain nights by booking ahead.

You've probably noticed that the best times of year to visit WDW are during the school year. A message for parents with kids: it's worthwhile to take your kids out of school to visit WDW if they can afford the short absence from the classroom. Otherwise, try for late May or early June, before the summer crowds hit their peaks.

Gay visitors take note: the unofficial "Gay Pride" day(s) are generally celebrated around the first weekend in June (check gaydays.com/calendar) and many celebrants visit the Magic Kingdom on Saturday of that weekend.

If you visit on or near your special day (birthday, anniversary, honeymoon, etc.) and want some special treatment, tell your meal reservationists, Guest Relations, or cast members at your resort and at all parks, restaurants, and other areas you visit. Get free birthday buttons from Guest Relations at the parks. You'll take home some magical memories. How about a birthday wake-up call from Mickey himself?!

Where to Stay

One of the most important decisions you'll make once you have picked dates for your visit is whether to stay "on property" or "off." Staying "on property," that is, at a Walt Disney World Resort hotel or campground, confers several important advantages.

Special privileges for on-property guests

On-property guests get Extra Magic Hours privileges at the theme parks on designated days of the week (see below), as well as free parking and free, generally efficient transportation to and from the theme parks and around WDW. Disney's free airport transportation service (see Disney's Magical Express in "Getting There," below) is an option for most on-property guests. They also get free delivery of theme park purchases to their rooms (except for some small items) and can charge most of those purchases to their hotel bill. They can reserve golf tee times (and receive a small discount) up to 90 days ahead – 30 days earlier than off-property guests – and qualify for free round-trip taxi rides between hotels and golf courses.

Note: Guests of the Downtown Disney Resorts on Hotel Plaza Boulevard (see below) are not eligible for all these benefits all the time. To avoid disappointment, ask which ones you'll get when you make your reservations.

Staying on property can be especially beneficial during very busy periods such as major holidays. During these periods, the crowds at one or more of the theme parks sometimes reach capacity. When that happens, the park's parking lot is closed and only Disney property guests arriving via Disney transportation are allowed to enter.

Note: Blizzard Beach and Typhoon Lagoon water parks can also fill to capacity, especially during the summer. But unlike the theme parks, they close to Disney property guests as well as the general public when that happens.

The most important reason for staying on property, however, is the property itself. When you stay on-property you are immersed in that magical Disney ambiance. Walt Disney World Resort hotels are themed, uniquely and beautifully. You'll feel transported far away from your everyday environment. In addition, most resorts have numerous activities for guests.

The downside is expense. Staying off property can be more economical, with lower hotel and food costs; 2008 rates on WDW property range from $82 a night for a double at Disney's All-Star or Pop Century Resorts (Fort Wilderness campsites can go for as little as $42 a night!) to more than $500 a night. In contrast, you can find off-property lodging within a reasonable driving distance from WDW for $50 a night and sometimes less. (Rates will vary seasonally wherever you stay.)

Tips: Always ask about any special rates or discounts that may be available when you book, for example, Annual Passholder, AAA, Disney Visa, Florida residents, etc. (Visit www.mousesavers.com to find Annual Passholder and other discount codes.) Wherever you book, be sure to note the hotel check-in time on your reservation confirmation form and plan your arrival accordingly. Then when you check in, inquire about complimentary room upgrades. Remember to ask for "connecting" rooms if you want a door between rooms.

Extra Magic Hours privileges

On-property guests are entitled to extra hours in the four major theme parks and the two water parks on certain days of the week, usually an hour

---

before the general public in the morning and up to three hours after park closing in the evening. Disney calls this privilege for its resort guests "Extra Magic Hours." During these hours, certain popular attractions will be open early or late in a designated park, giving resort guests a chance to experience them with minimal waits. The schedule for Extra Magic Hours (EMH) varies month to month, with different parks designated to host the early and late Magic Hours on any given day. As we go to press, for example, Magic Kingdom is open early on Thursday and late on Sunday. Each of the theme parks is open for extra morning and evening Magic hours at least once a week. The water parks' EMH schedule is more variable.

For current schedules, call 407-824-4321 or visit www.disneyworld.com six to eight weeks before your visit. (Click the calendar icon on the home page and then click on "Extra Magic Hours" on the calendar that pops up). Take advantage of the program while you're there if you qualify and the times agree with you.

WDW lodgings

The highest quality (and most expensive) hotel at Walt Disney World Resort is Disney's Grand Floridian Resort & Spa on the monorail to the Magic Kingdom. On the second tier, but not far behind in terms of quality, are Disney's three Epcot resort hotels, Disney's BoardWalk Inn and Villas, Disney's Beach Club Resort and Villas, and Disney's Yacht Club Resort, as well as Disney's Polynesian and Disney's Contemporary Resorts (both on the Magic Kingdom monorail), and Shades of Green (the last open exclusively to people connected with the U.S. military). In the same quality category, Disney's Old Key West Resort has nice studio rooms but is more isolated from the theme parks than the others.

The third tier of hotels, in quality terms, includes Disney's Animal Kingdom Lodge, Disney's Wilderness Lodge and Villas, Disney's Saratoga Springs Resort & Spa, and the WDW Swan and WDW Dolphin hotels (the last two are Epcot resort hotels popular with convention and meeting planners).

Moderate quality (and less expensive) hotels include Disney's Port Orleans–French Quarter, Disney's Port Orleans–Riverside, Disney's Coronado Springs, and Disney's Caribbean Beach Resorts. The budget hotels are Disney's All-Star Resorts and Disney's Pop Century Resort. These properties have smaller rooms with only one bathroom sink.

A brief rundown on the ambiance of each of the Disney resort hotels follows. See "Good Things to Know About," below, for reservations web sites and phone numbers. Rates are for 2008, before tax.

Deluxe resort hotels

(generally start at more than $225 per night)

- **Grand Floridian Resort & Spa** (over $385 per night). Serviced by the Magic Kingdom monorail, this hotel complex looks like a Victorian oceanside resort, complete with white wood buildings and red shingle roofs. In the center of the main building is a spacious lobby surrounded by several floors of elegant concierge rooms.

- **Polynesian Resort** (over $340 per night). Connected to the Magic Kingdom (MK) monorail, this complex of Pacific Island-themed buildings rests in a lush tropical landscape and is located next to the Transportation and Ticket Center, site of the MK's parking lot.

- **Beach and Yacht Club Resorts and Villas** (over $325 per night). Two of the five Epcot resort hotels, the Beach and Yacht Club Resorts are situated at the "back door" of Epcot. These wood-trimmed hotels are reminiscent of Atlantic coast resorts of the past. Ask about children's programs if you have kids with you.

- **BoardWalk Inn and Villas** (over $325 per night). BoardWalk shops and restaurants front this sprawling red, yellow, and pastel wood-trimmed hotel complex, located in the Epcot resort area across a lake from the Beach and Yacht Club Resorts.

- **Shades of Green** ($89 to $275 per night). If you're active duty or retired military, the Shades of Green Hotel is an exceptionally good deal. Located near the Grand Floridian, but not connected to the Magic Kingdom monorail, this secluded, recently renovated countryside hotel is surrounded by golf courses. The Shades of Green hotel is operated by the U.S. Military and is available only to military, Department of Defense, and Public Health Service personnel. Room rates are based on military or civilian grade; call 407-824-3400 for information or 888-593-2242 for current prices and reservations, or go to: shadesofgreen.org.

- **Old Key West Resort** (over $285 per night). Not far from the Port Orleans Resorts, Key West's pastel villas are spread about in clusters and decorated with Key West designs and landscaping. Guest rooms here are larger than average.

- **Contemporary Resort** (over $270 per night). Connected to the Magic Kingdom by monorail and a walking path, this A-frame futuristic hotel with adjacent garden buildings has a 15th-floor observation deck overlooking the Magic Kingdom.

- **Animal Kingdom Lodge** (over $225 per night). New in spring 2001 and modeled on an African game lodge, this resort is not far from Disney's Animal Kingdom theme park. Most of the rooms overlook an expansive, savanna-like preserve, which is home to birds, zebras, antelopes, giraffes, and other exotic creatures. (Ask for a savanna view when you make your reservations. The second or third floor Zebra Trail Section, 500 building, offers especially good views.)

- **Wilderness Lodge and Villas** (over $225 per night). Located on Bay Lake near Fort Wilderness, the Wilderness Lodge is a convincing rendition of national park lodges from the early 1900s, complete with a geyser and "mountain spring" swimming pool.

- **Saratoga Springs Resort & Spa** (over $285 per night). These Disney Vacation Club accommodations include studio units, one- and two-bedroom villas, and Grand Villa units (which sleep up to 12 guests). The resort is located across a lake from (and connected by a walkway to) Downtown Disney. Its Victorian architecture is reminiscent of Northeastern country resorts of the late 1800s.

- **WDW Swan and Dolphin Resorts** (over $359 per night). WDW handles their reservations, but the WDW Swan is owned by Westin and the WDW Dolphin by Sheraton. These sister Epcot resort structures are designed and decorated in a unique art deco style.

Moderate resort hotels

(approximately $149 to $215 per night; more for suites)

- **Port Orleans Resort–French Quarter.** Located next to Port Orleans Resort–Riverside and a relaxing boat ride away from Downtown Disney, this resort is reminiscent of the French Quarter of New Orleans pre-Katrina. In the center of the swimming pool is a water slide down a sea serpent's tongue.

- **Port Orleans Resort–Riverside.** A boat trip away from Downtown Disney, Port Orleans–Riverside looks like a sprawling plantation mansion in the rural South. Ol' Man Island is a recreational area with a playground, pool, and fishing hole. The food court sports a waterwheel that powers a cotton press.

- **Coronado Springs Resort.** A short bus ride from Disney's Animal Kingdom and Blizzard Beach, this resort brings to mind Mexico and the American Southwest. The guest buildings are spread around a lake, and water flows down a Mayan pyramid into the main swimming pool. Suites are available at higher rates.

- **Caribbean Beach Resort.** Five brightly colored guest villages named for Caribbean islands surround a large lake. The main swimming pool is themed after an old fort. The resort is a short bus ride away from Epcot and Disney's Hollywood Studios.

Value resort hotels

(approximately $82 to $121 per night; family suites $184 to $315)

- **All-Star Movies, All-Star Music, and All-Star Sports Resort.** This budget resort is amusingly themed with bright colors and oversized embellishments, such as huge Dalmatians, hockey masks, football helmets, baseball bats, soda cups, cowboy boots, guitars, a walk-through jukebox, and many other amazing sights. Although the ambiance is fun, each room is quite small with only one sink. The exceptions are the 192 family suites in All-Star Music. These sleep up to six people and come with two baths, a kitchenette, and a number of other amenities.

  All-Star Movies tends to be the quietest of the three, while All-Star Sports offers a big advantage if you're dependent on Disney buses: they pick up and drop off at Sports first. The All-Stars complex is a short bus ride away from both Disney's Animal Kingdom and Disney's Blizzard Beach water park. If you need a small refrigerator (at no charge), ask for one when you check in.

- **Pop Century Resort.** Located near the Caribbean Beach Resort, this budget resort celebrates twentieth-century American Pop Culture with such oversized icons as hula hoops and Rubik's Cubes. Classic phrases ("Boogie down," "You dig?") adorn the buildings. Rooms are small with only one bathroom sink. If you need a small refrigerator, ask for one when you check in. You won't pay extra for it.

- **Fort Wilderness.** One of the nicest campgrounds in the U.S., Fort Wilderness offers cabins for rent (they cost more than $255 per night), as well as sites for camping vehicles and tents (about $41 to $98 per night). The campground has biking and hiking trails, boating, fishing, swimming, horseback riding, hayrides, carriage rides, an evening campfire program, and courts for tennis, basketball, volleyball, and tetherball. The popular *Hoop-Dee-Doo Musical Revue* (separate admission) is here (see "Dinner Shows," below). The Magic Kingdom is a rather slow boat ride away.

Downtown Disney Hotel Plaza lodgings

Downtown Disney Hotel Plaza lodgings have the advantage of being on Disney property close to the Disney theme parks, but they do not confer all the advantages of staying "on property." They have their own free bus service to the theme parks, which is not as timely as the Disney bus service available elsewhere in WDW. And unlike the Disney's own resorts, they aren't Disney-themed.

There are seven hotels at the Downtown Disney Hotel Plaza:

- Best Western Lake Buena Vista Resort 407-828-2424, 800-348-3765
- Buena Vista Palace Hotel & Spa 407-827-2727, 866-397-6516
- DoubleTree Guest Suites Resort 407-934-1000, 800-222-8733
- Hilton in the Walt Disney World Resort 407-827-4000, 800-782-4414
- Holiday Inn (scheduled to reopen May 1, 2009, following major renovation) 407-828-8888, 888-465-4329
- Hotel Royal Plaza 407-828-2828, 800-248-7890
- Regal Sun Resort 407-828-4444, 800-624-4109

These range from value-priced to very expensive ($99 to $350-plus a night for a double). The Royal Plaza often advertises the lowest rates.

Nearby off-property lodgings

The highest quality hotels off WDW property but still nearby are the Ritz-Carlton Grande Lakes (407-206-2400), the Hyatt Regency Grand Cypress (407-239-1234), the Marriott Orlando World Center Resort (407-239-4200), the Peabody Orlando (407-352-4000), the Omni Orlando (407-390-6664), and the Gaylord Palms Resort (407-586-0000). These hotels are comparable in quality to the best WDW resorts but tend to be less pricey ($200 to $300 or more per night). Celebration Hotel (407-566-6000 or 888-499-3800), located in the quaint and scenic Disney-associated town of Celebration, Florida, is a fine lodging with an early 1900s' design and rooms priced at over $150 per night.

Some good quality, moderately priced hotels ($100 to $200 per night) off WDW property are Nickelodeon Family Suites Resort (407-387-5437), Radisson Resort Orlando Celebration (407-396-7000), Crowne Plaza Resort (407-239-1222), Westgate Resorts (800-925-9999), Cypress Pointe Resort (407-597-2700), Vacation Village Parkway (407-396-9086), and Celebrity Resorts Orlando (407-396-8300)..

Larger families might want to consider renting a "vacation home" offsite. Expect to pay about $200 or more per night.

You can order a free "Orlando Vacation Planning Kit" from the Orlando/Orange County Convention and Visitors Bureau. Call 800-972-3304 or 407-363-5872, or go to orlandoinfo.com. Either way, allow two to three weeks to receive your kit.

Getting There

Orlando is one of the country's top tourist destinations. You can drive there, bus there, train there, or fly there. Once there, you'll find it easiest to navigate the area and the many pleasures of Walt Disney World by car. If you plan to spend all your time at Disney, however, you can get by using the WDW buses, monorails, and boats. You'll just find it less convenient. Many visitors either drive their own cars or fly and then rent a car.

Disney's Magical Express. Guests of most WDW resorts can register (six weeks or more in advance to be safe!) for free airport shuttle service, luggage delivery, and return check-in at your resort for certain airlines. These services are free through the next few years at least. Book online at www.disneyworld.com or call 407-WDISNEY. Disney will mail you special luggage tags to put on your checked luggage. After you check in at your home airport, you won't see those bags again until they appear in your resort hotel room.

Tip: You can book Magical Express round-trip (to and from your WDW resort) or just one-way if you prefer.

Note: Pack a carry-on bag with essentials (overnight clothes, swimsuit, etc.) in case your checked luggage is delayed, or carry all your luggage on to the Magical Express bus yourself. Bus crowds may be lighter if you travel in off hours.

By air

WDW is just a 30- to 40-minute drive from the Orlando airport. If you don't want to rent a car, you can taxi to your hotel ($40 to $50 plus tip for up to eight people to lodgings in and near WDW). Less efficient than a taxi are the shuttle bus services operated by Mears (about $19 per person, children under 4 ride free). Or hire yourself a town car or limo ($55 to $120 for up to 14 riders) – very convenient! And many limos include a free stop for groceries if you want one.

Airlines to Orlando from the U.S.:

AirTran	800-247-8726	www.airtran.com
Alaska Airlines	800-252-7522	www.alaskaair.com
American	800-433-7300	www.aa.com
Continental	800-523-3273	www.continental.com
Delta	800-221-1212	www.delta.com
Frontier	800-432-1359	www.frontierairlines.com

Jet Blue	800-538-2583	www.jetblue.com
Midwest	800-452-2022	www.midwestairlines.com
Northwest	800-225-2525	www.nwa.com
Southwest	800-435-9792	www.southwest.com
Spirit	800-772-7117	www.spiritair.com
Sun Country	800-359-6786	www.suncountry.com
United Airlines	800-864-8331	www.united.com
US Airways	800-428-4322	www.usairways.com

Airlines to Orlando from Canada:

Air Canada	888-247-2262	www.aircanada.com
Air Transat	866-847-1112	www.airtransat.com
American Airlines	800-433-7300	www.aa.com
CanJet	888-201-2289	www.canjet.com
Continental	800-523-3273	www.continental.com
Delta	800-221-1212	www.delta.com
Northwest	800-225-2525	www.nwa.com
United	800-538-2929	www.united.ca
US Airways	800-428-4322	www.usairways.com
WestJet	888-937-8538	www.westjet.com

Airlines to Orlando from the UK:

Aer Lingus	0870-8765000	www.aerlingus.com
American	0207-365-0777	www.americanairlines.co.uk
British Airways	0844-4930-787	www.britishairways.com
Continental	0845-607-6760	www.continental.com
Delta	0845-600-0950	www.delta.com
United	0845-8444-777	www.unitedairlines.co.uk
Virgin Atlantic	0870-380-2007	www.virgin-atlantic.com

Charter Airlines to Sanford from the U.K.:

First Choice (Air 2000)	www.FirstChoice.co.uk
Flyglobespan (sched. flights)	www.flyglobespan.com
Monarch Airlines	www.FlyMonarch.com
Thomas Cook Airlines	www.ThomasCook.com
Thompsonfly	www.Thompsonfly.com
Travel City Direct	www.TravelCityDirect.com
XL Airways	www.XL.com

Note: Sanford, Florida is located about 50 minutes' to an hour's drive north of WDW.

By car

WDW is located close to Kissimmee, Florida, in Osceola county, just south of the city of Orlando, which is in Orange county. The area's major highway, Interstate 4 (I-4), runs east-west across the state, but roughly northeast to southwest through the Orlando metro area. WDW is located west of I-4 and north of US 192 (also called Hwy 192 and Irlo Bronson Highway), which runs east to west through Kissimmee, crossing I-4 at Exit 64.

Four exits from I-4 lead into WDW. Your choice will depend on your ultimate destination. The most northerly exit, 68, takes you onto Highway 535. Take a left to Hotel Plaza Boulevard and the Downtown Disney area. Exit 67 is your best route to Epcot. Exit 65 directs you to Disney's Wide World of Sports Complex and Disney's Animal Kingdom. The southernmost exits, 64 and 62, lead to Highway 192 and Disney's Wide World of Sports Complex, Disney's Animal Kingdom, Disney's Hollywood Studios, and further north to Magic Kingdom. If you're driving to WDW from the west, take the Western Way off Florida's Turnpike so you can avoid potential I-4 traffic.

From the airport: If you're driving a rental car from Orlando International Airport, take either the Beachline Toll Expressway (north airport exit) to I-4 or the longer and slightly more expensive Central Florida Greeneway (south airport exit) straight to Epcot Center Drive in the center of WDW. Bring several dollars in cash or quarters for either tollway and more cash for your return trip. The Beachline Expressway has colorful billboards advertising some of the exciting attractions of WDW and Universal Orlando. The Central Florida Greeneway is less congested and passes through uncluttered countryside.

Getting Around WDW

In most cases, the easiest method for navigating WDW is by private car. A car also gives you the freedom, time permitting, to visit some of Orlando's other stellar attractions, such as Universal Orlando, SeaWorld, and Discovery Cove. If you drive to WDW, no problem. If you fly into Orlando, plan to rent a car for the duration of your stay. To avoid disappointment, reserve your rental car prior to your arrival – well prior if you will be coming at a busy time of year (see "When to Go," above). Budget at least $50 a day or $240 weekly for a midsize car, or about $100 a day and $500-$600 per week if you visit over the Christmas holidays. Check mousesavers.com for discount codes.

Getting around WDW can be complicated. So ask your hotel Lobby

Concierge for a WDW map or get one before you arrive. You'll get a guide with a map which lists WDW buses, monorails, and boats. You'll find it especially useful if you don't have a car.

Note: Disney transportation begins about one to two hours before park opening times and continues to function two hours (and sometimes more) after the parks close. (See the introductions to the Touring sections in *Chapters Two* through *Five* for details on getting to each of the theme parks by car or Disney transport.)

Two exceptions to the navigate-WDW-by-car rule: You won't need a car if you are staying at the Polynesian, Grand Floridian, or Contemporary Resort and plan to spend most of your time at the Magic Kingdom (MK). You can ride the monorail to the MK directly from these hotels; you can also walk to the MK in about ten minutes from the Contemporary. You also won't need a car (though you will find it an advantage to have one) if your primary destination is Epcot and you stay in one of the Epcot resort hotels. These hotels are just a five- to ten-minute walk from the rear Epcot entrance.

Admission Tickets

WDW's "Magic Your Way" admission ticket program starts with a "base ticket" and lets you add options to it to suit your needs. Your choices will depend on how long you want to stay and how much freedom you want to move around within WDW. Child tickets are available to children 3 through 9 years of age; children under 3 are admitted free. Attendees of conventions held at WDW may qualify for discount tickets. Check with your convention coordinator.

Note: Prices listed are for fall 2008. They include sales tax unless noted and they may change at any time. They are likely to be raised sometime in 2009. Likewise, ticket options may change at any time. To verify prices and options for the dates of your visit, check online at www.disneyworld.com or call 407-WDISNEY.

Advance-purchase discounts (of anywhere from 3% to 10%) are available from time to time for multi-day ticket purchases. Check online at www. disneyworld.com. AAA members, Disney time-share owners, and military personnel receive discounts of 3% to 5% or more. Florida residents may also qualify for discounts or special tickets.

Note: All base tickets expire 14 days after their first use unless you add a No Expiration option (see below). You can upgrade or modify your base ticket (to add either more days and/or options) any time before the 14-day expiration, but you have to do it in person at WDW (at the parks, the resorts, or Downtown Disney). After the 14th day, you can't use or modify your base ticket but you can apply the dollar value of any unused major park days toward a new ticket.

One-Day base ticket

Adults	–	$80
Children (3 to 9)	–	$67

Good for one day only and for one park only (Magic Kingdom, Epcot, Disney's Hollywood Studios, or Disney's Animal Kingdom).

Multi-Day base tickets

Note: Advance purchase will save you 3% to 10%.

You can buy base tickets good for one to ten days. The more days you buy, the less you will pay per day. Unless you buy the Hopper option, however, you will still be able to visit only one park per day.

2-day base ticket: Adults – $159 Children (3 to 9) – $133
10-day base ticket: Adults – $252 Children (3 to 9) – $215

Ticket options

The three add-on options (ParkHopper®, Water Park Fun & More, and No Expiration) can be purchased any time before your base ticket expires (14 days after first use). The first two options cost the same whatever the length of your base ticket; the cost for the No Expiration option is based on the original length of the base ticket (i.e., one to ten days), regardless of how many unused days you have left when you purchase the option.

Prices listed include tax unless otherwise noted.

ParkHopper® option

Allows you to switch from one major theme park to another without limitation for the length of your base ticket. This option does not admit you to the minor parks and entertainment areas. The cost with tax is $53.25 per ticket for both adults and children and whether you want it for one day or ten.

Water Park Fun & More option

Admits you to WDW's water parks, Disney's nine-hole Oak Trail Golf Course (tee time reservations are required), DisneyQuest in Downtown Disney, and Disney's Wide World of Sports Complex. The cost with tax is a flat $53.25 for both adults and children. However, the number of options you get depends on the number of days on your base ticket. Each option admits you to one venue for one visit.

Length of base ticket	# of Fun & More options	Length of base ticket	# of Fun & More options
1 day	2	6 days	6
2 days	2	7 days	7
3 days	3	8 days	8
4 days	4	9 days	9
5 days	5	10 days	10

No Expiration option

When you add the no-expiration option, any unused days on your base ticket are good forever – or as close to it as WDW can arrange. Without this option, your ticket expires 14 days after first use; any unused days are wasted. The cost is the same for adults and children.

Length of base ticket	Cost for all	Length of base ticket	Cost for all
1 day	Not applicable	6 days	$ 85
2 days	$18	7 days	$117
3 days	$25	8 days	$154
4 days	$53	9 days	$181
5 days	$75	10 days	$213

Annual Passes

Theme Park Annual Pass:

Adults $499   Children (3 to 9) $441

Allows unlimited entry to the major theme parks for one year. The pass can be used in more than one park on the same day and includes use of the WDW transportation system and complimentary parking. Renewals are cheaper. Call 407-WDISNEY for current information.

Premium Annual Pass:

Adults $638   Children (3 to 9) $562

Allows unlimited entry to the major and minor parks, Disney's Wide World of Sports Complex, and WDW's entertainment areas (including DisneyQuest and Disney's Oak Trail Golf Course, a nine-hole walking course that's designed for the whole family. Otherwise, the Premium Annual Pass is just like the Theme Park Annual Pass.

Benefits. All Annual Passes confer a number of benefits in addition to the flexibility of unlimited entry to the parks. Passholders park free on WDW property. They qualify for a discounted "Tables in Wonderland" membership, which offers benefits such as a 20% discount at many WDW restaurants (call 407-566-5858 for more information). They receive seasonal discounts at selected resort hotels on property, as well as discounts (usually 10% to

15%) on food at certain restaurants, select merchandise at the Rainforest Café stores and numerous (but not all) shops in Downtown Disney, certain Disney backstage tours (you have to call 407-WDW-TOUR and ask which ones), Pleasure Island movie theaters, the PhotoPass system (occasionally; see page 63), and certain recreation (parasailing, waterskiing, wakeboarding, some boat rentals, miniature golf, and the *Richard Petty Driving Experience* packages). Passholders also get discounts for Disney's Pirate and Princess Party, "Night of Joy," Mickey's Halloween and Christmas parties, and, in some months, Cirque du Soleil. In addition, they get 10% off one Grand Floridian and one Saratoga Springs spa treatment each visit, 30% off golf fees at certain times, and a free subscription to the quarterly newsletter, *Mickey Monitor,* in which you will often find special, limited-time discount offers. Alamo offers passholders up to 20% off on car rentals, and passholders are occasionally invited to priority reviews of new attractions. Special Passholder merchandise and Limited Edition Pins are periodically offered for sale. Annual Passholders who do not have a Premium Annual Pass are also entitled to discounted admission to the water parks and DisneyQuest.

Note: Only one person in a group needs an Annual Pass to get certain benefits for the entire group, such as Annual Passholder discounts for resort rooms. The specific benefits change from time to time.

Specialty Annual Passes are available for the water parks, Disney-Quest, and other WDW activities. For current information, call 407-WDISNEY or check www.disneyworld.com.

Special tickets for Florida residents

WDW offers a number of incentives to Florida residents. They include: savings options on regular tickets; a Seasonal Ticket (good for entry to the major theme parks during slower times of the year); a "3-Day Play Pass"; resort discounts; and a Tables in Wonderland membership (call 407-566-5858), which offers benefits such as a 20% discount at many WDW restaurants. Floridians can also purchase Annual Passes at a discount (about 22% off the regular price) and qualify for Epcot After 4 [p.m.] passes. Call 407-939-6244 for current prices and information and be prepared to provide proof that you are a state resident.

Choosing your tickets

With so many options to choose from, selecting the ticket that's best for you can be tricky. Here are some things to think about:
- How many days do you have to devote to WDW?
- Are you interested in visiting every major and minor park plus the

entertainment areas, or are only some of them of interest to you?

• Do you plan to return to the area within the next year? Ever?

If you want to see a lot of WDW and won't be back within a year, base tickets with Hopper and Water Park Fun & More options for the minor venues are the best buys because they give you the most flexibility. For example, say the park you are visiting today gets too crowded for your comfort; you can use the Hopper option to switch to another park or use a Fun & More option to visit one of the minor venues.

Here are some guidelines for getting the best value for your time and money based on the number of days you have to spend:

If you have one day. Choose a park to visit. Buy a one-day base ticket and use the appropriate one-day touring plan (see *Chapters Two* to *Five*). Adding the Hopper option is expensive: about $48 with tax, and you'll find plenty to keep you well occupied in any one theme park. After the park closes, consider visiting Downtown Disney if you still have energy.

If you have two days. Choose two parks to visit and buy a two-day base ticket. Visit the parks of your choice and follow the appropriate one-day touring plans. If you add the Hopper option ($48), you can switch parks whenever you want. In fact, you can visit all four of the parks: simply pick up the touring plan for the park you're in at the appropriate place, based on the time of day. Consider visiting Downtown Disney the second night. You can add a Fun & More option to your base ticket and get into Disney's Oak Trail Golf Course (tee time reservations are required) and another minor venue "free," but the option will cost you $53.25.

If you have three days. Choose three parks to visit and buy a three-day base ticket. Tour the three parks (or all four if you add the Hopper option, $48, which lets you switch from park to park). Follow the appropriate touring plans. Consider visiting Downtown Disney the last night of your visit. You can add a Fun & More option to your base ticket and get into Disney's Oak Trail Golf Course (tee time reservations are required) and two other minor venues "free," but the option will cost you $53.25.

If you have four days. Buy a four-day base ticket. Visit all four major theme parks and follow the appropriate touring plans for each. You can switch parks as desired if you add the Hopper option ($48). I recommend purchasing it when you have four or more days on your base ticket because your base cost per day drops significantly at this point. Consider visiting Downtown Disney your last night. You can add a Fun & More option to your base ticket for $53.25 and get into Disney's Oak Trail Golf Course (tee time reservations are required) and three other minor venues "free."

If you have five days. Buy the five-day base ticket. Follow a two-day touring plan for either the Magic Kingdom or Epcot, depending on your interests, and one-day touring plans for the other three parks. Add the Hopper option ($48) and you can switch parks as you see fit. Or, if you'd like to see more of Orlando, buy a four-day base ticket and use a one-day touring plan for each park. Then buy separate admissions to other area attractions that interest you, such as Kennedy Space Center (about an hour's drive to the east), one of the Universal Orlando theme parks, SeaWorld, or Discovery Cove. On your last night, consider visiting Downtown Disney. Or add a Fun & More option to your base ticket for admission to Disney's Oak Trail Golf Course (tee time reservations are required) and four other minor WDW venues for $53.25

If you have six days. Buy a six-day base ticket. Visit the four major theme parks and switch parks as you please by adding a Hopper option ($48). Follow the two-day touring plans for the MK and Epcot and the one-day touring plans for the other two parks. Alternatively, buy a four- or five-day base ticket and work in visits to other area attractions during the remaining day or days. Consider visiting Downtown Disney the last night of your visit. Or add a Fun & More option to your base ticket for $53.25 for admission to Disney's nine-hole Oak Trail Golf Course (tee time reservations are required) and five other minor WDW venues.

If you have seven days. Buy a seven-day base ticket with a Hopper option so that you can switch parks at your pleasure. Follow the two-day touring plans for the Magic Kingdom and Epcot and the one-day plans for the other two parks. On the seventh day, visit a Disney water park (paying $42 for a water park ticket costs less than buying the Fun & More option), use the second day touring plan for Disney's Hollywood Studios, or revisit attractions at any of the other major Disney parks. Alternatively, buy a four-, five-, or six-day base ticket and visit other area attractions in your remaining time. Consider visiting Downtown Disney the last night of your visit. Or add a Fun & More option to your base ticket for $53.25 for admission to Disney's Oak Trail Golf Course (tee time reservations are required), a water park, and five more minor WDW venues.

If you have eight or more days. Buy an eight-, nine-, or ten-day base ticket with both the Hopper and Fun & More options to maximize your choices and mobility. Work in the two-day touring plans for the Magic Kingdom, Epcot, and Disney's Hollywood Studios and the one-day touring plan for Disney's Animal Kingdom. Swim in Disney's water park(s), revisit your favorite attractions, and review *Chapter Seven* for insider information about other fun things to do at WDW. Visit Downtown Disney one evening. Alternatively, buy shorter tickets and spend the rest of your time exploring other area attractions. Isn't it great to have so many choices?

Note: For information about other area attractions, see my publisher's books, *Universal Orlando* and *SeaWorld, Discovery Cove & Aquatica*. Or check out my publisher's web site: www.TheOtherOrlando.com.

When the No Expiration option makes sense

If you have one or more unused day(s) on your ticket at the end of your stay and you plan to return to WDW in the future, the No Expiration option *may* make financial sense for you. But do the math before buying the option. At current prices, if you have only one day left on your ticket, the No Expiration add-on costs less than buying a one-day ticket *if* you are adding on to a two- to five-day base ticket. If you have two unused days, the No Expiration option makes financial sense if you are adding it to a two- to eight-day base ticket. If you have three or more unused days, a No Expiration option will pay off for any length base ticket.

When an Annual Pass makes sense

You will probably come out ahead with an Annual Pass in these two circumstances: (1) you live in Florida, visit frequently, and want to take advantage of the discounts or (2) assuming the benefits now offered stay in effect, you visit WDW at least twice in a 12-month period and spend a total of six or more days in the theme parks, with a minimum of two days in the parks on each visit. If you visit for a total of five days or fewer in the 12-month period, you'll spend less on admissions (and be able to do more) if you buy a base ticket with Hopper and Fun & More options (instead of an Annual Pass). You'll also come out ahead financially with the base ticket and options (including No Expiration) if you want to make two or more visits (for a total of 10 days or fewer) over a period longer than a year.

Note: These calculations do not take Passholder discounts (including discounts on resort rooms) and free parking privileges into consideration. Parking at the theme parks costs $11 per day as we go to press and discounts on lodging can be significant.

Buying your tickets

You can purchase Magic Your Way tickets and Annual Passes before your trip over the Web (www.disneyworld.com), or by phone (407-WDISNEY), or three- to seven-day Magic Your Way tickets by mail (Walt Disney World, Box 10140, Lake Buena Vista, FL 32830-0030, ATTN: Ticket Mail Order). You'll pay a $3 shipping charge on the above orders. Make checks payable to Walt Disney World Company and allow three to four weeks for delivery. You can also purchase select tickets from your travel agent or at your local Disney Store.

Note: You don't necessarily have to have your tickets mailed to you. You can arrange to pick up some types of tickets at your Disney resort, at any theme park ticket booth, or any Guest Relations area upon your arrival.

In Florida, tickets can be bought at a number of sites. They include the two Disney Stores in Orlando International Airport (call 407-825-2339), Character Outlet Malls near WDW, the WDW hotels, the Transportation and Ticket Center (TTC) near the Magic Kingdom, Downtown Disney Guest Relations, and the park and entertainment-area entrances. You can also buy Magic Your Way tickets (but not Annual Passes) from a number of vending machines at the Transportation and Ticket Center, just outside the Magic Kingdom, and at a few other places in WDW.

Tip: You'll save time and maybe money (advance purchase discounts are available for some tickets) by buying your tickets before you get to the parks, where ticket lines are often long.

Note: Not all types of tickets are available at every location. Call 407-WDISNEY to confirm availability of the ticket or pass you want.

Some tickets are also available from ticket brokers at a slight or no discount. Look for the broker's license to be sure you are dealing with a legitimate agent. And be sure you know what you'd pay in the park or at a Disney Store before you plunk down your money. Check for ticket discount information at mapleleaftickets.com or mousesavers.com.

Package deals

Vacation packages appeal to many visitors. They're simple and you can save money if you take advantage of all the elements. But that's a big "if." Often, you won't have the slightest interest in some of the elements, or if interested, won't have the time for all of them. When that's the case, the package is likely to cost you more than buying separately the elements you really want. So if you're interested in a package vacation to WDW, be prepared to do some studying. A variety of packages is available. Sit down with several that look appealing, do the budget arithmetic, factor in the convenience offered by the package, and make certain that you're willing and able to take advantage of all the features you're paying for. Furthermore, read the fine print to make sure you aren't paying too much. Some packages are loaded with features that few families or individuals could reasonably use during their vacation because of time and energy limitations. At a minimum, check the cost of any package you're seriously considering against the cost of purchasing separately the elements you're really after.

WDW vacation packages. If you're interested in a WDW package, get a free "Walt Disney World Resort Vacation Brochure" from your travel agent. Or order it (two or more months in advance of your visit) from the Walt Disney Travel Company by calling 407-934-7639, which can also provide you with information on Disney dining plans and special events such as fireworks parties and cruises you may want to reserve. Or go online to disneyworld. com for that information and to order Disney's free vacation planning kit. If your group numbers eight or more, check into Disney's Magical Gatherings at www.disneyworld.com/magicalgatherings or by calling 407-WDWPLAN.

If you have a large family of big eaters, or if you want to dine in upscale table-service restaurants that are normally not part of your budget, consider the "Magic Your Way Plus Dining" package (or the more expensive Premium or Platinum packages, which are packed with options). With these dining plans, you'll save money if you indulge in the higher-priced cuisine items. Call it your culinary WDW vacation! (And note, you still have to make reservations.)

Good Things to Know About

You will have the best time – and fewest hassles – if you know a bit more about your options ahead of time.

Budgeting

What does it cost to visit WDW? It depends on the choices you make. A family of four (two adults, one teenager, one child) may spend about $450 per day at WDW **excluding** lodging and transportation. This cost includes tickets, a light breakfast and lunch, a $100 dinner, a few light snacks in the parks, and a few souvenirs. A couple could get by on $200 a day per person (**including** admission tickets and lodging) with some careful budgeting. You'll minimize your expenditures by staying in a hotel off property and eating light food from hotel snack areas and from vendors and fast food eateries in the theme parks. You can order food online (and save money) at wegoshop.com, gardengrocer.com, or goodings.com, and have it delivered to your hotel. However, part of the unique magic of Walt Disney World Resort exists in the on-site hotels and restaurants (character meals, for example). You'll pay more for these experiences, but you'll take home many more special memories. Share meals (if the portions are large enough) to save money.

Note: Whenever you buy something at WDW, be sure to ask if any discounts apply.

Car rentals

Call the agency of your choice and reserve a car well ahead of your trip – three to six months ahead if you are coming at Christmastime. A good rule of thumb is to book your car when you book your hotel. Budget at least $50 a day or $240 weekly for a midsize car; twice that during Christmas week. Check mousesavers.com for rental car discounts.

Character meals

Eating breakfast, lunch, or dinner with a Disney character – or better yet, two or more of them – is a very popular activity. To avoid disappointment, book your seats when you make your hotel arrangements or up to 180 days prior to your desired meal date. by calling 407-WDW-DINE. See pages 54 to 56 for more about "Where to Dine with Your Favorite Character."

Child care

As you'd expect, child care is readily available to Orlando area visitors from a number of reputable agencies. You can drop your children off or arrange for in-room care. Most agencies that offer in-room services charge a four-hour minimum plus a travel fee for the babysitter, with the hourly rate determined by the number of children. Expect to pay $12 to $16 per hour for one child plus $1 to $2 per hour more for each additional child. Travel fees range from $10 to $12. Some agencies charge extra for care that begins after 9:00 p.m. Check with your hotel concierge for a list of reputable services.

Here are a few services and phone numbers to get you started:

- All About Kids   (in-room)   407-812-9300 or 800-728-6506
- Fairy Godmothers   (in-room)   407-277-3724
- Kid's Nite Out   (in-room)   800-696-8105 or 407-828-0920
- KinderCare   (drop-off)   407-827-5437

A few of these services will also accompany kids to the theme parks (for a fee) and can be hired by families who feel the need for an extra adult to help manage the little ones.

WDW provides evening fun for resort guests ages 4 (potty-trained) to 12 through several resort-property children's clubs: The Never Land Club at the Polynesian Resort (very popular); The Cub's Den at Wilderness Lodge; Simba's Cubhouse at the Animal Kingdom Lodge; The Sandcastle Club at the

Yacht and Beach Club Resorts; The Mouseketeer Club at the Grand Floridian Resort, and Camp Dolphin at the Swan and Dolphin Resorts. Call 407-939-3463 for information and reservations (407-934-1621 for Camp Dolphin). Hourly rates run about $10 per child. At times, at some resorts, the charges may be waived if the parents eat at one of the resort's restaurants.

During the day, WDW offers various educational and fun youth programs; call 407-939-8687 for information and reservations (for example, for Magic Kingdom children's tours) or 407-939-3463 for the Wonderland Tea Party (at the Grand Floridian), the Albatross Treasure Cruise at the Yacht Club, and the Pirate Adventure Cruises at Grand Floridian, Port Orleans–Riverside, and the Caribbean Beach resorts. Check "Activities for kids" in the *Index* for additional children's activities.

Extra Magic Hours (EMH)

WDW Resort guests get early entry into one of the theme parks every morning and can stay up to three hours in a designated theme park after it closes to the general public in the evening, giving on-property guests a chance to experience some of the most popular attractions when the parks are relatively uncrowded. Each park is scheduled for both morning and evening EMH at least once a week, but no park hosts both on the same day. Off-property guests should check the EMH schedule carefully (at www.disneyworld.com) and avoid visiting any park on a day that it's scheduled for morning EMH. By the time it opens to the general public, it will already be crowded. See pages 18-19 and 44 (#4) for more details and tips.

FASTPASS and singles lines

Consider using these timesavers whenever theme-park lines start to lengthen. **FASTPASS** is available for a number of popular attractions in each of the four major theme parks (check the park Guidemaps for attractions marked with an FP). This option saves you time in line by giving you a ticket now for later admission to the attraction with a shorter wait. To get one, place your admission ticket through the slot in the FASTPASS turnstile near the entrance to the attraction you've chosen. You will receive a slip of paper with a time period for you to come back (e.g., 1:20 p.m. to 2:20 p.m.). You simply return to the separate FASTPASS entry line at any time during that period and your wait will be shorter than the general admission queue. You won't be admitted earlier than your allotted time range but usually the attendant will admit you later.

You can get a FASTPASS for another attraction when your current time window begins or two or more hours after your current FASTPASS was issued, whichever comes sooner. But the rules change periodically. For example, the two-hour wait requirement may be cut to as little as five minutes for certain attractions during your visit. Check your FASTPASS ticket for the latest information.

Note: FASTPASS tickets are often unavailable during the late afternoon or evening hours.

Tip: If someone wants to sit out an attraction, send him or her with everyone's park tickets to get FASTPASSes for another attraction.

Single-rider lines (aka, singles lines) are sometimes available for popular attractions such as *Test Track, Mission: SPACE* and *Soarin'* at Epcot, *Rock 'n' Roller Coaster* at Disney's Hollywood Studios, *Expedition Everest* at Disney's Animal Kingdom, and the *ChairLift* at Blizzard Beach water park. Your park Guidemap marks these attractions with an "S" for Single Rider Queue; or ask a Disney attendant at the park's Tip Board. These lines are used to fill the empty seats in ride vehicles. Singles lines have shorter waits, but your party will usually be split up to fill the seats as they become available.

Guests with disabilities

WDW is fully accessible to persons with disabilities. For a free copy of Disney's "Walt Disney World Guidebook for Guests with Disabilities," call 407-939-6244 two or more months in advance of your visit and talk with a Disney operator. Better yet, pick up a copy of *Passporter's Open Mouse for Walt Disney World and the Disney Cruise Line: Easy Access Vacations for Travelers with Special Challenges* by Deb Wills and Debra Martin Koma (Ann Arbor, MI: Passporter Travel Press, ©2008). It has detailed information for those who suffer from just about any kind of disability, from allergies to mental health disorders to mobility, hearing, and vision problems. Any Guest Services area in WDW can also provide information about accommodations for guests with disabilities.

Important web site addresses

You can gather information, investigate vacation packages, buy theme park admission tickets, and make hotel and restaurant reservations with your computer if you use the Internet. The following sites are especially helpful:

- www.disneyworld.com – A comprehensive Disney web site, especially good for park and event hours to assist in trip planning.
- www.allears.net – An unofficial but comprehensive source of Disney advice and information.
- www.wdwinfo.com – A more personal site for WDW updates that's maintained by Disney aficionados; includes bulletin boards full of advice.

- www.hiddenmickeysguide.com – My expanding site of Hidden Mickey photos and sightings.
- www.pages.prodigy.net/stevesoares – Schedules for live entertainment throughout WDW.
- www.theotherorlando.com – Objective information on virtually all of Orlando's non-Disney attractions.
- www.floridakiss.com – Site of the Kissimmee Convention and Visitors Bureau with many links. (Kissimmee is the town closest to Walt Disney World)
- www.orlandoinfo.com – Site of the Orlando/Orange County Convention and Visitors Bureau, with many links.
- www.eventservices.disney.go.com/pintrading/index – If you collect and trade pins, check out this site!
- www.mousesavers.com – Searching for Disney discounts? Pay this site a visit.
- www.mouseforless.com – Good travel tips and aids. For example, go to "For the Kids" to download school excuse letters.
- www.disneyworldtrivia.com – Browse this site for answers to all your trivia questions.

Motion sickness

Roller coasters, spinning rides, and simulator rides (especially the last) can cause motion sickness in those prone to it. If that's you and you'd like to give the rides a try, take an over-the-counter motion-sickness remedy before you head for the parks (follow the directions on the label). Alternatively, opt for the "no-motion" version of the ride when one is available.

Mouse talk

Disney calls its theme park employees **cast members**. The **Disney Imagineers** are the folks who dream up and build WDW's wonderful environments and attractions. Guests staying at WDW's resort hotels and campground are **on-property** guests.

If you want to commend a cast member, write to Walt Disney World Communications, P.O. Box 10040, Lake Buena Vista, FL 32830-0040 or email to:guest.mail@wdw.disneyonline.com.

Park hours

Theme park hours are subject to change. Call 407-824-4321 or 407-824-4500 (or check www.disneyworld.com) a few days before you arrive for park and event (parades, fireworks, etc.) hours during your visit and to find out what Extra Magic Hours (EMH, see above) will be in effect. Then reconfirm the schedules with your hotel Lobby Concierge after you arrive.

Tip: Again, be sure to check the EMH schedule even if you aren't a WDW resort guest and, therefore, can't take advantage of the program. If you are staying off property and the program is in effect when you visit, schedule your park visits carefully. Avoid any park on days that it is open for morning EMH; it will already be crowded by the time it opens to non-WDW resort guests.

Note: The theme parks often admit guests earlier than the "official" hours you'll be given when you check for park hours. For example, if the official opening time for the Magic Kingdom (on a non-EMH day) is listed as 9:00 a.m., you may be admitted to Main Street, U.S.A. at 8:30 a.m.; the remainder of the park will open at 9:00 a.m. Occasionally when the official opening time is 9:00 a.m., you'll be admitted to Main Street as early as 8:00 a.m. and to the rest of the park at 8:30 a.m. If you don't know this nuance of Disney magic and arrive "on-time" at 9:00 a.m., you may find Main Street already buzzing.

Parking

Parking at the four major theme parks is free for WDW property guests and Annual Passholders, $11 per day for others. Once you've paid for the day at one park, you can leave and reenter the same lot or switch to the lot at another major WDW park without paying again (simply show your parking receipt). Parking is free for everyone at Downtown Disney, the water parks, Disney's Wide World of Sports Complex, the five golf courses, and the two miniature golf courses.

Pets

Can't bear to leave your pet at home? Call 407-824-6568 for WDW boarding information and vaccination requirements. WDW does not allow pets in its hotel rooms, but pets can stay with you for an additional fee of $10 per day per pet if you camp at certain sites in the Fort Wilderness Campground. Overnight pet kennel stays for dogs cost $20 as we go to press (WDW Resort hotel guests pay $18), and day stays cost $15. Prices for cats are $15, $13, and $10, respectively. Disney expects to add to its five current kennels a "luxury pet resort" in mid-2009, promising amenities such as nature walks, "playgroups," grooming, and even TVs for Fido and Fluffy. No pricing available as we go to press.

Resting places

Busy as they are, each of the major theme parks offers some inviting places to sit and relax. I list them for you in the appropriate chapters. Enjoy!

Switching off

Disney provides this option for parties with two or more adults and one or more children who are too young or frightened to experience a particular attraction. Initially you wait in line together. When the group reaches the loading area, one adult rides while the other adult and the kid(s) are directed to a specific area to wait. When the first adult disembarks and takes the kid(s), the second adult gets on the ride without a wait. A third adult (and the older children) in the group can ride twice, once with each of the other adults, if there's space.

Switching off is available at some attractions in all the parks; they are listed in the "Attractions That May Frighten Children" sections of *Chapters Two, Three, Four,* and *Five.* If you want to take advantage of it, tell all the Disney attendants you encounter as you move through the queue that you want to switch off.

Visiting other area attractions

If you plan to check out Universal Studios Florida or Islands of Adventure during your stay, call ahead (407-363-8000) for park hours and to find out if any movie or TV production is scheduled during your stay. You may also want to pick up a copy of my publisher's book *Universal Orlando,* by Kelly Monaghan, for a complete guide to Universal's attractions (see www.TheOtherOrlando. com for more information).

WDW (and related) phone numbers

Use these numbers to get the information you need before you head out and while you're in Orlando:

General All-Purpose Number	407-824-2222
General Information	407-824-4321 / 407-934-3344
General Lobby Concierge	407-824-4500
Hotel Reservations	407-934-7639 / 407-824-8000
or for the Swan & Dolphin	
(not operated by Disney)	800-227-1500
Dining Reservations	407-939-3463
All-Star Resorts:	
Sports	407-939-5000
Music	407-939-6000
Movies	407-939-7000
Animal Kingdom Lodge	407-938-3000
Atlantic Dance	407-939-2444
Beach Club Resort	407-934-8000

WDW (and related) phone numbers, cont'd.

Blizzard Beach	407-560-3400
BoardWalk Resort	407-939-5100
Caribbean Beach Resort	407-934-3400
Centra Care (walk-in medical clinic and 24-hour hotel in-room services)	407-238-2000
Cirque du Soleil	407-939-7600
Contemporary Resort	407-824-1000
Coronado Springs Resort	407-939-1000
Disabled Guests Special Requests	407-939-7807
Disney Cruise Line	407-566-3500 / 800-951-3532
Disney Vacation Club (DVC)	800-500-3990
Dolphin Resort	407-934-4000 / 800-227-1500
Fantasia Gardens Miniature Golf	407-939-7529
Florist	407-827-3505 / 877-608-0066
Fort Wilderness Campground	407-824-2900
Golf Reservations and Information	407-939-4653
Grand Floridian Resort & Spa	407-824-3000
Group Sales & Convention Info	407-828-3200
Guided Tour Information	407-939-8687
Guided VIP Tours	407-560-4033
Honeymoons	407-828-3400 / 800-370-6009
House of Blues Information	407-934-2583
Lost and Found	
lost yesterday and before	407-824-4245
lost today at Magic Kingdom	407-824-4521
lost today at Epcot	407-560-7500
lost today at the Studios	407-824-4245
lost today at Animal Kingdom	407-938-2785
lost today at Fort Wilderness	407-824-2726
lost today at Downtown Disney	407-828-3058
Magic Your Way Dining Plans	407-934-7639
Mail Order and Merchandise Return	407-363-6200
Old Key West Resort	407-827-7700
Outdoor Recreation Reservations	407-939-7529
Pleasure Island Information	407-939-2648
Polynesian Resort	407-824-2000
Pop Century Resort	407-938-4000
Port Orleans Resort–French Quarter	407-934-5000
Port Orleans Resort–Riverside	407-934-6000

Saratoga Springs Resort & Spa	407-827-1100
Shades of Green (U.S. Military) Hotel	407-824-3400
Swan Resort	407-934-3000 / 800-227-1500
Tennis Reservations and Lessons	407-939-7529
Typhoon Lagoon Information	407-560-4141
Weather Information	407-827-4545
Weddings	407-828-3400
Wide World of Sports Complex	407-939-4263
Wilderness Lodge Resort	407-824-3200
Winter Summerland Miniature Golf	407-560-3000
Yacht Club Resort	407-934-7000

What to do on arrival day

If you have an Annual Passport, you can go to a major park (follow the afternoon and evening parts of the appropriate touring plan; see *Chapters Two, Three, Four,* and *Five*). Otherwise don't burn a day of your other passes. Instead, try one or more of the following options: swim – don't sunburn!; spa; play miniature golf; visit DisneyQuest, a water park, Fort Wilderness (boating, horseback riding, hayride, carriage ride, campfire show), Cirque du Soleil, a dinner show, or Downtown Disney; explore your hotel or other hotels; enjoy afternoon tea at the Grand Floridian Resort; ride the monorail; rent a boat or a BoardWalk surrey bike; sing along at Jellyrolls; dance at Atlantic Dance; enjoy a hotel or character dinner; watch the Electrical Water Pageant; look for Hidden Mickeys in the hotels or other WDW areas; get married or renew your vows at the Wedding Pavilion! See *Chapters Six* and *Seven* for additional ideas and information.

If you stay on property, sample the TV channels that describe WDW attractions the first night of your stay, if you have the energy.

What to do on departure day

Schedule a character breakfast; revisit favorite attractions (if your ticket allows); look for more Hidden Mickeys; consider arrival day options you haven't yet tried.

What to do when it's really crowded

For most visitors, especially first-timers, the WDW theme parks will likely feel crowded even on an average day – particularly the Magic Kingdom and Disney's Hollywood Studios, which are the least spacious. Follow the touring plans in *Chapters Two* to *Four* and you should be fine. However, if you plan to visit during Christmas week, Spring Break, on July 4, or on any holiday weekend, the crowds will be enormous. You can still have a wonderful time; you just have to plan a little more carefully.

If you want to ride the most popular attractions on ultra-crowded days:

1. Arrive before the official opening time and head for the more popular attractions before the crowds build.

2. Use the FASTPASS and singles line options when available and convenient for you. Your park guidemap notes the attractions that have FASTPASS ("FP") and working single riders queues ("S"). You must walk to the attraction to get a FP, and remember that on busy days FPs may no longer be available by early afternoon.

3. If you have the ParkHopper® option and the crowd in the park you're visiting gets too heavy for you, try switching to another park – one that did not offer morning Extra Magic Hours. Epcot is usually a good choice since it's spread out and can handle large crowds with less congestion.

4. Take advantage of Extra Magic Hours (EMH) if you're staying on property. Even during busy season, you can usually enjoy several popular attractions with minimal waits in the early morning before the crowds build. Evening EMH is usually a great time for efficient touring in any of the parks. (The Magic Kingdom may be crowded on some evening EMH days, but the crowds do tend to thin out in the last hour.)

5. If all the theme parks and water parks are crowded and you have the time for other Disney attractions, spend some time in Fort Wilderness, Downtown Disney, the BoardWalk area, a miniature golf course, or one or more of the beautiful WDW Resorts, which schedule their own fun on-site activities. Many of these are open to all WDW Guests, not just those staying at the WDW Resorts.

What to Bring

1. An over-the-counter analgesic, such as Aspirin, Tylenol, Advil, or Aleve, plus an over-the-counter motion-sickness remedy if you are prone to motion sickness (you may need it for simulator rides).

2. Sunburn protection (SPF 15 or higher) and insect repellent if you react to bug bites.

3. Lip balm.

4. Bandage strips and first-aid cream.

5. Two pairs of cotton or other thin socks for each foot if you tend to blister.

6. Moleskin (buy at a pharmacy) to place over "hot spots" on feet before they blister. If the tender spot is already blistered, cut a hole in a square of moleskin and place the hole over the blister; if the tender area is just a red spot, cover the entire spot with moleskin.

7. Small scissors to cut moleskin (packed in checked luggage if you fly).

8. Hats or caps (the Florida sun is very strong).

9. Swimsuits if your family likes to swim, and also to wear under clothes for wet rides (like the one at Disney's Animal Kingdom) and the interactive fountains you'll find at some of the theme parks. Remove your (or your kids') regular clothes before the drenching experiences and you'll have dry clothes to wear the rest of the day.

10. Small towels to dry wet skin and a cloth for cleaning spectacles. (You will get wet on certain rides and in the interactive fountains).

11. Broken-in walking shoes (you'll walk several miles or more daily in the parks). Bring two pairs of shoes, if you can, so you'll have a dry pair available if your shoes get drenched on a wet ride or in a sudden downpour.

12. Aqua shoes if you're a water park fan.

13. Compact ponchos for rain protection. Also consider small umbrellas for rain and sun protection, especially if you're visiting in summer.

14. Lightweight jackets or sweaters for indoor air-conditioning and outdoors during the cooler months (November through March, especially in the evenings).

15. Brightly colored, loud shirts/blouses if you like to volunteer for shows.

16. Nice clothes (jackets for men) if you plan to eat at Victoria & Albert's at the Grand Floridian. (Tie optional.)

17. A fat pen for autographs. (Fat pens are easier for the Disney characters to handle.)

18. Autograph book (or buy one at your hotel or in the parks). Write your name and address in it.

19. A pen and note paper for writing down your parking locations plus a unique object to hang from your rear view mirror or antenna to help you find your car (if you plan to have a car at WDW).

20. Adhesive labels, so you can label items you carry into the parks (film, cell phones, etc.) with your name and address. That way if you lose them, you'll have a good chance of getting them back.

21. Camera with batteries, and plenty of film if you use film. (Film and disposable cameras are available in the parks, but you'll generally pay more there than you would at home.) Use your adhesive labels to put your name and both your home address and your resort or hotel and length of stay on the camera(s) and every roll of film.

22. Clear plastic water bottles.

23. A Walt Disney World Resort map if you're driving. (Check with your local bookstore or download a map from one of the WDW-related web sites.)

24. Several dollars (preferably in quarters) for the tollway if you plan to fly in and rent a car at the airport.

25. A few more dollars for tipping the hotel baggage handlers.

26. Your pet's vaccination record if you bring a pet.

27. Your admission tickets! (if purchased ahead of time). Write down and keep your ticket codes in case you lose your tickets. You'll find the codes (a combination of numbers and letters) on the back of the tickets at the bottom.

28. A small bag or fanny pack to carry your goodies. (Add a self-seal plastic bag inside if you're worried about waterproofing.)

29. Email addresses of friends and family if you want to send messages from WDW (for example, from ImageWorks in Epcot). If you're bringing a cell phone, you may also want to program in the phone numbers of anyone you might want to call from WDW.
    Note: While in WDW, keep your cell phone on vibrate mode!

30. Earplugs if you don't like loud noises at some of the attractions.

31. Photo IDs for everyone in your party.

32. A letter of medical necessity for a special need that isn't obvious.

33. This book.

34. My *Hidden Mickeys* book.

Where to Eat

WDW offers plenty of choices when it comes to food and eateries. You'll find restaurant recommendations for the theme parks in the following pages, followed by recommendations for restaurants outside the parks, and then by my ratings of each of WDW's full-service eateries. To give you an overview of the wide range of choices and prices available to you at WDW's full-service restaurants, and also to make it as easy as possible for you to compare them, I group my ratings together alphabetically instead of separating them by theme park or other venue. The touring plans for each park (see *Chapters Two* to *Five*) include additional recommendations.

Advance dining reservations

"Advance dining reservations," or ADRs, (formerly called "priority seating reservations") are recommended for most full-service restaurants in WDW, so plan ahead if you can. You can book up to six months in advance, and you'll need to if your heart's set on eating at one (or more) of WDW's most popular eateries during busy seasons. Call 407-WDW-DINE. If you can't get an ADR at the time and/or restaurant of your choice, call back later and try to nab a cancellation.

Note: With ADRs, you don't actually have a reservation in the sense that a table will be held for your arrival, but you'll be seated as close as possible to the assigned time and ahead of walk-ins. During busy periods, ADRs work best near popular restaurants' opening times; that's why my touring plans for each park emphasize eating early lunches and dinners if possible.

Another big advantage to dining early is that prime tables are more often available to early diners. Some of the prime locations you may want to try for are window seats at the California Grill in the Contemporary Resort, seats close to the aquarium glass wall (in the first three rows of tables) at the Coral Reef Restaurant in Epcot's The Seas with Nemo & Friends Pavilion, and seats overlooking the *Gran Fiesta Tour* attraction at the San Angel Inn Restaurant in Epcot's Mexico Pavilion.

Character meals

Dining with Disney characters is a must for many guests, especially families with young children.. You'll find a section on character meals, "Where to Dine with Your Favorite Disney Characters," below following my restaurant ratings. It includes some general notes and two at-a-glance charts. Check the first to see where you can share a meal with Mickey, Cinderella, or any of

29 other Disney characters. Check the second to locate character meals by restaurant and theme park or resort.

A few general notes

Restaurant hours, menus, and prices change periodically, and eateries may be refurbished or replaced.

A child's meal is available for ages 3 to 9 in most WDW restaurants.

Gratuities: Most full-service restaurants (the ones included in my rating chart, below) automatically add an 18% gratuity. Be sure to take this into consideration when estimating what you'll probably spend in a given restaurant.

Money-saving tip: Eat light food for breakfast (most hotels have a snack area with cereals, fruit, etc.). Then buy from vendors and counter-service eateries in the theme parks. Share meals if portions are large. Big eaters may want to look into Disney's various dining plans (see "packages," page 35).

Healthy eating: All the parks have fresh fruit stands and fast food is available in abundance. The health-conscious can ask for carrots in place of french fries.

Caution: Don't sit under trees near food areas; birds might find you a tempting target.

A final note: The tastiest (and safest) seafood is served in restaurants that specialize in seafood.

Restaurant recommendations

Magic Kingdom

The Plaza Restaurant at the end of Main Street has decent food, and you can get seated quickly if you're at the door when it opens for lunch at 11:00 a.m. even if you don't have advance reservations. Tony's Town Square Restaurant near the Main Street Train Station also has decent food; try the specialty pizza for lunch (noon-2:45 p.m.). Reservations are recommended for the generally good character meals at The Crystal Palace buffet and Liberty Tree Tavern, and they are essential if you want to break bread with the characters at Cinderella's Royal Table.

Fast food abounds in the Magic Kingdom. You might try the apple pie in the restful surroundings of Aunt Polly's Dockside Inn (open seasonally on Tom Sawyer Island in Frontierland) or the pineapple soft serve ice cream at Aloha Isle in Adventureland (eat in the covered patio nearby). The upstairs area of Columbia Harbour House restaurant is usually relaxing and quiet.

Note: If you're already at Magic Kingdom and want advance dining reservations, walk to City Hall in Town Square or to the restaurant of your choice and see what's available.

Epcot

Epcot serves some of WDW's best park food. All eleven World Showcase countries (see *Chapter Three*) have restaurants. Ten are full-service eateries, while the one at the American Adventure Pavilion offers counter service. The full-service restaurants are picturesque and worthwhile. In Canada, Le Cellier Steakhouse reservations go fast, and Teppan Edo in Japan serves tasty food prepared before your eyes by entertaining chefs. Restaurant Marrakesh in Morocco offers entertainment (music and belly dancing) with lunch and dinner. The Biergarten in Germany has musicians performing afternoons and evenings. In the Coral Reef Restaurant (expensive) in The Seas with Nemo & Friends Pavilion, you sit and eat near floor-to-ceiling windows that allow you to see the marine life in the huge aquarium. Character meals are available in The Garden Grill Restaurant in The Land Pavilion and in Akershus Royal Banquet Hall in Norway.

Note: If you're at Epcot and want advance dining reservations, talk with the personnel at Guest Relations (to the left – east – of *Spaceship Earth*) and see what's available.

Disney's Hollywood Studios

The Hollywood Brown Derby, named for the original Brown Derby in Hollywood, California, cooks up this park's tastiest food. The Sci-Fi Dine-In Theater Restaurant and the 50's Prime Time Café offer good food with unique and memorable ambiance. At Sci-Fi, you sit in small convertible cars at a "drive-in" movie theater and watch trailers from old science fiction films while you eat. At Prime Time, a motherly server brings your food ("Better clean your plate!") while you watch 1950s' sitcom segments on small TVs. Mama Melrose's Ristorante Italiano offers decent Italian fare. Character meals are available at the Hollywood & Vine buffet. For fast food, try the Backlot Express for burgers and sandwiches or the Toy Story Pizza Planet for pizza and lemonade.

Note: If you're at Disney's Hollywood Studios and want dining reservations, walk to the service window near the corner of Hollywood and Sunset Boulevards and see what's available.

Disney's Animal Kingdom

This park boasts two full-service restaurants, the Rainforest Café at the park entrance and the Yak & Yeti Restaurant in Asia. Rainforest Café serves good food in a jungle atmosphere. It's a fun place to eat, and you don't even have to buy park admission to eat here because you can enter the restaurant from inside or outside the park. The Yak & Yeti, named after a famous hotel in Kathmandu, Nepal, offers an Asian-inspired menu. A character breakfast buffet is available at Tusker House Restaurant. Fast food eateries are scattered around the park, and the food and ambiance in them are generally good (especially at Flame Tree Barbecue and the Yak & Yeti Local Food Cafes, which are separate from the full-service Yak & Yeti Restaurant).

Elsewhere in WDW

You'll find plenty of worthwhile WDW restaurants outside of the theme parks. The three best restaurants in WDW are Victoria & Albert's at the Grand Floridian Resort & Spa, the California Grill at the Contemporary Resort, and (newer and not far behind) Todd English's bluezoo at the Dolphin hotel. All three are expensive. The Marketplace at Downtown Disney has a second Rainforest Café (moderate) equal in quality to the one in Disney's Animal Kingdom. Il Mulino restaurant (expensive) at the Swan hotel offers good Italian food. Other very good eateries include: Kimonos (Japanese) at the Swan hotel; the Flying Fish Café (seafood) and Spoodles (Mediterranean fare) at the BoardWalk Resort; Citricos (Mediterranean fare) and Narcoossee's (seafood) at the Grand Floridian Resort; Artist Point (seafood) at Wilderness Lodge; Shula's Steak House at the Dolphin hotel; Yachtsman Steakhouse at the Yacht Club Resort; Cape May Café (seafood buffet) at the Beach Club Resort; Fulton's Crab House and Raglan Road (Irish fare) at Pleasure Island; Olivia's Café (American) at Old Key West Resort; Jiko and Boma (both African) at the Animal Kingdom Lodge; Wolfgang Puck Café (American) at Downtown Disney West Side. The Whispering Canyon Café at Wilderness Lodge (good American fare) gets diners (especially kids) involved in fun games during meals.

Dinner shows

The best dinner show at WDW is *Hoop-Dee-Doo Musical Revue*, an energetic song and dance show with tongue-in-cheek humor at Fort Wilderness Pioneer Hall. You can reserve one of three nightly performances (5:00 p.m., 7:15 p.m., or 9:30 p.m.). The show is popular, so make reservations months in advance; you can book up to 180 days ahead. Your other option is *The Spirit of Aloha* show at the Polynesian Resort. It's entertaining and has decent food. The price is the same for either: Adults $51 to $59, children $26 to $30, depending on your seating category (a 2007 innovation). Category 1 seats are closest to the action, but Category 2 and 3 seats still afford good views. Book by calling 407-WDW-DINE. Full payment is required when you book.

WDW Full-Service Restaurants Rated

- Rating: * to * * * * *
- Price: (the approximate cost of soup or salad and a main course, without drinks, dessert, or WDW's automatic 18% gratuity):
  - Expensive ($36 and over per person; over $100 per person at California Grill and Victoria & Albert's)
  - Moderate ($15 to $35.99 per person)
  - Inexpensive (less than $15 per person)
- Meals Offered: Breakfast (B), Lunch (L), Dinner (D)
- † Next to the meal designation, for example (B†), means the restaurant offers an "all you can eat" buffet at that meal
- nyo: Not yet open as we go to press

Notes: Restaurant opening hours, menus, and prices change periodically, and eateries may be closed for refurbishment or replaced. Be sure to include the 18% gratuity that most WDW restaurants automatically add when calculating meal costs.

Tip: Call 407-WDW-DINE and your restaurant of choice if you have specific diet requests. Disney chefs will happily accommodate you!

Restaurant	Location	Cuisine	Rating	Price
Akershus (B†,L†,D†)	Norway, Epcot	Norwegian	* * *	Moderate
All-Star Café (L,D)	Wide Wld of Sports	American	* *	Moderate
Andiamo Italian Grille (D)	Hilton Resort	Italian	* *	Moderate
Artist Point (D)	Wilderness Lodge	Seafood	* * * *	Expensive
Beaches & Cream (L,D)	Beach Club	American	* *	Inexpensive
Benihana (D)	Hilton Resort	Japanese	* * *	Moderate
Biergarten (L†,D†)	Germany, Epcot	German	* * *	Moderate
Big River Grille (L,D)	BoardWalk	American	* *	Moderate
Bistro de Paris (D)	France, Epcot	French	* * *	Expensive
Boatwright's (B,D)	Port Orleans/Rvsd	Cajun	* *	Moderate
Boma (B†,D†)	Animal Kngdm Ldg	African	* * * *	Moderate
Bongo's (L,D)	Disney West Side	Cuban	* *	Moderate
California Grill (D)	Contemporary	American	* * * * *	Expensive
Cape May Café (B†,D†)	Beach Club Resort	Buffet	* * *	Moderate
Cap'n Jack's (L,D)	Disney Marketplace	Seafood	* * *	Moderate
Captain's Grille (B†,L,D)	Yacht Club Resort	American	* * *	Moderate
Chef Mickey's (B†,D†)	Contemporary	Buffet	* * *	Moderate
Chefs de France (L,D)	France, Epcot	French	* * *	Moderate
Cinderella's Royal Table (B,L)	Magic Kingdom	American	* *	Expensive
Citricos (D)	Grand Floridian	Mediterran.	* * * *	Expensive

Restaurant	Location	Cuisine	Rating	Price
Concourse Steakhouse (B,L,D)	Contemporary	Steak	* * *	Moderate
Coral Reef (L,D)	The Seas, Epcot	Seafood	* * *	Expensive
Crystal Palace (B†,L†,D†)	Magic Kingdom	Buffet	* * *	Moderate
Dolphin Fountain (L,D)	Dolphin Resort	American	* *	Inexpensive
El Dolbe	Downtown Disney	nyo	nyo	nyo
ESPN Club (L,D)	BoardWalk	American	* *	Moderate
Evergreen Cafe (B†,L,D)	DoubleTree Suites	American	* * *	Moderate
50's Prime Time Café (L,D)	the Studios	American	* *	Moderate
Flying Fish Café (D)	BoardWalk	Seafood	* * * *	Expensive
Fresh (B†,L†)	Dolphin Resort	American	* * *	Moderate
Fulton's Crab Hse (L,D)	Pleasure Island	Seafood	* * *	Expensive
Garden Grill (L,D)	The Land, Epcot	American	* * *	Moderate
Garden Grove (B†,L†D†)	Swan Resort	American	* *	Moderate
Giraffe Diner (B†,L,D)	Royal Plaza Resort	American	* *	Moderate
Grand Floridian Café (B,L,D)	Grand Floridian	American	* *	Moderate
Hollywood & Vine (B†,L†,D†)	the Studios	American	* * *	Moderate
Hollywood Brown Derby (L,D)	the Studios	American	* * * *	Expensive
House of Blues (L,D)	Disney West Side	American	* * *	Moderate
Il Mulino (D)	Swan Resort	Italian	* * * *	Expensive
Jiko (D)	Animal Kngdm Ldg	African	* * * *	Expensive
Kimonos (D)	Swan Resort	Japanese	* * *	Moderate
Kona Cafe (B,L,D)	Polynesian Resort	Asian	* * *	Moderate
LakeView (B,L,D)	Regal Sun Resort	American	* *	Moderate
Le Cellier Steakhse (L,D)	Canada, Epcot	Steak	* * * *	Moderate
Liberty Tree Tvn (D)	Magic Kingdom	American	* * *	Moderate
Mama Melrose's (L,D)	the Studios	Italian	* * *	Moderate
Marrakesh (L,D)	Morocco, Epcot	Moroccan	* * *	Moderate
Maya Grill (B†,D)	Coronado Springs	Mexican	* *	Expensive
Narcoossee's (D)	Grand Floridian	Seafood	* * * *	Expensive
Nine Dragons (L,D)	China, Epcot	Chinese	* * *	Moderate
1900 Park Fare (B†,D†)	Grand Floridian	Buffet	* * *	Moderate
'Ohana (B,D)	Polynesian Resort	Polynesian	* * *	Moderate

Restaurant	Location	Cuisine	Rating	Price
Olivia's Café (B,L,D)	Old Key West	American	* * *	Moderate
The Outback (D)	Buena Vista Palace	Steak	* * *	Expensive
(**Note:** not part of the Outback Steakhouse restaurant chain)				
Planet Hollywood (L,D)	Disney West Side	American	* *	Moderate
Plaza (L,D)	Magic Kingdom	American	* * *	Moderate
Raglan Road (L,D)	Pleasure Island	Irish	* * *	Moderate
Rainforest Café (B,L,D)	Animal Kingdom	American	* * *	Moderate
Rainforest Café (L,D)	Disney Marketplace	American	* * *	Moderate
Rose & Crown (L,D)	UK, Epcot	English	* * *	Moderate
San Angel Inn (L,D)	Mexico, Epcot	Mexican	* * *	Expensive
Sand Trap (B,L)	Eagle Pines/Osprey Ridge Golf Club	American	* *	Inexpensive
Sci-Fi Dine-In (L,D)	the Studios	American	* *	Moderate
Shula's (D)	Dolphin Resort	Steak	* * * *	Expensive
Shutters (D)	Caribbean Beach	Caribbean	* *	Moderate
Spoodles (B,D)	BoardWalk	Mediterran.	* * *	Moderate
Streamers (B†,L,D)	DoubleTree Suites	American	* *	Moderate
T-Rex Café	Disney Marketplace	American	nyo	nyo
Todd Eng.'s bluezoo (D)	Dolphin Resort	Seafood	* * * *	Expensive
Teppan Edo (L,D)	Japan, Epcot	Japanese	* * * *	Expensive
Tokyo Dining (L,D)	Japan, Epcot	Sushi	* * * *	Expensive
Tony's Town Sq (L,D)	Magic Kingdom	Italian	* *	Moderate
Traders (B,L.D)	Lake Buena Vista	American	* *	Moderate
Trail's End (B†,L†,D†)	Fort Wilderness	Buffet	* * *	Moderate
Turf Club Grill (L,D)	Saratoga Springs	American	* *	Moderate
Tuscan Country Trattoria (L,D)	Pleasure Island	Italian	nyo	nyo
Tusker House (B†,L†D†)	Animal Kingdom	Buffet	* * *	Moderate
Tutto Italia Ris. (L,D)	Italy, Epcot	Italian	* * *	Expensive
Victoria & Albert's (D)	Grand Floridian	Gourmet	* * * * *	Expensive
Watercress Café (B†,L)	Buena Vista Palace	American	* *	Moderate
Whispering Canyon (B,L,D)	Wilderness Lodge	American	* * *	Moderate
Wolfgang Puck (L,D)	Disney West Side	Californian	* * *	Expensive
Yachtsman Steakhse (D)	Yacht Club Resort	Steak	* * * *	Expensive
Yak & Yeti (L,D)	Animal Kingdom	Asian	* * *	Moderate

Where to dine
with your favorite characters

You'll find decent character meals both inside and outside the theme parks. They're popular, so you'll want to make advance reservations for them if possible. By far, the hardest to get into is the breakfast at Cinderella's Royal Table in the Magic Kingdom with Cinderella and friends. Call 407-WDW-DINE for reservations 180 days in advance several minutes before 7:00 a.m. Eastern time and hit redial until the center opens. Have your credit card handy. The price of all Cinderella's Royal Table meals include photos of your group. In contrast, the Saturday and Sunday breakfasts with Goofy, Pluto, and Chip and Dale in the Swan Resort's Garden Grove Café are usually not too crowded.

Note: The specific characters at character meals change from time to time. So call ahead to be sure you'll be dining with your favorites.

Note: Be sure to arrive on time. Most character meals have waiting lines of Guests who called too late to snag a seat, and latecomers are apt to find they've lost their places to them.

Character meals by character

- B - breakfast; L - lunch; D - dinner
- † Next to the meal designation, for example (B†), means the restaurant offers an "all you can eat" buffet at that meal
- * next to the restaurant name means that the character is one of several who may dine with you
- MK - Magic Kingdom, E - Epcot, DH - Disney's Hollywood Studios, AK - Disney's Animal Kingdom, R - Resort (see above for specifics)

Character	Restaurant / (location)	Meal(s)
Belle	Akershus Royal Banq Hall* (E)	B†,L†,D†
	Cinderella's Royal Table (MK)	B,L
Chip 'n' Dale	Cape May Café (R)	B†
	Chef Mickey's* (R)	B†,D†
	Garden Grill (E)	L,D
	Garden Grove Café (R)	B† (Sat, Sun), D† (M-Th, Sat)
	Liberty Tree Tavern (MK)	D
Cinderella	Cinderella's Royal Table (MK)	B,L
	1900 Park Fare (R)	D†
Daisy Duck	Tusker House (AK)	B†
Donald Duck	Chef Mickey's* (R)	B†,D†
	Tusker House (AK)	B†

Character	Restaurant / (location)	Meal(s)
Eeyore	Crystal Palace (MK)	B†,L†,D†
Esmeralda	Akershus Royal Banq Hall* (E)	B†,L†,D†
Goliath (from *Jojo's Circus*)	Hollywood & Vine (DH)	B†,L†
Goofy	Cape May Café (R)	B†
	Chef Mickey's* (R)	B†,D†
	Garden Grove Café (R)	B† (Sat, Sun)
		D† (M-Th, Sat)
	Liberty Tree Tavern (MK)	D
	Tusker House (AK)	B†
Jasmine	Akershus Royal Banq Hall* (E)	B†,L†,D†
	Cinderella's Royal Table (MK)	B,L
JoJo (from *Jojo's Circus*)	Hollywood & Vine (DH)	B†,L†
Leo (from *Little Einsteins*)	Hollywood & Vine (DH)	B†,L†
Lilo	'Ohana (R)	B
Mary Poppins	Akershus Royal Banq Hall* (E)	B†,L†,D†
	1900 Park Fare (R)	B†
Meeko (from *Pocahontas*)	Liberty Tree Tavern (MK)	D
Mickey	Chef Mickey's (R)	B†,D†
	Garden Grill (E)	L,D
	'Ohana (R)	B
	Tusker House (AK)	B†
Minnie	Cape May Café (R)	B†
	Chef Mickey's* (R)	B†,D†
	Liberty Tree Tavern (MK)	D
Mulan	Akershus Royal Banq Hall* (E)	B†,L†,D†
Piglet	Crystal Palace (MK)	B†,L†,D†
Pluto	Cape May Café (R)	B†
	Chef Mickey's* (R)	B†,D†
	Garden Grill (E)	L,D
	Garden Grove Café (R)	B† (Sat, Sun),
		D† (M-Th, Sat)
	Liberty Tree Tavern (MK)	D
	'Ohana (R)	B
Jasmine	Cinderella's Royal Table (MK)	B,L
Pocahontas	Akershus Royal Banq Hall* (E)	B†,L†,D†
Pooh	Crystal Palace (MK)	B†,L†,D†
Rafiki	Garden Grove Café (R)	D† (Fri, Sun)
Sleeping Beauty	Akershus Royal Banq Hall* (E)	B†,L†,D†
Snow White	Akershus Royal Banq Hall* (E)	B†,L†,D†

Character meals by character (cont'd.)

Character	Restaurant / (location)	Meal(s)
Snow White, cont'd.	Cinderella's Royal Table	B,L
Stitch	'Ohana (R)	B
Tigger	Crystal Palace (MK)	B†,L†,D†
Timon	Garden Grove Café (R)	D† (Fri, Sun)

Character meals by location

Magic Kingdom

Cinderella's Royal Table	B,L	Cinderella, Snow White, Belle, Jasmine
Crystal Palace	B†,L†,D†	Pooh, Tigger, Piglet, Eeyore
Liberty Tree Tavern	D	Minnie, Goofy, Chip 'n' Dale, Pluto Meeko

Epcot

Akershus Royal Banq Hall (Cinderella does not appear here)	B†,L†,D†	Four or more of the following: Snow White, Sleeping Beauty, Mary Poppins, Belle, Jasmine, Pocahontas, Esmeralda, Mulan
Garden Grill	L,D	Mickey, Pluto, and Chip 'n' Dale

Disney's Hollywood Studios

Hollywood & Vine	B,L	JoJo, Goliath, Leo

Disney's Animal Kingdom

Tusker House	B†	Donald, Daisy, Mickey, Goofy

Resorts

Cape May Café (Beach Club)	B†	Minnie, Goofy, Chip 'n' Dale, Pluto
Chef Mickey's (Contemporary)	B†,D†	Five of the following: Mickey, Minnie, Goofy, Donald, Chip 'n' Dale, Pluto
1900 Park Fare (Grand Floridian)	B†	Mary Poppins and variable others
	D†	Cinderella and variable others, e.g., Stepsisters, the Mad Hatter
'Ohana (Polynesian)	B	Lilo, Stitch, Mickey, Pluto
Garden Grove Café (Swan)	B† (Sat, Sun)	Goofy, Chip 'n' Dale, Pluto
	D† (M-Th, Sat)	Goofy, Chip 'n' Dale, Pluto
	D† (Fri, Sun)	Rafiki and Timon

Basic Rules for Touring

1. **Don't try to do everything.** Each theme park, with the possible exception of Disney's Animal Kingdom, is too large to experience fully in one day. If you come to WDW intending to experience every attraction, you'll probably be disappointed. Furthermore, you'll quickly reach sensory overload, that point during the day when the kids are crying and you're no longer having fun.

2. **Get to the park early, and take a break in the afternoon** either back at your hotel for a rest or swim – or in the park itself (see touring plans). This approach will provide the most time-efficient method for visiting the more popular attractions and let you recharge during the afternoon break. Furthermore, you'll prevent sensory overload and avoid the worst of the afternoon heat. If you decide to sleep in, just pick up the appropriate touring plan later in the morning (a few steps before lunchtime) and try to catch the more popular attractions with FAST-PASS (see "Good Things to Know About," above), during the parades, and/or in the hour before closing.

3. **If you go later. . .** If you're visiting WDW to play golf or attend a conference, go to the parks after your morning recreation and follow the afternoon and evening portions of the appropriate touring plan(s). To avoid the longest lines, try to experience the more popular attractions during parades or in the hour before the park closes. Also, use the FASTPASS or singles line options when available (see above) to minimize your waits for some popular attractions.

4. **Don't wait in long lines**. A long wait is more than 15 to 20 minutes. Current attraction wait times are posted on park Tip Boards (sometimes inaccurate) and in front of most attractions (usually accurate), or you can ask the Disney attendant. Waiting in queues can be exhausting, especially for children. As you follow the touring plans, the lines may become unbearably long later in the morning or early afternoon. At this point, you have several alternatives: You can use the FASTPASS and singles line options; you can skip down the touring plan to less congested attractions, or you can leave the park you're in and switch to another (if your ticket allows), in essence combining touring plans for different parks on the same day. Just pick up the next park's touring plan at an appropriate point. The act of switching parks will also provide a break of sorts, by offering you a change of scenery.

5. **Relax!** You'll encounter many hyperkinetic vacationers in the theme

parks, running to and fro, dragging crying kids behind them, jostling for position before parades and character greetings. Some of these folks don't get to WDW very often and are trying to pack too much into too short a time. Are these people really having fun? Avoid them if you can and seek quieter surroundings.

6. **Avoid sunburn, dehydration, and exhaustion.** If you start losing steam, seek a rest area (consult the list of rest areas for each park in the appropriate chapters), take some refreshment in a cool place, or leave the park for your hotel. Drink frequently, even if you or your kids don't feel thirsty. Bring or rent a stroller for kids six and under.

   Note: The larger double strollers are more difficult to maneuver around the parks (especially when the parks are crowded).

7. **Don't tote bulky purchases around with you.** All the shops in the theme parks will send bulky and heavy purchases to a "package pickup" area near the park exit at no extra charge. If you're staying on property, they'll deliver them right to your door, again at no charge.

7. **Bring small snacks**, such as gum or mints, into the parks in your shoulder bag or fanny pack. They come in handy between meals.

8. **Use the touring plans.** Convince your family, *before* you enter the parks, of the benefits of following the plans you'll find in the upcoming chapters. They will minimize waiting while offering maximum opportunities for experiencing the best of WDW. They should also prevent time-consuming and sometimes emotional arguments and discussions about what everyone wants to do next.

   Convince your kids that they will meet plenty of Disney characters during their visit, so hopefully they won't stop in their tracks every time they spot one. On the other hand, if your child seems desperate at times and the line for the character isn't too long, go ahead and queue up. If there's a specific character you want to find, ask at any Guest Relations.

   Strategies: The touring plans take busy periods into account and suggest strategies for dealing with them whether you are staying on property or off. One strategy is to arrive early, visit until the park becomes too crowded for comfort, and then switch to another, less crowded park if your ticket allows. Another is to give yourself a "time out" by taking a rest break in the park itself. Either way, later in the day your time is best spent enjoying the least crowded attractions (see "Attractions with Minimal Waits (Usually)" in *Chapters Two to Five*).

   Tip: On really crowded days, plan to visit Epcot. It is large enough and offers enough shows to accommodate crowds enjoyably even when Walt Disney World is packed.

Note: Some children do better if they visit Magic Kingdom last. If they experience it first, they may not enjoy the other parks quite as much because they may expect all of WDW to be just like the MK.

9. **Keep your camera readily available.** Consult the park Guidemaps for "picture spot" locations that you may come upon as you follow the touring plans. Be alert for the many special picture moments that will inevitably happen.

   Note: See "Bringing the Magic Home," below, for photo-taking tips.

10. **If you get around WDW by car** (recommended), write down your parking location on a piece of paper that you keep with you. Or take a digital photo of your car's row number and section. Do this *every* time you park your car, even at the hotels.

11. **Be ready for surprises**. Attractions are periodically updated, changed, or closed for refurbishment. Times, schedules, shows, and parades vary continually. Furthermore, attractions occasionally break down, and inclement weather may cause cancellation of parades or temporary closing of certain rides. If you paid for any special show that was cancelled or shortened because of bad weather, always ask at Guest Relations for a ticket refund or a voucher for a future show.

    Note: This book is current as we go to press, but don't be dismayed if you encounter a few surprises during your vacation. Even the Guidemap you pick up at the park entrance occasionally has erroneous information. Ask a cast member (Disney employee) if you have questions.

Hidden Mickeys

A long tradition with Disney's Imagineers (see "Mouse Talk," above) is to build or paint the silhouette of Mickey Mouse into rides and attractions. Most of these silhouettes are not obvious, thus the "hidden Mickey" term. Some Disney fans become experts at hidden Mickey lore, and some web sites cover this arcane area. When Disney cast members are hired, certain of them are given review sheets that list the location of some hidden Mickeys.

A few such locations are listed in each of the next four chapters. If you're interested, try to find them when you're in the parks. Most Disney cast members will happily point out nearby hidden Mickeys if you ask. Better yet, get my book *Hidden Mickeys: A Field Guide to Walt Disney World's Best Kept Secrets,* (Branford, CT: The Intrepid Traveler). It provides six scavenger hunts for searching out over 700 Hidden Mickeys at WDW, complete with clues and points to be scored, plus an index that lets you locate them wherever you happen to be.

Attraction ratings explained

In the following four chapters, you'll find ratings of each park's attractions, along with descriptions of each ride or exhibit. Here is what the stars mean:

The Very Best	🐭🐭🐭🐭🐭
Outstanding	🐭🐭🐭🐭
Very Good	🐭🐭🐭
Good	🐭🐭
Average But Still Fun	🐭

Using the touring plans

The touring plans are the heart of this book. They are customized to the preferences of adults and teens, families with younger children, and seniors, and they work – better than you could ever imagine. I've tested and perfected them over a number of years with the help of numerous friends, friends of friends, and other visitors who turned to me (the WDW fanatic) for help in making their WDW visits as magical as possible. BUT the plans aren't intended for armchair reading. If you've never visited the WDW theme parks and simply read the touring plans, you're likely to find them a little confusing.

Trust me. Once you are in the parks, you'll find these touring plans a breeze to follow. Visitors who've used them tell me they are like having your own personal tour guide. Follow them and you'll avoid the long lines and the exhaustion and frustration that can set in when you don't know what to do first or how to pace yourself. If you're visiting WDW for the first time, using these plans will help to ensure a truly magical experience. And if you are a repeat visitor, they will help you savor the magic as you never have before.

Accuracy and other impossible dreams

I have tried to be as accurate and up-to-date as possible. But complete accuracy is an unattainable goal. As noted in #11, above, Walt Disney World is always changing – tweaking attractions, adding new lodging, restaurants, and entertainment venues, and adjusting prices and ticket options. Most likely to change are the prices and ticket options. Like any business, WDW reserves the right to change these at any time without notice. So it is possible, even probable, that there will be changes after this book is printed. Just to be on the safe side, visit Disney's web site (www.disneyworld.com) when you are planning your trip to check the latest price information.

A special word about closings

It is likely that one or more of the attractions described in this book will be closed when you visit, because WDW closes attractions periodically for routine maintenance and refurbishing. It lists these closings on its web site to help you with your planning. It also replaces attractions from time to time. If an attraction that's listed in one of the touring plans in *Chapters Two* through *Five* has been replaced, you'll probably find the new attraction as good – or even better – than its predecessor. Simply note its name and include it in your touring plan in place of the old attraction.

Bringing the Magic Home

Nearly every visitor to WDW tries to capture the magic in photos, but all too often the results fall short of the goal. Here are some tips to help you get shots you'll enjoy viewing for years to come. Special thanks to my colleague Mark Ahrens, ER Nurse and photography enthusiast, for his help with this section.

1. We're in the digital camera age. Not only do digitals let you check the pictures you take almost instantly and erase those you don't like, but also many let you record video with sound. Expect to pay a list price of $75 and up – to thousands of dollars if you insist on the best digital money can buy with all the bells and whistles. However, you won't need anything that sophisticated to take good pictures.

2. If you'd prefer not to invest in a digital or don't want to bring yours (or your old-fashioned film camera) along, you can get decent pictures with a simple disposable (single-use) camera. The disposable's fixed-focus lens is usually set to photograph subjects four to six feet away. So long as you keep that in mind, you're likely to find the image quality acceptable. If you decide to go this route, buy several disposables at a discount store before your trip (they're more expensive at WDW).

3. For higher quality photos or more flexibility, opt for an auto-focus digital or a 35 mm range finder, auto-focus (film) camera. Both provide good image quality for their $100 to $200 cost and offer such features as a zoom lens and a built-in flash. The 35 mm cameras will also be self-loading and self-winding. Choose a camera you find comfortable to hold, with buttons that are easy to operate. The zoom feature will help you capture images in the distance – exotic animals at Disney's Animal Kingdom, for example.

4. Test your camera before your vacation (unless, of course, it is a disposable). Read the owner's manual (especially important if you get a digital). Shoot a number of digital photos or a roll of film in the store to test all the features (flash, zoom lens, and so on), and ask for instruction if you need help. If your digital photos don't turn out well, consult with the salesperson immediately and then shoot some more to be sure you can do what you want with the camera. If you've bought a film camera, leave the store, have the film developed at a one-hour processing center, and then return to the store for advice if the pictures don't turn out well. In either case, you may want to exchange your purchase for a different camera if the one you've selected and tested isn't satisfactory.

5. Come to WDW prepared. If you've opted for disposables, bring plenty and store the extras in a locker at the parks to lighten your load when touring. If you're using a digital, bring plenty of batteries, and don't forget the charger if they are rechargeable. If you're using film, make sure it is fresh by checking the expiration date on each roll, and bring along extra camera batteries. Store the extra batteries and film cartridges in a park locker. You may want to stash exposed film there, too.

6. Put your name and address on your camera(s) and film canisters with adhesive mailing labels or the like. That way if you drop one, you're likely to get it back. (Theme park guests tend to turn in found objects.)

7. Take a number of pictures of the subject if you can. Professional photographers take numerous photos to get the few that stand out. If you feel a photo op coming on, start clicking away! Try different angles and perspectives, sometimes tilting the camera to a 45-degree angle, for example, for variety.

8. Always include close-ups, and be sure your subject isn't wearing a hat or sunglasses in every shot; both can obscure the face. Use the flash in daylight hours to fill in shadows, for example, under your subject's chin or in architectural recesses. The flash range of most cameras is about 10 feet. If your subject is farther away, your flash photo may be too dark.

9. Take some pictures when your subject isn't posing. One trick is to stand behind a character to capture the spontaneous facial expressions of your child approaching and greeting the character. If you're alert – and lucky – you may get a photo of a first-time visitor's glimpse of Main Street and Cinderella Castle as he or she comes out from under the Train Station arches.

10. Include yourself! Ask strangers or cast members (especially PhotoPass cast members, see below) to take photos of you with your group. You can take self portraits, too. Use the delayed-action shutter button on

fancy cameras or just hold your disposable at arm's length.

11. Come up with a theme. For example, your kids trying on different hats or posing with their favorite characters or character merchandise. Try arranging your subjects in unique formations or with unusual props. Offbeat themes can be fun. My teenage son once took pictures of his friends coming out of each restroom in the World Showcase countries at Epcot!

12. Keep your cool. If your kids, pals, or significant other get tired of posing or waiting while you do elaborate set-ups, be content with snapping them in action for a while. Remember, those candid shots are often the most magical.

13. You can take your digital camera memory cards to photo centers around WDW to transfer photos to CD. Check the CD before erasing your memory card!

Disney's PhotoPass system

If you want your whole party to be in the photo, or you're not confident of your abilities as a photographer, make use of Disney's PhotoPass system. PhotoPass cast members are available in most "picture spot" areas. They'll take your photo (if you ask) and give you a coded plastic PhotoPass card. This personal card can be used for photos for the rest of your trip – and even for future visits. (Write down your card ID number in case you lose the card.) You can view your PhotoPass photos at www.disneyphotopass.com from a Photo Center in WDW or online from your resort, home, or wherever you choose. At WDW Photo Centers, cast members can advise you about modifying your photos (crop, add logos, etc.), and you can delete, modify, and email your photos online. So far, you haven't spent a penny! It goes almost without saying that you can purchase prints of the photos you like and have them mailed to you, but there is no obligation to do so.

If you like lots of photos, the PhotoPass CD costs about $125 (less if you order one before your visit at www.disneyphotopass.com/previsitcdplan. aspx). You can store up to 300 photos on the CD, which includes a copyright release that allows you to reprint your photos when you return home. You can purchase the CD at WDW (or online from www.disneyphotopass.com).

Note: It's a good idea to take conventional photos at WDW in case none of the PhotoPass ones appeal to you. If you ask them, the PhotoPass photographers will snap a photo of you with your camera, so that you can get yourself with the rest of your group in your own photos as well as in the PhotoPass shots.

Cinderella Castle, icon of the Magic Kingdom.

Chapter 2

The Magic Kingdom

One of the most visited theme parks on earth, the Magic Kingdom (MK) is the original place of magic and fantasy at Walt Disney World Resort, and it never disappoints its visitors. There's something here for everyone, although the parent will likely leave the MK with a list of favorite attractions different from the list of his or her teenager or tot.

Attractions Described and Rated

Main Street, U.S.A.

Guests pass through the MK entrance turnstiles, under the arches of the overhead *WDW Railroad* tracks, and into Town Square, which funnels folks onto Main Street. The Main Street shops open a half-hour before the rest of the Magic Kingdom and close up to an hour after the park's official closing time.

Main Street, U.S.A. is a re-creation of a small town American street of the early 1900s. As you enter **Town Square**, City Hall will be to your left, with a fire station and shop next door. At City Hall, you can pick up Guide-maps (in seven languages) and get information about dining, character greeting opportunities, lost and found, and other topics of interest from helpful

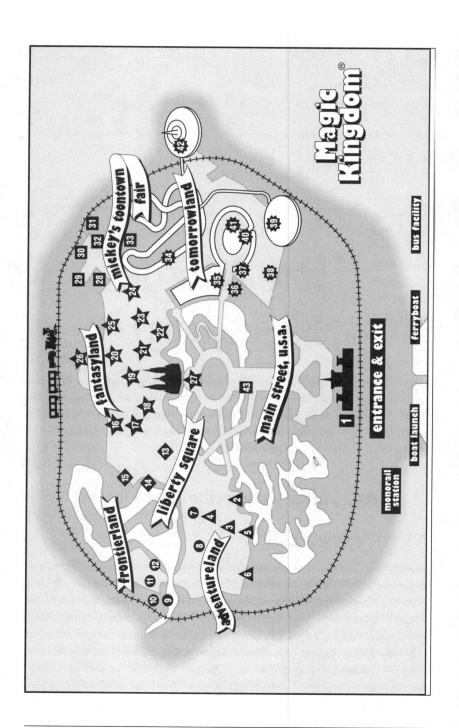

1 WDW Railroad, Entrance

adventureland

2 Swiss Family Treehouse

3 The Enchanted Tiki Room Under New Management

4 The Magic Carpets of Aladdin

5 Jungle Cruise

6 Pirates of the Caribbean

frontierland

7 Frontierland Shootin' Arcade

8 Country Bear Jamboree

9 Splash Mountain

10 WDW Railroad

11 Big Thunder Mountain Railroad

12 Raft to Tom Sawyer Island

liberty square

13 The Hall of Presidents

14 Liberty Square Riverboat

15 The Haunted Mansion

fantasyland

16 "it's a small world"

17 Peter Pan's Flight

18 Mickey's PhilharMagic

19 Cinderella's Golden Carrousel

20 Dumbo the Flying Elephant

21 Snow White's Scary Adventures

22 Fairytale Garden

23 The Many Adventures of Winnie the Pooh

24 Mad Tea Party

25 Pooh's Playful Spot

26 Ariel's Grotto

27 Castle Forecourt Stage

mickey's toontown fair

28 Minnie's Country House

29 Toontown Hall Of Fame

30 Mickey's Country House

31 WDW Railroad

32 Donald's Boat

33 The Barnstormer at Goofy's Wiseacre Farm

tomorrowland

34 Tomorrowland Indy Speedway

35 Stitch's Great Escape!

36 Monsters, Inc. Comedy Club

37 Buzz Lightyear's Space Ranger Spin

38 Galaxy Palace Theater

39 Walt Disney's Carousel of Progress

40 Tomorrowland Transit Authority

41 Astro Orbiter

42 Space Mountain

main street, u.s.a.

43 Guest Information Board

Disney cast members. Inside the Exposition Hall, next to Tony's Town Square Restaurant, you'll find interesting **interactive photography exhibits**.

Along Main Street are places to eat, shops, and an old-time barber shop. You can ride a fire engine or a horse-drawn trolley from Town Square down Main Street to the central hub in front of Cinderella Castle (and back to Town Square if you get off and queue up again).

Look up at the store windows above the street. The "proprietors" are people who were actually involved in the early Disney company or people Walt Disney used as "front names" so he could secretly buy at market value the property on which he built WDW. Look back at the window above the Plaza Ice Cream Parlor and find the name of the man himself, Walter E. Disney. Walt wanted guests to see his name as they were leaving the main part of the Magic Kingdom.

Walt Disney World Railroad

Rating: 🐭🐭
Type: Gentle train ride with audio tour guide
Time: About 20 minutes to circle the park
Steve says: A great way to relax and rest your legs

Take a pleasant, scenic journey around the MK, and keep your eyes and ears open for the Audio-Animatronics frontier and American Indian scenes along the way. The three stops are Main Street, Frontierland, and Mickey's Toontown Fair. You can ride for as long as you want. Be aware, though, that folks in the first car are occasionally subjected to engine exhaust fumes.

Adventureland

The flower-covered bridge to Adventureland suggests you're entering an exotic paradise. The environment here evokes the Pacific and Caribbean Islands with a sprinkling of Africa and Asia. Adventureland has shops, eating places, and attractions.

Swiss Family Treehouse

Rating: 🐭🐭🐭
Type: Outdoor walk-through exhibit
Time: 10 - 15 minutes, but dally longer if you wish
Steve says: Kids of all ages should have a treehouse like this!

You pass through the entry turnstile into an imaginative trail that winds up and through a replica of the treehouse built by the shipwrecked Robinson family. It's fun to visually explore the fascinating details of the various "rooms" of the house. Try to follow the intricate water delivery system throughout the huge tree.

Note: If you want to linger at sights in the *Swiss Family Treehouse*, move to the side of the walkway and let those behind you pass by.

The Magic Carpets of Aladdin

Rating: ♥♥
Type: Flying, steerable carpets
Time: Less than 2 minutes
Steve says: Eye-pleasing circle ride

Colorful, four-seater carpets whiz around in lofty circles. However, these magical carpets have a bit more zing than other circle rides: the two riders in the front control vertical movement, while the two rear riders can tilt the carpet nose up or nose down. It's rather like sitting on a real flying carpet! Fly high to avoid the water-squirting camel.

The Enchanted Tiki Room – Under New Management

Rating: ♥♥
Type: Musical show with singing robotic birds
Time: 16 minutes
Steve says: The Tiki Goddess can frighten some young children

The first Disney Audio-Animatronics attraction, this amusing show takes place above your head as you sit in a dark, cool room. The attraction was updated to add Iago (from *Aladdin*) and Zazu (from *The Lion King*) to the veteran choir of brightly colored birds. Even the flowers and tiki statues sing!

Note: Ask a cast member where to sit during the show to catch a feather from an overhead bird (usually about two-thirds down the first row on the left as you enter).

Jungle Cruise

Rating: ♥♥♥♥
Type: Outdoor boat tour
Time: 9 - 10 minutes
Steve says: Fun for all; the boat skipper has everyone smiling

A classic Disney attraction, *Jungle Cruise* takes you gently down the great jungle rivers of the earth. Along the way, you pass Audio-Animatronics elephants, hippos, and other animals. The boat skipper's jokes are corny yet still amusing and seem perfectly in tune with the ride. Be sure to marvel at the "back side of water."

Tip: After the early morning, the lines at *Jungle Cruise* are usually long for the rest of the day, especially during busy seasons.

At the exit is **Shrunken Ned's Junior Jungle Boats**, which are miniature boats navigated by your remote control around a pond studded with various jungle obstacles. They're not free; you have to buy a $1.00 token to make the boats operate for about two minutes.

Tip: Save *Shrunken Ned's* for downtime. It's fun but if you've only one day in the MK, you'll want to spend it experiencing more exciting attractions.

Pirates of the Caribbean

Rating: 🐭🐭🐭🐭🐭

Type: Indoor boat ride past pirate scenes

Time: About 8 minutes

Steve says: A classic attraction; not scary except for one small boat drop

The queue area and the boat ride take you back in time to pirates searching for island treasures. Along the right entrance queue, notice the skeletons of pirates who died while playing chess; the game was a stalemate! Your boat initially passes pirate skeletons, then swooshes down a mild water drop back to the time when those pirates were alive and pillaging. You float by incredibly detailed sets and Audio-Animatronics figures as the pirates invade and conquer an island town. Captain Jack Sparrow and his nemesis Barbossa (from the Disney *Pirates* movies) make appearances along the way; they're racing to find the treasure at the end of the ride! Look for the hairy pirate leg dangling from a bridge above you and the jail-door lock shaped like Mickey Mouse's head. The waiting lines generally move quickly, but even this ride can be a long wait during afternoons in busy seasons.

Frontierland

Frontierland's main thoroughfare takes you back in time to the days of the Old West. The frontier ambiance is so realistic, a Western movie could be filmed here! Frontierland has its own unique shops and eating places.

Note: The *Walt Disney World Railroad* makes one of its three stops in Frontierland. The station is right by *Splash Mountain*.

Country Bear Jamboree

Rating: 🐭🐭🐭

Type: Indoor theater show with singing bears

Time: 15 minutes

Steve says: Toe-tapping country-hillbilly style music

These Audio-Animatronics bears bring smiles to just about everyone as they sing a series of humorous country and hillbilly songs from a stage facing the theater. Many in the audience will clap and sing along. A special holiday show usually runs for several weeks during the Christmas season.

Frontierland Shootin' Arcade

Rating: ♥♥
Type: Shooting gallery
Time: A few minutes per session
Steve says: A fun diversion

This arcade will entertain children and teenagers until they run short of money. (There is a $1.00 charge for every 35 shots.) The guns shoot infrared beams at targets scattered around an Old West town. Expect humorous, unique visual and sometimes auditory effects (tombstones that rise up or spin, a howling coyote, a galloping ghost rider in the sky) as your rifle scores direct hits on the hapless bull's-eyes.

Splash Mountain

Rating: ♥♥♥♥♥
Type: Log flume ride through a mountain
Time: 10 - 11 minutes
Steve says: A fun feast for the eyes and ears and a gut check
                 for the stomach

This attraction is the favorite of some folks. Hollowed-out log boats take you on a more than half-mile journey inside the mountain and past riverside scenes that showcase singing and talking Audio-Animatronics characters from the Disney movie *Song of the South*. Brer Fox chases Brer Rabbit to the "Laughing Place," while other Brer characters regale you with song as you float by. Several small drops prepare you for the big 52-foot drop into a "briar patch" (the "Laughing Place") near the end of the ride.

On the way down the big drop, you'll be photographed, and you can check out the picture at the end of the ride. You may want to buy your picture at least once, since these *Splash Mountain* photos are some of the best mementos of WDW vacations.

Tip: To enhance the thrill of the drop, some riders raise their arms straight up on the way down. Unfortunately, these high hands can block the faces of riders in the seats behind them. If you sense a hand raised in front of you, tilt left in your seat before the flash to preserve your frightened mug for posterity.

Splash Mountain's big drop often gets riders wet, especially those in the front seat. Riders on the right side of the boat will also frequently get wet during the journey. Since the boat seats are usually moist, you'll notice that just about everyone exiting in front of you will have a damp derriere!

Note: See "The Dash to Splash," page 91, for insider directions on the fastest way to get to *Splash Mountain* at opening time.

Height restriction: Kids must be 40" or taller to ride.

Big Thunder Mountain Railroad

Rating: ❤❤❤❤

Type: Outdoor roller coaster

Time: 3 - 4 minutes

Steve says: Moderately fast coaster with dips and turns, no loops

BTMR is a roller coaster that winds and dips around and through a big mountain past various mining and desert scenes, including mountain animals, falling rocks, and geysers. The sights from the train are humorous and entertaining. The roller coaster ride itself is tame for teenagers, but many older folks will find it jarring enough. The experience is more thrilling if you hold your arms straight up during drops and turns. You can study the flooded mining town scene at a more leisurely pace from the *WDW Railroad* train as it passes by Big Thunder Mountain.

Height restriction: Kids must be 40" or taller to ride.

Tom Sawyer Island

Rating: ❤❤❤

Type: Elaborate outdoor playground

Time: As long as you want, minimum 20 minutes

Steve says: A place where kids and adults become excited explorers

Take a raft over to *Tom Sawyer Island* and enter the world of Mark Twain's famous character. This forested island has caves, bridges, a frontier fort, winding trails, and other interesting discoveries. Don't miss the escape tunnel from the back of the fort. If you're flagging a bit in the early afternoon, head over to Aunt Polly's Dockside Inn (open seasonally) for rest and refreshment while the youngsters explore the island. *Tom Sawyer Island* closes in the early evening.

Liberty Square

This small but beautiful section of the park re-creates colonial America at the time of the Revolutionary War. In the middle of Liberty Square, you'll find the Liberty Tree. This large spreading live oak (it is real) has 13 lanterns hanging from its branches, representing the 13 original colonies. You'll also see a replica of the cracked Liberty Bell (the original is in Independence National Historical Park in downtown Philadelphia). Liberty Square has its own shops and eateries, including the moderately priced Liberty Tree Tavern.

The Hall of Presidents

Rating: 🐭🐭🐭
Type: Indoor historical theater show
Time: 23 minutes
Steve says: Moving and patriotic; a fitting attraction for Liberty Square

The first part of the show is a patriotic movie-screen review of important moments in American history. The show ends with an impressive on-stage presentation of all the U.S. presidents (thanks to Audio-Animatronics). Each president responds with a nod as his name is called and, during the roll call, the presidents act almost like real people: they fidget and even whisper to each other! Their clothes and furniture are historically accurate, so the history buffs in the audience can get deeply absorbed in the details. Your kids might even learn something. But don't use the word "educational" in front of them beforehand or they might want to skip this attraction. The show starts every 30 minutes, usually on the hour and the half-hour.

Liberty Square Riverboat

Rating: 🐭🐭🐭
Type: Outdoor gentle boat ride
Time: 16 - 18 minutes
Steve says: A relaxing tour around *Tom Sawyer Island*

This paddle-wheel steamboat, called the **Liberty Belle**, tracks through the half-mile long Rivers of America on an underwater rail. The journey is laid-back and pleasant, and the boat passes a variety of frontier and Old West scenes on the riverbanks. Stand at the front or rear of the boat toward the center on any level for the best view of both riverbanks. Listen to the recorded spiel and learn some river lore of the American past, like the meaning of "mark twain": two fathoms or twelve feet deep ("mark one" is one fathom). "Mark twain" is deep enough for safe passage for these riverboats. You'll also hear some humorous aphorisms from famed writer Mark Twain himself.

Note: You won't hear the spiel as well if you stand at the rear of the boat on the lower level near the paddle wheel; the noise of the wheel muffles the speaker.

The "Liberty Belle" usually leaves the dock on the hour and the half-hour. This attraction sometimes closes at dusk.

The Haunted Mansion

Rating: ♥♥♥♥

Type: "Dark ride" through a haunted house

Time: About 9 minutes

Steve says: Not scary, except for small children

Inside this imposing old house, Disney visits Halloween tongue-in-cheek. Your lighthearted journey begins in a dark room where the walls and pictures stretch. (Actually, the ceiling moves up!) Then you step onto a "doom buggy" which takes you past all manner of ghosts and spooky (but humorous) special effects, such as a banquet hall with dancing ghosts and a cemetery where the dead come alive and drink tea. In fact, there's so much to see, it's difficult to take it all in on just one ride through. Look for the "hidden Mickey" in the arrangement of dishes in one of the individual place settings on the large dinner table, and read a few of the humorous tombstone epitaphs on the left side of the walkway on your way in or out. Just before the mansion entrance doors, a lady on a tombstone opens her eyes every few minutes! After you exit, marvel at the pet cemetery outside on your left.

Fantasyland

An imaginative and dreamy place, Fantasyland is what some people conjure up when they think of the Magic Kingdom. This land sits just behind Cinderella Castle, so it's easy to see why some folks are drawn to Fantasyland as one of their first stops. It has its own unique shops and places to grab a bite.

Cinderella Castle

There's no ride in the Castle, but Cinderella's Royal Table (a restaurant) is here. While walking through the Castle, note the beautiful mural along the walls that tells the Cinderella story. (One stepsister's face is red with anger, while the other's is green with envy.) Before the evening fireworks, an acrobatic woman performs **Tinker Bell's Flight** as she "floats" down a wire stretching from a high point on Cinderella Castle to a rooftop in Tomorrowland (weather and wind permitting).

"it's a small world"

Rating: ♥♥♥

Type: Indoor boat ride

Time: 11 - 12 minutes

Steve says: A family favorite; try to guess the different cultures

Inside a cool and restful building, a boat floats you gently past singing and dancing dolls representing the dress and culture of many nations of the Earth. You'll sing along with German oompah bands, scarlet-garbed Tower of London guards, Japanese kite fliers, Don Quixote tilting at windmills, and much more. The melodic theme song is soothing and easily learned, and repetitive enough that it will probably remain locked in your subconscious for the rest of your life. This ride is a good choice if you're feeling hot and need a rest because the lines are often short and the boats load quickly.

Peter Pan's Flight

Rating: ♥♥♥♥
Type: "Dark ride" in suspended boats
Time: 3 - 4 minutes
Steve says: A classic theme ride

This short indoor flight in soaring ships is a perennial favorite of many guests, including me. A sprinkling of pixie dust allows you to fly from Wendy's house out over London (the cars on the streets far below really move), past the Big Ben clock, and then to Never Land. The atmosphere is absorbing and delightful as Peter Pan and his friends eventually vanquish Captain Hook and his pirates.

Mickey's PhilharMagic

Rating: ♥♥♥♥
Type: 3-D theater show
Time: About 12 minutes
Steve says: Delightful animated graphics

Mickey's PhilharMagic stars Donald Duck, Mickey Mouse, and other Disney characters. The show is a "3-D film spectacular" complete with in-theater effects, a 150-foot wide screen, and plenty of Disney music. Donald suddenly finds himself leading the PhilharMagic orchestra, but, as you might expect with Donald at the podium, things quickly spiral out of control!

Tip: Avoid the last two rows of the theater; the view isn't as good there.

Cinderella's Golden Carrousel

Rating: ♥
Type: Carousel ride
Time: 2 - 3 minutes
Steve says: Slow loader; not worth a long wait

Every horse is different on this colorful and intricate merry-go-round. Notice the Cinderella story pictures above the horses. The ride is fun, but the real beauty is in the details of the carousel itself.

Dumbo the Flying Elephant

Rating: 🐭🐭 for most visitors
🐭🐭🐭🐭🐭 for young children

Type: Flying, steerable elephants

Time: About 2 minutes

Steve says: A must for young children

Most folks have been on rides of this type at local carnivals and fairs. However, this circular ride in Disney elephant vehicles is frequently represented in pictures of the Magic Kingdom, and it's the favorite ride of many young children who visit WDW. Your joystick controls the height of the elephant vehicle.

Note: The lines are long all day, except early in the morning just after the park opens. Even if the queue is long, however, you will be giving your child a long-lasting and cherished memory by waiting patiently for your turn to fly with Dumbo.

Ariel's Grotto

Rating: 🐭

Type: Elaborate character greeting area and water playground

Time: About 1 minute, once you get to her

Steve says: Fun for little ones; memorable photo for your album

This small area tucked away at the back of Fantasyland is a combination spurting water playground and greeting area for an autograph and picture with Ariel, the mermaid. WDW has placed several of these **interactive fountains** around the theme parks since the first one, near Epcot's central walkway, became an instant hit. Each consists of a soft matted area with holes from which water spurts randomly to various heights and shapes. It's delightful to observe children completely lose themselves in innocent play here as they dart in and out among the water spurts. In fact, these playgrounds are magnets for young children. If you turn your head for only a second as you and your child approach the area, your young one will be dripping wet before you can utter a sound.

Get in line whenever you want to meet Ariel.

Snow White's Scary Adventures

Rating: 🐭🐭🐭

Type: "Dark ride"

Time: 2 - 3 minutes

Steve says: Revisit some classic characters

The Dwarves' diamond mine car takes you winding along a track past indoor scenes of Snow White in peril. The Dwarves try to help as Snow White runs from the evil Queen. The wicked Witch pops out several times and frightens some young children, but the story ends happily as you wave goodbye to Snow White and the Prince. Nevertheless, some youngsters remember only the scary Witch.

Caution: If you're concerned about your child's reaction, please prepare him or her before the ride or skip it altogether; it may not be worth the risk of spoiling the rest of your day at the Magic Kingdom.

The Many Adventures of Winnie the Pooh

Rating: ♥♥♥♥
Type: "Dark ride"
Time: 4 - 5 minutes
Steve says: A must ride for children; fun for adults, too

Your "Hunny Pot" vehicle moves indoors through scenes from *Winnie the Pooh* stories. You meet Pooh, Kanga, Roo, and Owl coping with the wind on a "Blustery Day," then your car bounces along with Tigger deeper into the Hundred Acre Wood. The next scene is the inside of Pooh's house, where you enter Pooh's dream about Heffalumps and Woozles. Your "Hunny Pot" bobs through the "Floody Place," where Piglet is saved from going over a waterfall. Final scenes are the "Hero Party" with Pooh's friends, then Christopher Robin and Pooh skipping into the horizon. The attraction is happy and uplifting and is accompanied by classic *Winnie the Pooh* music.

Mad Tea Party

Rating: ♥♥
Type: Outdoor spinning ride
Time: About 2 minutes
Steve says: A favorite for teenagers (and for adults who like to whirl)

These teacups spin you as the entire floor rotates. You can spin even faster by turning the wheel at the center of the teacup. When the ride stops, you may feel like the dizzy mouse that periodically pops out of the teacup at the center of the ride.

Pooh's Playful Spot

Rating: ♥
Type: Outdoor playground
Time: As long as you want

Steve says: Not as elaborate as other WDW kid's playgrounds

Pooh's Playful Spot is a good place to watch your kids let off some steam, although this small grotto can get hot in the afternoon. You can play inside the large tree that towers over the grotto.

Mickey's Toontown Fair

This small, colorful land is truly a haven for kids. They can meet Mickey here (as well as a slew of other characters), tour Mickey's and Minnie's houses, ride a cool kiddies' roller coaster, and get wet in *Donald Duck's Boat*. You can shop at the *Toontown Hall of Fame* tent and then quell the munchies with a stop at the snack area. Your kids can even get their faces painted for about $8 to $10 and up. (Face painting is offered at several locations around WDW.)

To get to Mickey's Toontown Fair, ride the *Walt Disney World Railroad* or walk the short path from Fantasyland or the little-used path from the side of the Tomorrowland Arcade.

Minnie's Country House

Rating: ❤❤❤

Type: Walk-through house exhibit

Time: 5 - 10 minutes, sometimes longer for young children

Steve says: Worth a visit no matter what your age

Walk at your own pace through this wonderfully detailed house, filled with interesting pictures and knickknacks. Her kitchen is really cool, especially after you open the refrigerator door and feel the frosty air.

Toontown Hall of Fame

Rating: ❤❤

Type: Indoor area for meeting characters

Time: Up to 10 minutes for each group greeting (not counting the time waiting in line)

Steve says: A great place for adding to the autograph books, but it can be time-consuming

Located between Mickey's and Minnie's houses, this big tent is where you and your kids can meet a bunch of characters who cluster at the end of three different queues. For example, one recent grouping had classic Disney characters in one room (Minnie Mouse, Goofy, Pluto, Chip 'n' Dale, Daisy Duck, Donald Duck, Uncle Scrooge or Roger Rabbit), Winnie the Pooh and pals in a second room (Tigger, Piglet, and Winnie), and Disney princesses

(Snow White, Aurora, Belle, Ariel, etc.) in the third room.

Note: Only three characters may be present at any given time, and one or more change(s) every half hour.

You will be ushered into the room with 10 to 15 other guests for about a 10-minute visit with the characters. You have to queue up all over again for each of the other rooms.

Mickey's Country House

Rating:	❤❤❤
Type:	Walk-through house exhibit
Time:	About 10 minutes. Add 10 - 30 minutes (depending on the crowd) if you want to meet Mickey Mouse in the Judge's Tent out back
Steve says:	Mickey's home is fun for all ages, but unless the waiting line at the Judge's Tent is short, it's easier to meet Mickey at one of his character meals.

Walk through Mickey's house and revel in the detail. The Imagineers must've had great fun designing these rooms, along with the backyard and garage. Mickey's friends are still working at remodeling the kitchen, which is quite a mess. Don't miss Pluto's doghouse in the back, and note that the vegetables in the garden magically grow Mickey ears! The sidewalk behind the house leads to **Mickey's Judge's Tent**, where you and your children can line up and meet the Main Mouse in person.

Tip: If you don't want to enter the Judge's Tent, exit through Mickey's garage.

Donald's Boat

Rating:	❤❤
Type:	Spurting water playground
Time:	As long as you want; your kids may not want to leave
Steve says:	Your kids will get wet

Like *Ariel's Grotto*, this spurting fountain playground provides a wet antidote to hot afternoons. Kids love to explore the boat while trying in vain to dodge the random spurts from the sides of the leaky vessel.

The Barnstormer at Goofy's Wiseacre Farm

Rating:	❤❤❤
Type:	Short, outdoor roller coaster for kids
Time:	Less than one minute
Steve says:	Adults enjoy this one, too

The Barnstormer roller coaster zips you up and around, then through the walls of Goofy's barn. The ride is short but fun, especially for kids.

Height restriction: Children less than 35" tall cannot ride.

Tomorrowland

This glistening, futuristic land should rightfully be entered from above, preferably along a beam of light from a hovering spaceship. If you don't command such a vehicle, stand in the middle of Tomorrowland, near the *Astro Orbiter* ride, and turn slowly around. You'll feel as if you are on an old sci-fi movie set. Tomorrowland, colorful during the day, is especially striking after dark with its bright neon lights. Like the MK's other lands, it has its own themed shops and eating places.

Tomorrowland Indy Speedway

Rating:	🐭🐭
Type:	Outdoor miniature raceway
Time:	4 - 5 minutes
Steve says:	Great fun for children, but be wary; you can get rammed from behind

Slow-moving gasoline-powered miniature cars putter over guide rails along a winding track. The cars are painted and decorated to resemble racing cars. Preschool and elementary school children enjoy this ride, and the fun is enhanced by the loud car engine noises. Teens and adults find it less exciting.

Height restriction: You have to be 52" or taller to drive by yourself.

Stitch's Great Escape!

Rating:	🐭🐭
Type:	Indoor special effects fun-fest
Time:	12 minutes (not counting a 5 - 6 minute pre-show)
Steve says:	A more lighthearted show in contrast to its predecessor, the gruesome *Alien Encounter*

The Galactic federation captures "Experiment 626" (whom we know as Stitch). During the show, Stitch escapes his containment cell in the middle of the theater and has fun with the audience. You'll hear and feel Stitch up close and personal! Unfortunately, this attraction is not particularly kid-friendly. In fact, children of all ages, especially those age 6 and under, can find it frightening. And if you haven't seen the movie or TV series, *Lilo and Stitch*, you may not "get" the Stitch character.

Height restriction: Kids have to be at least 40" tall to see Stitch here.

Monsters, Inc. Laugh Floor

Rating: ♥♥♥♥
Type: Animated interactive show
Time: About 15 minutes
Steve says: Clean comedy, well done!

One-eyed Mike Wazowski from the *Monsters, Inc.* movie is the host for a comedy show. He hopes to funnel the energy from the audience's laughter (including yours) to power his city of Monstropolis. So feel free to hold your belly and let your laughs ring out; the monsters will appreciate it!

Note: The monsters on screen react to changing audiences, so no show is exactly like the next.

Buzz Lightyear's Space Ranger Spin

Rating: ♥♥♥♥
Type: Indoor, interactive track ride
Time: About 5 minutes
Steve says: Great fun for all ages

This indoor ride is more interactive than most: you can turn and even spin your car and shoot simulated laser guns at multiple targets. Your mission is to help Buzz Lightyear save the universe from the villainous Emperor Zurg and his warriors. At the end of the ride, your total shooting score is displayed in front of you on the dashboard. The cars seat two, and your fellow soldier's shooting score is tallied separately from yours.

Tip 1: To maximize your score, hold down the firing button while you turn the laser gun and car for the best target angles.

Tip 2: As you pass the orange robot in the first room, turn your car around and fire at the targets on his arms and chest. One of them is worth 100,000 points!

Walt Disney's Carousel of Progress

Rating: ♥♥♥
Type: Indoor theater show with changing tableaus
Time: About 18 minutes
Steve says: Especially interesting for adults

This attraction has endured well. You sit in a comfortable indoor theater which revolves around stage sets of an Audio-Animatronics family as they grow older gracefully. The theme here is progress, especially the evolution of the American home with its ever more complicated appliances and entertainment gadgets. The scenes take you from the early part of the 20th century all the way forward to the computer age. The 1950s' kitchen is reminiscent of the 50's Prime Time Café at Disney's Hollywood Studios. As at *The Hall of Presidents*, your kids might actually learn something here while having fun!

Note: Carousel of Progress is open seasonally, typically during busy periods, and it may close early (consult your Times Guide).

Tomorrowland Transit Authority

Rating: ♥♥
Type: Gentle tram ride
Time: 10 - 12 minutes
Steve says: A unique view of Tomorrowland from above

A slow-moving tram takes you on a restful, scenic journey around Tomorrowland, both outdoors and inside the various attraction buildings. The overhead spiel during the ride is entertaining. There's rarely a long wait, so this is a good bet during hot or crowded times of the day.

Tip: The rear seats provide the best vantage.

Astro Orbiter

Rating: ♥♥♥
Type: Flying, steerable rockets
Time: Less than 2 minutes
Steve says: Grand panoramic view over the Magic Kingdom

You ride an elevator up to the loading platform, then climb into a small rocket that flies you in circles high in the air. It's a futuristic *Dumbo* ride, as a control stick allows you to select and adjust the height of your rocket. The view from the ride is a large part of the fun. Be prepared to get dizzy, unless you're accustomed to rides that move in rapid circles.

Space Mountain

Rating: ♥♥♥♥♥
Type: Indoor roller coaster
Time: About 3 minutes
Steve says: Exhilarating, worth riding again and again

This roller coaster ride in the dark is the favorite attraction of many visitors to the Magic Kingdom. The long entrance path inside the futuristic cone-shaped building winds past visual effects about astronomy that set the mood for your blastoff into space. The coaster ride is filled with dips and spiraling turns (no loops), as asteroids whiz by overhead. If you can hold your gaze upwards long enough, you'll spot galaxies and other space matter moving through the blackness. *Space Mountain* is not as terrifying as well-known roller coasters at other theme parks, but the ride is great fun if your neck, back, and inner ear are up to it.

Height restriction: Kids have to be 44" or taller to ride.

Note: See "The Race to Space," page 90, for insider tips on the fastest way to get to *Space Mountain* first thing in the morning.

Special Attractions

Parades. The Magic Kingdom usually offers two parades, one in the afternoon and, on most days, another in the evening. In busy seasons, it adds a second evening parade. Different characters appear in the afternoon and evening, so parade fans will want to catch both.

Fireworks. Weather permitting, most evenings end with **Wishes**, a fireworks display that offers a magical conclusion to your day in the MK.

Attractions with Minimal Waits (Usually)

- *Swiss Family Treehouse.* On crowded days, you may have a wait.
- *The Enchanted Tiki Room.* The wait is usually the time until the next show, except on really crowded days.
- *Shrunken Ned's Junior Jungle Boats.* You may have to wait for the next available remote control stand. It costs money to play – $1 per short session.
- *Frontierland Shootin' Arcade.* You may have to wait a short time for the next available gun. Again, the cost is $1 per short round.
- *The Hall of Presidents.* The wait is usually the time until the next show, except on very crowded days.
- *Liberty Square Riverboat.* The wait is usually the time until the next "voyage."
- *"it's a small world."* On really crowded days, you may have a wait.
- *Donald's Boat.* This interactive fountain usually has room for a few more young guests.
- *Walt Disney's Carousel of Progress.* You usually wait until the next show.
- *Tomorrowland Transit Authority.* If this ride has a wait, chances are the entire park is very crowded.

Attractions That May Frighten Children

Remember that "switching off' is available at some of these attractions; see *Chapter One*, "Good Things to Know About," and the Family touring plans, in the Touring section that follows "Hidden Mickeys," below.

- *The Enchanted Tiki Room.* The Tiki Goddess and some loud special effects may frighten toddlers.
- *Pirates of the Caribbean.* May frighten toddlers.
- *Splash Mountain.* The drop at the end of this ride can frighten anyone. Switching off is available.
- *Big Thunder Mountain Railroad.* This roller coaster is fast enough to frighten children and seniors. Switching off is available.
- *The Haunted Mansion.* The mansion's dark ambiance may frighten young children.
- *Snow White's Scary Adventures.* This ride has a history of frightening preschoolers.
- *The Barnstormer at Goofy's Wiseacre Farm.* This zippy roller coaster can frighten young children.
- *Stitch's Great Escape!* The special sound and tactile effects in the show may spook young children.
- *Space Mountain.* Intense roller coaster in the dark can frighten anyone. Switching off is available.
- *Mad Tea Party.* Can cause motion sickness in anyone.

Least Crowded Restrooms

- The restrooms to the left off Main Street in a small alcove between Casey's Corner and The Crystal Palace restaurant.
- The restrooms on the right side of *Pirates of the Caribbean.*

Especially Attractive at Night

- *Big Thunder Mountain Railroad*
- *Cinderella's Golden Carrousel*
- *Astro Orbiter*

Resting Places

- The quiet and shady park in Liberty Square behind Ye Olde Christmas Shoppe.
- The benches in the small alcove to the right of the entrance to *Pirates of the Caribbean*.
- The benches under the shed at the edge of the rose garden between the two entrance bridges to Tomorrowland.
- The chairs at the end of the cul-de-sac to the right, halfway down Main Street as you're entering the park.
- The small theater at the back of Town Square Exposition Hall.

Hidden Mickeys

Here are just a few of the hidden Mickeys you may want to look for in the Magic Kingdom:

- *"it's a small world."* As you are floating through the tropical segment, look up and find the hanging vines that curve down from the ceiling. One of the vines has leaves shaped like a silhouette of Mickey's head, with the round head and two round ears.
- *The Haunted Mansion.* As you are passing by the ghostly dining room, observe the left end of the large banquet table below. One of the place settings (a plate and two small dishes) is usually arranged like a silhouette of Mickey's head.
- *Splash Mountain.* Toward the end of the ride after the big drop, look to your right as you float toward the riverboat with singing fowl. A white cloud on the wall is shaped like Mickey reclining on his back with his head on the right. You can also see this Hidden Mickey from the *WDW Railroad* train as it passes by.
- *Walt Disney's Carousel of Progress.* In the last scene, a pepper grinder on the kitchen counter has Mickey ears.
- *Tomorrowland Transit Authority.* Toward the end of the ride, your car will pass a woman getting her hair done. Her belt buckle sports a Mickey head.

Touring
The Magic Kingdom

Getting to the Magic Kingdom can be a less than magical experience, especially if you are staying off property and want to arrive early, as I recommend. The following tips will help you arrive with minimal frustration. Once you're there, follow the appropriate touring plan for a hassle-free visit.

Note: The park opens an hour early to Disney property guests for "Extra Magic Hours" (EMH; see *Chapter One*) at least one day a week. By the time it opens to other visitors on these Early Entry EMH days, it is already crowded. I strongly advise visiting on another day of the week if you are not eligible for Early Entry or choose not to take advantage of it.

Getting to the entrance turnstiles if you are staying on property

Guests staying on Disney property have a major advantage over those staying elsewhere because they can take Disney transport directly from their hotels to the MK turnstiles. Grand Floridian and Polynesian Resort guests can hop a resort monorail or a boat (the boats are usually slower), while guests of the Contemporary Resort can take a resort monorail or a special walkway to the Magic Kingdom; the walk takes about 10 minutes. The other Disney properties (except Fort Wilderness and the Wilderness Lodge) provide bus service directly to the entrance turnstiles (see "Caution," below). Fort Wilderness and the Wilderness Lodge provide boat service to the entrance turnstiles but bus service only to the Transportation and Ticket Center (TTC) across the Seven Seas Lagoon from the MK. Ask your hotel Lobby Concierge how long it will take you to get to the Magic Kingdom entrance.

Caution: WDW buses that arrive prior to one hour before the park's official opening time will drop you at the Transportation and Ticket Center (TTC), where you will be stuck waiting with all the off-property guests for the monorail and ferry to begin running. Ask the bus driver where you will be dropped before you board to avoid any unpleasant surprises.

Getting to the entrance turnstiles
if you are staying off property

You cannot go directly to the turnstiles, but will enter the MK by way of the Transportation and Ticket Center (TTC), where the parking lot is located. Once you've parked, you will hop a tram to the boarding area for transport to the MK. Your choices are the express monorail or the ferryboat. (Note that the ferries don't always operate in the afternoons during slower times of the year.) The monorail is a few minutes faster (the trip takes four to five minutes), but it often has a longer wait than the ferry (which takes six to seven minutes). If the monorail entry ramp is packed with people, take the ferry if it is in or approaching the dock. Also take the ferry if a magical approach is more important to you than a speedy one. Budget a total of 15 to 25 minutes for your entire trip from parking lot to entrance turnstiles.

In the early morning hours when you're striving to arrive early, the ferries and express monorail from the TTC often do not even begin to operate until 30 minutes before the official opening time. That happens to be about when the Magic Kingdom begins to admit guests at the entry turnstiles! Message: WDW clearly favors its resort guests at times like these.

Insider tip #1: During slow seasons, guests staying off property can sometimes gain the Disney resort-guest advantage. Drive early to the Contemporary or another monorail resort and tell the parking lot guard that you're having breakfast at the hotel. Then eat an early breakfast (especially if you haven't eaten already), leave your car in the lot, and walk (about 10 minutes from the Contemporary) or ride the hotel monorail (budget 10 to 25 minutes) to the MK entrance. If you decide to try this strategy, be sure to make dining reservations before your arrival. WDW hotel parking areas are gated to keep out non-guests. The guard may check your name against the restaurant's reservations list before letting you in. Don't be too disappointed if you can't get in. WDW employees (cast members) who are off duty and visiting the Magic Kingdom often park their cars in a lot at the Contemporary Resort to the left of the guard gate and close to the walkway to the Magic Kingdom. During busy periods, the guard turns them away from this lot, presumably to keep it clear for Contemporary Resort guest use.

Another option for off-property guests is the bus. Some public and hotel shuttle buses make regular runs to the TTC during MK operating hours.

Insider tip #2: If your admission ticket allows you to switch from one WDW theme park to another without penalty and you'd like to combine a morning visit to the Magic Kingdom with an afternoon visit to Epcot, you have another transportation option. Park your car in the morning at Epcot. Then take the Epcot monorail to and from the MK via the TTC. Allow about 20 to 30 minutes one way. You'll save yourself the considerable hassle of having to retrieve your car from the MK parking lot and re-park it at Epcot. And when you leave for the day, your car will probably be more conveniently located than it would have been had you parked it at Epcot in mid afternoon.

How early should you arrive?

Whatever your mode of transport, plan to arrive early in the day, preferably before opening time, so that you can experience the major rides and attractions with minimal waits. If you are a Disney property guest, plan to arrive at the entrance turnstiles about 30 minutes before the official opening time (or at least 75 minutes ahead if you're an EMH Early Entry guest). If you're not staying on Disney property, plan to arrive at the Transportation and Ticket Center 50 to 60 minutes before the official opening time if you already have your admission tickets, and an hour or more before the official opening time if you have to purchase your tickets. If you follow this advice, you will be able to ride at least two and possibly four or more popular attractions before the lines become long. But don't despair if you aren't an early riser; the touring plans below can be picked up any time of the day. Just be aware that you will have to make some hard choices about what to skip.

Note: If you are visiting on or near a major holiday, add 30 minutes to each of the above times.

Tip: If you have young children, make a dining reservation (on a non early-entry day) in the MK for breakfast at 8 a.m., then enter Fantasyland with the touring plan at 9 a.m. when the park opens.

Entering the Magic Kingdom

After passing through the security checkpoint, survey all the entrance turnstiles on the left and right sides to spot the shortest lines. A turnstile is "green" (admitting guests) if a cast member is standing next to it. If the morning lines are long at all entrance turnstiles, line up in an outside queue. Sometimes an attendant will open up a nearby turnstile at the last minute, and you may be positioned to move with other excited guests to the new and shorter queue.

Have your admission ticket ready (plus your hotel room key for Early Entry privileges). If you don't have a park Guidemap and Times Guide yet (they are available at the WDW hotels), pick them up as soon as you can.

Sometimes they are piled on the entry turnstiles for entering guests, or pluck one from a container on the walls beneath the arched walkways under the Main Street train station. Otherwise, you can pick them up at City Hall to the left of Town Square or at the counters of the stores and outside merchandise stands along Main Street.

What you ride first will depend on your interests. I recommend *Dumbo the Flying Elephant* for parties with preschoolers (although older children may also place this ride high on their lists). For others, I recommend *Space Mountain* or *Splash Mountain*. If it's a tie between *Mountains*, head for *Space Mountain* first.

Getting to the 'Mountains'

Two fascinating rituals occur each morning at the Magic Kingdom as visitors to the MK attempt to be first in line at two of the park's most popular rides, *Space Mountain* and *Splash Mountain*. When the park opens on non Early Entry days (usually 30 minutes before the official opening time), or if you arrive near the official opening time on any day, you're admitted through the entrance turnstiles and onto Main Street. The rest of the park is roped off and will not admit guests until the official opening time. Some otherwise sane folks gather at the rope at the end of Main Street with impatient anticipation of that exhilarating first-of-the-morning ride on *Space Mountain*. Others line up at the ropes to Adventureland giddy with anticipation of the *Splash Mountain* experience. By the time the overhead welcoming announcements end and the hapless Disney cast members begin to pull the ropes back, the nervous excitement of the early morning crowd has reached a fever pitch.

Now there's no holding back. The stampede that ensues can be unstoppable, despite Disney's best intentions. Make no mistake about it, these are no walks in the park. In fact, if you are walking to either *Mountain*, prepare to get bumped and jostled. Parents with strollers, beware! Wild-eyed and breathless *Mountain* junkies of most ages (anyone who can jog or run) will be hurtling by you. For the safety of everyone, parents with strollers or those in wheelchairs should stay at the fringes of the frantic rush. On a crowded day, inadvertent jostles and sometimes collisions between people are not unusual. Folks may drop sunglasses or caps, stop to retrieve them, and risk a rugby-style encounter from behind.

These morning races are unique and memorable, and you can enjoy them firsthand even if you just walk fast. However, don't overexert yourself in the excitement. You have a long fun day ahead; don't spoil it with an untimely injury or exhaustion. Even if you are not among the first in line, you won't have a very long wait if you head to the *Mountain* of your choice first thing.

Note: On Early Entry days, *Splash Mountain* will be closed till the park's official opening time and *Space Mountain* will usually be open.

Tip: WDW periodically attempts to control these morning dashes. You may be instructed to walk briskly behind a Disney cast member to the *Mountain* entrances. If you encounter this method of crowd control, follow instructions but be prepared to dash with other excited guests when the entrance is in sight. Even Disney can't always prevent these last-second dashes.

Here are my tips for putting yourself near the front of the crowd to the Mountain of your choice:

The Race to Space

The closest rope to *Space Mountain* is *either* the one at the end of Main Street to the right past the Plaza Ice Cream Parlor and near the Tomorrowland Terrace Noodle Station *or* the rope at the first bridge to Tomorrowland. The exact position of these ropes varies from time to time. Ask the Disney attendant if the bridge rope will be moved forward (a few minutes before the official opening time) to the edge of Tomorrowland at the far end of the bridge. If the answer is yes, or if the rope has already been moved, line up at this rope. *Space Mountain* is slightly to the left past *Stitch's Great Escape!* and then straight ahead. Disney began this rope-moving maneuver to counteract the advantage that the rope near the Tomorrowland Terrace Noodle Station offered joggers to *Space Mountain*.

If the answer is no, the rope near the Tomorrowland Terrace Noodle Station is the closest rope for the race to *Space*. You will power walk, jog, or run toward and through the left side of the Tomorrowland Terrace Noodle Station restaurant and into Tomorrowland. Pass *Monsters, Inc. Laugh Floor* on your right, then pass *Stitch's Great Escape!* on your left. Be careful not to get entangled in the waiting area chains at *Stitch's Great Escape!*; take a wide berth around the last posts of this waiting area. Now you can see the *Space Mountain* building. Head straight for it and you'll spot the entrance. Unless you're a fast sprinter with some endurance and get to *Space Mountain* ahead of them, you can easily follow the speedy teenagers to the entrance.

If you're pushing a stroller, you can still move briskly, but please don't move along beside other strollers. This will inadvertently create an obstacle for the out-of-control sprinters who may be coming up behind you – a potentially dangerous situation. For safety's sake, strollers and wheelchairs should move along the sides of the paths to *Space Mountain* and not in the midst of the mayhem.

Once you arrive, slow down a bit and try to sense where people are.

The inside queue area is long and dark, so it's easy to collide with someone in front of you. If you have time, note the interesting astronomical exhibits and photographs along the walls of the entrance queue area.

Tip: *Space Mountain* has two coaster tracks. Generally only one will be operating at opening. If you have a choice between the right or left tracks, choose the side that seems less crowded or the side that you haven't been on before. At the end of the ride, feel free to ride the moving sidewalk (instead of walking or jogging) and view the interesting and humorous science fiction exhibits along the side.

Note: If you're staying on Disney property and Early Entry Extra Magic Hours are in effect (see page 18), most attractions in Fantasyland and Tomorrowland will be operating when you enter early. The rest of the park will be closed until the official opening time. *Space Mountain* may or may not be operating initially. Check with the Lobby Concierge in your WDW hotel or look for an explanatory placard inside the entrance turnstiles to find out which attractions (specifically *Space Mountain*) are open. Or ask the turnstile attendant at the entrance.

If *Space Mountain* is open, you have to hustle down Main Street with the rest of the early entrants. For the shortest route, remember to turn right off Main Street at the Plaza Ice Cream Parlor so you can head through the Tomorrowland Terrace Noodle Station as described above. However, in the early morning this route is sometimes blocked by a rope and a Disney attendant! If so, continue on to the first open route to Tomorrowland on your right, jog past *Stitch's Great Escape!* and angle slightly left to *Space Mountain*.

If *Space Mountain* is not open initially, ask the entrance turnstile attendant (he or she may not know) or any attendant near Tomorrowland when it will open. Take in other attractions in Fantasyland or Tomorrowland while you wait (consult the appropriate Early Entry tour plan below), then line up as close as you can to *Space Mountain* 15 minutes before opening. (You'll usually be able to line up past the *Tomorrowland Indy Speedway* entrance within sight of the *Space Mountain* entrance.) When the attendant says "go," you can dash the short distance to the entrance.

The Dash to Splash

When the Magic Kingdom turnstiles open (usually 30 minutes before the official opening time), line up at the ropes to Adventureland. For the shortest route, stand close to the rope in front of the Crystal Palace Restaurant. In front of this restaurant is a bridge to Adventureland. When the rope drops after the welcome spiel at the official opening time, walk fast, jog, or sprint across this bridge and turn left into Adventureland. When you spot the *Swiss Family Treehouse* on your left, slow down, and look right to find a passageway to Frontierland. Go through this passageway, veer left, and look for *Splash Mountain*; it's left of *Big Thunder Mountain Railroad*. Go straight to the end of the wide path through Frontierland and turn right to the *Splash Mountain* entrance.

Note: If Early Entry is in effect, *Splash Mountain* will not be operating at first. Follow the Early Entry tour plan (if you are eligible for it) until 15 minutes before the park's official opening time, then buy some coffee or other refreshments in Fantasyland and line up at the rope between Fantasyland and Liberty Square. When the rope drops, hightail it through Liberty Square to the Frontierland path to *Splash Mountain*.

Caution: Occasionally, the speaker near the Liberty Square rope doesn't work, so the Disney attendant there can't hear the park opening spiel and therefore doesn't drop the rope when the park officially opens. When this happens, you may not have a chance of being at the front of the *Splash* line! By the time you get to it, the Frontierland path may already be clogged with folks who waited at the Main Street ropes (where the attendant could hear the spiel and dropped the ropes on time). So be sure to ask the attendant if the speaker has been functioning lately. If there is any doubt, leave Liberty Square and line up at the rope near Cinderella Castle. You'll find it at the entrance to the small walkway to Liberty Square (just past the Cinderella fountain). Even if the speaker isn't working at this location, you'll have a better vantage point to sense when the Main Street ropes drop. When your rope drops, hustle down this path, turn right into Liberty Square at the Sleepy Hollow eatery, then veer sharply left just before the Liberty Tree. Follow the path around the left side of the big tree and into Frontierland.

Note 1: The dash to *Splash* is longer than the race to *Space*. Unless you're in excellent aerobic shape, you need to pace yourself. Don't worry about the competition; although many folks start out sprinting, you'll pass by tiring joggers whose legs and lungs gave out toward the end of the Frontierland path.

Note 2: Some folks take the first *WDW Railroad* train from Main Street to Frontierland at opening time. The joggers (but not the casual walkers) will beat the train riders to *Splash Mountain*.

Note 3: Lines to *Splash Mountain* remain long all day, and big rushes occur after parades as people in Frontierland make a beeline to the entrance. If you don't ride it first thing, plan on getting a FASTPASS for it at the appropriate time (see the touring plan of your choice, below).

One-Day Touring Plans for Adults and Teens

You won't be able to experience every attraction in the Magic Kingdom in a single day, but following this plan will ensure that you'll experience the best the MK has to offer adults and teens.

This plan assumes you will arrive at or before opening time. If you want to sleep in, just pick up the non Early Entry plan around step 5. If the park is crowded and you arrive late, consider skipping the afternoon break and use the time to visit attractions that usually have minimal waits (see page 83); or consult your Times Guide for stage shows. Use FASTPASS or the singles line option (when available) for crowded attractions.

Note: I consider a wait of more than 15 to 20 minutes "too long."

Adults and Teens One-Day Plan for Extra Magic Hours' Early Entry Days

(WDW property guests only)

Note: During evening Extra Magic Hours, the crowds are sometimes lighter. You can use the non Early Entry day touring plan for attractions that are open or simply tour at leisure with your own itinerary.

1. Ride *Space Mountain.* (See "The Race to Space," page 90, for the best way to get to it.) If the Main Street ropes are up, line up at the one by the Plaza Ice Cream Parlor or at the first bridge to Tomorrowland. (Remember: this rope may be moved up to the far end of the bridge.) Resist the urge to ride it again; there's a lot more fun stuff ahead.

   If *Space Mountain* is not open initially, ask a Tomorrowland attendant when it will open. Then continue with the touring plan and line up near *Space Mountain* about 15 minutes before it opens.

2. Exit straight ahead. Pass *Astro Orbiter* on your left, and ride *Buzz Lightyear's Space Ranger Spin* if it's open.

3. Exit *Buzz,* turn left, and take the route to Fantasyland past *Tomorrowland Indy Speedway.* Walk into Fantasyland past *Mad Tea Party* and ride *The Many Adventures of Winnie the Pooh.*

4. If you have more than 25 minutes before the official opening time, turn left, head past *Cinderella's Golden Carrousel* on your left, and ride either

Peter Pan's Flight or *Snow White's Scary Adventures* if the wait is five minutes or less.

5. 15 minutes before the official opening time, line up at the rope between Fantasyland and Liberty Square. Ask the Disney rope attendant if the speaker is working so you can hear the park opening spiel. If there's any doubt, walk back through Fantasyland, turn right just before Cinderella Castle, pass by the Cinderella fountain, and line up at the rope on the small walkway to Liberty Square. If you have a few minutes, buy some coffee or refreshments to enjoy while you wait at the rope.

6. When the rope drops, hurry through Liberty Square to Frontierland. Or, if you're at the second rope by Cinderella Castle, go down the Liberty Square path and turn right at the Sleepy Hollow eatery and then left before the Liberty Tree to enter Frontierland. Hustle to the end of the Frontierland path and turn right to ride *Splash Mountain*.

7. Ride *Big Thunder Mountain Railroad*.

8. Pick up the following plan at step 4. Skip any steps you've already done today.

Adults and Teens One-Day Plan for Non EMH Early Entry Days

1. Ride *Space Mountain*. (See "The Race to Space," page 90, for the best way to get to it.) Resist the urge to ride it again; there's a lot more fun stuff ahead.

2. Walk back through Tomorrowland past *Stitch's Great Escape!* on your right. Walk to the left side of the central hub and onto the path to Adventureland. Turn right just past *Swiss Family Treehouse* and pass through a tunnel to Frontierland. Turn left and walk to the end of the Frontierland path, then get a FASTPASS for *Splash Mountain* to ride later. Turn left to the nearby entrance to *Big Thunder Mountain Railroad* and ride. Skip ahead to steps 5, 6, etc. if you have time before you do *Splash Mountain*.

3. Return to ride *Splash Mountain* at your allotted time.

4. Exit *Splash Mountain* and cross over the bridge to your right to the Frontierland walkway. Walk to Adventureland and ride *Pirates of the Caribbean*.
    Tip: Choose the left queue if it's open; it's often shorter.

5. Retrace your steps to Frontierland then walk to Liberty Square. Keep to the left and ride *The Haunted Mansion*.

6. Consider an early lunch. The Plaza Restaurant at the end of Main Street usually opens at 11:00 a.m. and is a good place to lunch. Fast food eateries like Pecos Bill Café in Frontierland are also a good bet.

7. After lunch, walk to the *Country Bear Jamboree* and enjoy the show.

8. Pass by *Splash Mountain* and turn left to *Walt Disney World Railroad*. Ride the train around the entire park. Exit at Mickey's Toontown Fair on your second pass.

9. Visit *Mickey's Country House* and *Minnie's Country House* and enjoy the colorful details of Mickey's neighborhood.

10. If you're staying on Disney property and feel tired, consider leaving the park at this point (via the train to Main Street) to refresh yourself at your hotel for a few hours. Keep your parking receipt handy if you paid for parking so that you can re-enter the lot without paying again. Return to the park when you feel re-energized and pick up the touring plan where you left off. If the timing is right, eat an early dinner in your hotel (or at the park on your return) and then resume the touring plan after dinner if the park is open late.

    Alternative: If you need a rest but are staying off property, leaving may be more trouble than it is worth. Simply rest in a shady spot for a while in mid-afternoon. The quiet park across from the Sleepy Hollow eatery behind Ye Olde Christmas Shoppe in Liberty Square is a good place.

    Note: If the park is too crowded for your comfort and your ticket allows, switch to a non Early Entry Disney park at this point and start with the afternoon or evening section of the appropriate touring plan.

11. Walk to Tomorrowland. Get a FASTPASS for *Buzz Lightyear's Space Ranger Spin*, then see *Monsters, Inc. Laugh Floor*, which is across from *Stitch's Great Escape!*

12. Exit *Monsters, Inc. Laugh Floor*. Ride *Buzz Lightyear's Space Ranger Spin* at your allotted time.

13. Cross Tomorrowland to go to *Walt Disney's Carousel of Progress*. Enjoy the show.

14. Exit the show. Cross Tomorrowland past *Monsters, Inc. Laugh Floor* on your left, and walk through or around the central hub on the right. Enter Liberty Square and walk to *The Hall of Presidents* on your right. Enjoy the show.

15. Exit the show. Turn right to the *Liberty Square Riverboat* (it sometimes closes at dusk). If the wait is 10 minutes or more, grab a snack from a vendor in Liberty Square or Frontierland and refresh yourself as you wait. On the riverboat, listen to the overhead spiel for some humorous Mark Twain aphorisms.

16. Disembark. Turn left and walk past Columbia Harbour House eatery to Fantasyland. Walk to *Mickey's PhilharMagic* on your right side. Enjoy the show if the line's not too long.

17. Most Fantasyland attractions are crowded in the afternoon and early evening. If the wait for *Peter Pan's Flight*, *Snow White's Scary Adventures*, or *The Many Adventures of Winnie the Pooh* is 15 minutes or less, go ahead and ride one or all of them now. Use FASTPASS for one of the rides if it is available (consult your Guidemap).

18. Ride *"it's a small world"* across from *Peter Pan's Flight*. The wait for *"it's a small world"* is usually not too long.

19. Leave Fantasyland through Cinderella Castle and enjoy the elaborate mosaic mural inside on the Castle wall. Turn left and walk to the second entrance to Tomorrowland. Walk past *Monsters, Inc. Laugh Floor* and see *Stitch's Great Escape!* if the wait isn't too long. Then ride *Tomorrowland Transit Authority*. While you're enjoying the *Tomorrowland Transit Authority*, consider your dinner options if you don't already have advance reservations. The Crystal Palace buffet is a good bet if you can get there early; Disney characters visit your table. Or eat upstairs at Columbia Harbour House counter-service restaurant.

20. Eat dinner.

21. How you spend your remaining time will depend on when the park closes. At a minimum, plan to see one of the evening parades and the fireworks show. If there is time before the parade, consider visiting one or more of the following attractions: *Swiss Family Treehouse* (requires climbing stairs), *The Enchanted Tiki Room* (lighthearted musical fare, but skippable for many folks) or *The Magic Carpets of Aladdin*.

    20 to 30 minutes before parade time, find a viewing spot in Frontierland. Ask a Disney cast member where the parade is starting from. If it begins at Main Street, you have 15 or more minutes after starting time before the parade hits Frontierland. Send someone for refreshments if you wish.

    Later, watch the fireworks from the main bridge to Tomorrowland. At the beginning of the fireworks, Tinker Bell floats down from near the top of Cinderella Castle to a rooftop in Tomorrowland (weather and wind permitting).

    After dark and during one of the evening parades (preferably the early one if there are two), check out *Jungle Cruise* (use FASTPASS if it's available; consult your Guidemap). Check the Tip Board across from Casey's Corner for approximate attraction wait times (but be aware that it's not always accurate).

22. Close down the park with any last-minute attractions you want to see (such as *Astro Orbiter* and *Mad Tea Party*) and shop on Main Street on your way out. Check out the virtual games at the Main Street Cinema, if available, and enjoy the Disney window scenes at the Emporium shop.

One-Day Touring Plans for Families with Young Children

You won't be able to experience every attraction in the Magic Kingdom in a single day, but following this plan will ensure that you'll experience the best the MK has to offer you and your children.

Tip: Some children do better if they visit Magic Kingdom last. If they experience it first, they may not enjoy the other parks quite as much because they may expect all of WDW to be just like the MK.

This plan assumes you will arrive at opening time. If you want to sleep in, just pick up the non Early Entry plan around step 5. If the park is crowded and you arrive late, consider skipping the afternoon break and use the time to visit attractions that usually have minimal waits (see page 83); or consult your Times Guide for stage shows. For crowded attractions, use FASTPASS or the singles line option (if you and your children are comfortable with it) when available.

Be aware that only collapsible strollers are allowed on the *WDW Railroad*. Leave any noncollapsible stroller at the station and retrieve it later, or get a replacement stroller with your rental receipt at your destination.

Note: I consider a wait of more than 15 to 20 minutes "too long."

Families One-Day Plan for Extra Magic Hours' Early Entry Days

(WDW property guests only)
Note: During evening Extra Magic Hours, the crowds are sometimes lighter. You can use the non Early Entry day touring plan for attractions that are open or simply tour at leisure with your own itinerary.

1. Rent strollers, if needed, past the entrance turnstiles and under the *Walt Disney World Railroad*.
2. Line up at the rope nearest Cinderella Castle. When the rope drops, or if the rope is not up, head up either walkway and through Cinderella

Castle to Fantasyland and ride **Dumbo the Flying Elephant** (photo right). If your kids enjoyed the ride, get back in line and soar again!

3. Exit and walk left to ride *The Many Adventures of Winnie the Pooh*.
4. Turn left at the exit and ride *Peter Pan's Flight*, or get a FASTPASS and ride later if the wait is too long.
5. Turn right at the exit, cross to the right of *Cinderella's Golden Carrousel*, and ride *Snow White's Scary Adventures* if you can (it may not be open yet).

   Caution: This ride can frighten children age 6 and under. If your child is the squeamish type, skip the ride.
6. Across from *Peter Pan's Flight* is *"it's a small world."* If you have 15 minutes or more before the official opening time, enjoy the ride and the song. If it's not open, hop on *Mad Tea Party*.
7. After *"it's a small world,"* take some refreshment from one of the Fantasyland vendors.
8. When the park officially opens to the general public, ride *Cinderella's Golden Carrousel*.
9. Next, get in line for *Mickey's PhilharMagic*.
10. Ride *Snow White's Scary Adventures* and *Mad Tea Party* if you haven't yet.
11. If your kids want autographs (and what kids don't), exit and walk past *Dumbo*, then line up to meet Ariel at *Ariel's Grotto* at the rear of Fantasyland on the lagoon. The queue passes by an interactive fountain. If you don't mind your kids getting wet, strip them down to their bathing suits or other essentials (hopefully you brought along dry clothes for them) and let them go crazy! If the line for *Ariel's Grotto* is short, get Ariel's autograph before loosing your kids in the fountain.
12. After 10 minutes or so in the fountain, dry the kids off. Then go to step 8 of the following plan and skip any steps you've already done today.

Families with Young Children
One-Day Plan for Non Early Entry Days

1. Rent strollers, if needed, past the entrance turnstiles and under the *Walt Disney World Railroad*.
2. Line up at the rope nearest Cinderella Castle. When the rope drops, or if it's not up, head up either walkway and through Cinderella Castle to Fantasyland. Ride *Dumbo the Flying Elephant*.
3. Exit and walk left to ride *The Many Adventures of Winnie the Pooh*.
4. Turn left at the exit and ride *Peter Pan's Flight*, or get a FASTPASS and

---

ride later if the wait is too long now.

5. Turn right and line up for *Mickey's PhilharMagic* (next door). Ask the attendant how long the wait is for the next show. Someone in your party can acquire refreshments if the wait is long enough.

6. Line up to meet Ariel at *Ariel's Grotto* at the rear of Fantasyland on the lagoon. The queue passes by an interactive fountain. If you don't mind your kids getting wet, strip them down to their bathing suits or other essentials and let them go crazy! (Hopefully you brought along an extra set of clothes for them.)

7. Exit right and leave Fantasyland for Liberty Square. Take a right after entering Liberty Square and ride *The Haunted Mansion*. The ride isn't all that scary, but the darkness and loud sounds may frighten some squeamish youngsters.

8. If you have 25 minutes or more before your advance reservations for lunch, walk across Liberty Square and into Frontierland. Turn left into the passageway just past the *Frontierland Shootin' Arcade*. Enter Adventureland and turn right to ride *Pirates of the Caribbean*.
   Tip: Choose the left queue if it's open; it's often shorter.

9. If you haven't made plans for lunch, eat after *Pirates* at Pecos Bill Café in Frontierland, or better yet at The Crystal Palace Character Buffet if the wait isn't too long.

10. After lunch, leave the Magic Kingdom and return to your hotel for a swim and naps if you're staying on property. Keep any parking and stroller receipts so that you won't have to pay again when you return.

Alternative: If you're not staying on property or if you can't bring yourself to leave the park, find a resting spot (such as the Liberty Square park across from Sleepy Hollow and behind Ye Olde Christmas Shoppe). Park your family for a respite and maybe even naps for the kids.

Note: If the Magic Kingdom is too crowded for your comfort and your ticket allows, switch to a non Early Entry Disney park at this point and start with the afternoon or evening section of the appropriate touring plan.

11. Return to the Magic Kingdom at around 2:30 p.m. Pick up a stroller with your receipt and claim a position for the 3:00 p.m. parade. Find a shady spot along the rope in Frontierland. (One good place to stand is between the columns that line the covered walkway next to the Liberty Tree Tavern.) Ask a Disney cast member where the parade is starting from. If it begins at Main Street, you have 15 or more minutes after starting time before the parade hits Frontierland. Send someone for refreshments if you wish. While you're waiting for the parade, check your Times Guide for any live shows that interest you. Insert them into your post-parade touring plan as time permits.

    Warning: People can get a bit pushy at parade time, so protect your viewing spot to prevent any potential irritation.

12. After the parade, walk toward *Splash Mountain*. If your kids have been asking about *Splash Mountain* and if they're tall enough (40" or more), go get in line or use "switching off." But be aware that the wait will be long. Use the FASTPASS option if it's available.

13. Walk to the *Tom Sawyer Island* raft loading dock. Ride the raft to *Tom Sawyer Island* and spend 30 to 40 minutes or so exploring the island's caves, trails, bridges, and interactive playthings.

14. The park may close early or late. Spend your last hour in the park at Mickey's Toontown Fair. If you have time before then, leave *Tom Sawyer Island*, turn left, and exit Frontierland to Tomorrowland's main entrance bridge. Ride *Buzz Lightyear's Space Ranger Spin* or get a FAST-PASS if available and ride later if the wait is too long.

15. Whenever it's appropriate, honor any reservations you may have for dinner. Check your Times Guide to see when *The Enchanted Tiki Room* and *Country Bear Jamboree* close. Try to fit them in.

16. If your kids are intrigued by the loud car noises, check out the line for the *Tomorrowland Indy Speedway*. If it's not too long (10-minute wait or less), go ahead and ride. While in the car, a parent can work the foot pedal while the child steers.

    Tip: The right queue to the first loading area is a shorter distance and thus may have a shorter wait.

Height alert: You must be at least 52" tall to ride alone.

17. Exit left and go through the passageway to Frontierland. Turn left and see the *Country Bear Jamboree* if the wait isn't too long (15 minutes or less).

18. Go to Adventureland. Enjoy *The Magic Carpets of Aladdin* (if the wait isn't too long) and then *The Enchanted Tiki Room* show.

    Caution: The Tiki Goddess can scare little ones!

19. Ride *"it's a small world"* if you haven't already.

20. Play awhile in *Pooh's Playful Spot* (across from *Winnie the Pooh*).

21. Leave time to see the evening parade. Stake out a viewing spot 20 minutes before parade time along the ropes in Frontierland or on Main Street. Get some refreshments to enjoy while you wait.

22. In Tomorrowland, see *Monsters, Inc. Laugh Floor* then walk around *Astro Orbiter* and relax aboard the *Tomorrowland Transit Authority.*

23. Walk to Mickey's Toontown Fair. Visit *Mickey's Country House.* Pass through Mickey's backyard to a big tent to get Mickey Mouse's autograph and a picture of him with your kids.

24. Walk down the street a bit and visit *Minnie's Country House.*

25. Next stop is the *Toontown Hall of Fame* between Mickey's and Minnie's houses. Here your kids can meet more characters. They can choose one of three queues, each leading to a different set of characters. If time allows, let the kids wait through all three lines if they're up for it.

26. After the characters, cross the street to *The Barnstormer at Goofy's Wiseacre Farm.* This short roller coaster may be too zippy for some young kids, but other kids 6 and older may like it.

    Height alert: You must be at least 35" tall to ride.

27. The final stop in Mickey's Toontown Fair is *Donald's Boat.* Kids go wild in this interactive fountain, and they can get drenched. Hopefully, you're prepared for wet munchkins.

28. Is everyone still awake? Plan to see the nightly fireworks show, *Wishes.* At the beginning of the fireworks, Tinker Bell floats down from near the top of Cinderella Castle to a rooftop in Tomorrowland. You can enjoy the show from the street in Mickey's Toontown Fair or (better) from the main bridge to Tomorrowland.

29. If you're in Toontown after the fireworks, board the train to Main Street if it's still running. Retrieve your stroller if necessary, and leave the park with everyone else. Or shop on Main Street until the crowds thin out. If you dawdle, be sure to enjoy the Disney window scenes at the Emporium shop.

One-Day Touring Plans for Seniors

These plans include no fast, scary, or spinning attractions. If you enjoy such rides, follow the touring plan for adults and teens.

This plan assumes you will arrive at opening time. If you want to sleep in, just pick up the non Early Entry plan around step 5. If the park is crowded and you arrive late, consider skipping the afternoon break and use the time to visit attractions that usually have minimal waits; or consult your Times Guide for stage shows. Use FASTPASS or the singles line option (when available) for crowded attractions.

Note: I consider a wait of more than 15 to 20 minutes "too long."

Seniors One-Day Plan for Extra Magic Hours' Early Entry Days

(WDW property guests only)

Note: During evening Extra Magic Hours, the crowds are sometimes lighter. You can use the non Early Entry day touring plan for attractions that are open or simply tour at leisure with your own itinerary.

1. Line up at the rope nearest Cinderella Castle. When the rope drops, or if the rope is not up, head up either walkway and through Cinderella Castle to Fantasyland. Walk past *Snow White's Scary Adventures*, turn right and ride *The Many Adventures of Winnie the Pooh*.

2. Turn left at the exit. Cross to the other side of Fantasyland and ride *Peter Pan's Flight*.

3. Turn right at the exit and ride *Snow White's Scary Adventures* if it has opened (it may not be open yet).

4. Walk back towards *Peter Pan's Flight* and ride *"it's a small world"* or *Cinderella's Golden Carrousel*.

5. 15 minutes before the official opening time, line up at the rope between Fantasyland and Liberty Square. If you have a few minutes, buy some coffee or refreshments to enjoy while you wait.

6. When the rope drops, walk at a leisurely pace into Liberty Square. Pass under the overpass and then turn right to ride *The Haunted Mansion*.

7. Pick up the following plan at step 6. Skip any steps you've already done and move on to 9 and 10 if you have time before lunch.

Seniors One-Day Plan
for Non Early Entry Days

1. Line up at the rope nearest Cinderella Castle. When the rope drops, or if it is not up, head up either walkway and through Cinderella Castle to Fantasyland. Walk past *Snow White's Scary Adventures*, turn right, and ride *The Many Adventures of Winnie the Pooh*.

2. Turn left at the exit. Cross to the other side of Fantasyland and ride *Peter Pan's Flight*.

3. Turn right at the exit and ride *Snow White's Scary Adventures*.

4. Cross into Liberty Square. Grab some refreshment in Liberty Square or Frontierland and take a break.

5. When you're hydrated and rested, visit *The Haunted Mansion* in Liberty Square.

6. Walk across Frontierland to the *Country Bear Jamboree* on your left and enjoy the show.

7. Turn right at the exit. Walk to the *Liberty Square Riverboat* and board at the next departure. On the riverboat, listen to the overhead spiel for some humorous Mark Twain aphorisms.

8. Consider an early lunch. The Plaza Restaurant on Main Street usually opens at 11:00 a.m. and is a good place to lunch.

9. Cross to Adventureland and ride *Pirates of the Caribbean*.
   Tip: Choose the left queue if it's open; it's often shorter.

10. Exit *Pirates of the Caribbean* and turn left. Pass by *Splash Mountain* and turn left to the *Walt Disney World Railroad*. Ride the train around the entire park and exit at Mickey's Toontown Fair on your second pass.

11. Visit *Mickey's Country House* and *Minnie's Country House*. Enjoy the colorful details of Mickey's neighborhood.

12. If you're staying on Disney property and you start feeling tired, consider leaving the park (via the train to Main Street) to refresh yourself at your hotel for a while. Keep any parking receipts so that you don't have to pay for parking twice in the same day. Return to the park when you feel re-energized and pick up the touring plan where you left off. If the timing is right, eat an early dinner in your hotel or at the park and resume the touring plan after dinner if the park is open late.
   Alternative: If you are staying off property or just don't feel like leaving the park, rest in a shady spot for a while in mid-afternoon when the sun is hottest. One such option is the park across from the Sleepy Hollow eatery behind Ye Olde Christmas Shoppe in Liberty Square.

Note: If the Magic Kingdom is too crowded for your comfort and your ticket allows, switch to a non EMH Early Entry Disney park after your break and start with the afternoon or evening section of the appropriate touring plan.

13. Walk to Tomorrowland, and enjoy the show at *Walt Disney's Carousel of Progress*.

14. See *Monsters, Inc. Laugh Floor*, across from *Stitch's Great Escape!*

15. Leave Tomorrowland and walk through or around the central hub on the right. Enter Liberty Square and catch the next show at *The Hall of Presidents*.

16. Turn right at the exit and walk past Columbia Harbour House eatery to Fantasyland. Walk to *Mickey's PhilharMagic* on your right. Enjoy the show if the line is not too long.

17. Ride *"it's a small world"* across from *Peter Pan's Flight*. The wait for *"it's a small world"* is usually not too long.

18. Leave Fantasyland through Cinderella Castle and enjoy the elaborate mosaic mural inside on the Castle wall. Turn left and walk to the second entrance to Tomorrowland. Walk past *Monsters, Inc. Laugh Floor* and *Astro Orbiter* on your left to *Tomorrowland Transit Authority*. While you're enjoying the *Transit Authority*, consider your dinner options if you don't already have advance reservations. The Crystal Palace buffet is a good bet (Disney characters visit your table) though it's usually crowded. Or try good counter-service food at Tomorrowland Terrace Noodle Station.

19. See the show at *The Enchanted Tiki Room* in Adventureland.

20. Ride *Jungle Cruise* in Adventureland. If the wait is long, use a FASTPASS if available. Or if two evening parades are scheduled, get in line during the early evening parade.

21. Plan to see one of the evening parades and the fireworks show. Find a viewing spot in Frontierland 20 to 30 minutes before parade time. Ask a Disney cast member where the parade is starting from. If it begins at Main Street, you have 15 or more minutes after starting time before it hits Frontierland. Send someone to get refreshments if you wish.

    Later on, watch the fireworks from the middle of the main bridge to Tomorrowland. As they start, Tinker Bell floats down from near the top of Cinderella Castle to a rooftop in Tomorrowland (weather and wind permitting).

22. Close down the park with any last-minute attractions you want to see, and shop on Main Street on your way out. Enjoy the Disney window scenes at the Emporium shop.

Two-Day Touring Plans for Adults and Teens

These plans assume you will arrive at opening time on both days. If you want to sleep in, just pick up the non Early Entry plan around step 3 or 4. If the park is crowded and you arrive late, consider skipping the afternoon break and use the time to visit attractions that usually have minimal waits (see page 83), or consult your Times Guide for stage shows. Use FASTPASS or the singles line option (when available) for crowded attractions. Bear the following in mind:

• I consider a wait of more than 15 to 20 minutes "too long."

• Because guests generally take advantage of the Extra Magic Hours' Early Entry privilege (when available) only once at each park – or want to do the same popular rides again if they do two Early Entry days in the MK – the Early Entry tour plans are similar for Days One and Two. I include them under both days so that you won't have to flip back and forth in the book.

• A few Magic Kingdom attractions are not included in this touring plan because they are not generally that popular with adults. If some of them appeal to you, check out one of the "Families with Young Children" touring plans to see when you might best fit them into your schedule.

Adults and Teens Day One Plan for Extra Magic Hours' Early Entry Days

(WDW property guests only)

Note: During evening Extra Magic Hours, the crowds are sometimes lighter. You can use the non Early Entry day touring plan for attractions that are open or simply tour at leisure with your own itinerary.

1. Ride *Space Mountain* (see "The Race to Space," page 90, for the fastest way to get there). Resist the urge to ride it again; there's a lot more fun stuff ahead. If *Space Mountain* is not open initially, ask a Tomorrowland attendant when it will open. Then continue with the touring plan and line up near *Space Mountain* about 15 minutes before opening.

2. Exit straight ahead, pass *Astro Orbiter* on your left, and visit *Buzz Lightyear's Space Ranger Spin* if it is open.

3. Exit *Buzz*. Turn left and take the route to Fantasyland past *Tomorrowland Indy Speedway*. Walk into Fantasyland past *Mad Tea Party* and ride *The Many Adventures of Winnie the Pooh*.

4. If you have more than 25 minutes before the official opening time, turn left, head past *Cinderella's Golden Carrousel* on your left, and ride *Peter Pan's Flight* and *Snow White's Scary Adventures* if the wait is five minutes or less.

5. 15 minutes before the official opening time, line up at the rope between Fantasyland and Liberty Square. Ask the Disney rope attendant if the speaker is working so you can hear the park opening spiel. If there's any doubt, walk back through Fantasyland, turn right just before Cinderella Castle, pass by the Cinderella fountain, and line up at the rope on the small walkway to Liberty Square. If you have a few minutes, buy some coffee or refreshments to enjoy as you wait at the rope.

6. When the rope drops, hurry through Liberty Square to Frontierland. Or, if you're at the second rope by Cinderella Castle, go down the Liberty Square path and turn right at the Sleepy Hollow eatery and then left before the Liberty Tree to enter Frontierland. Hustle to the end of the Frontierland path and ride *Splash Mountain*.

7. Ride *Big Thunder Mountain Railroad*.

8. Pick up the following plan at step 4. Skip steps you've already done.

Adults and Teens Day One Plan for Non Early Entry Days

1. Ride *Space Mountain* (see "The Race to Space," page 90, for the fastest way to get there).

2. Exit straight ahead. Pass *Astro Orbiter* on your left, and ride *Buzz Lightyear's Space Ranger Spin*.

3. Exit *Buzz*, turn left, and take the route to Fantasyland past *Tomorrowland Indy Speedway*. Walk through Fantasyland past *Mad Tea Party* and *Dumbo the Flying Elephant* and ride *Peter Pan's Flight*. Get a FASTPASS if the wait is too long.

4. Exit and turn right to *Mickey's PhilharMagic*. Enjoy the show if the lines aren't too long.

5. Exit and turn left to Liberty Square. Make a hard right and experience *The Haunted Mansion*.

6. Eat an early lunch to beat the crowds. Try the Plaza Restaurant (it usually opens at 11:00 a.m.) or Pecos Bill Café.

7. After lunch, go to the middle of Liberty Square to *The Hall of Presidents*. Consult the sign out front or ask the attendant at the door when the next show is. If it's more than 20 minutes away, walk to the *Liberty*

Square Riverboat to find out if you can board within five minutes or so. If not, browse around the shops in Liberty Square and catch the next show of *The Hall of Presidents*.

8. At this point, if you're staying on property consider returning to your hotel for a rest or swim. Keep any parking receipts for free re-entry to the parking lot when you return. Come back to the park when you feel re-energized and pick up the late afternoon or evening part of the touring plan.

    Alternative: If you need a rest but are staying off property, leaving may be more trouble than it's worth. Simply rest in a shady spot inside the park for a while. The park in Liberty Square, across the road from the Sleepy Hollow eatery, or the end of the cul-de-sac off Main Street are good resting spots.

    Note: If the park is too crowded for your comfort and your ticket allows, switch to a non Early Entry Disney park at this point and start with the afternoon section of the appropriate touring plan.

9. At about 2:40 p.m. (20 minutes ahead of time), stake out a shady spot along the rope in Frontierland or along Main Street for the 3:00 p.m. afternoon parade. A good bet is to stand between the columns along the covered walkway next to the Liberty Tree Tavern. Ask a Disney cast member where the parade is starting from. If it begins at Main Street, you have 15 or more minutes after starting time before the parade hits Frontierland. Send someone for refreshments if you wish. Enjoy the parade!

10. After the parade, follow the Frontierland waterfront to the first bridge and on to the loading area for the raft to *Tom Sawyer Island*. Spend an hour or so enjoying the creative nooks and crannies scattered over the island. Get a lemonade or other refreshment at Aunt Polly's Dockside Inn (open seasonally).

11. Return on the raft to Frontierland and keep to the right to enter Adventureland. Cross to the other end of Adventureland and visit the *Swiss Family Treehouse* on your right. This attraction requires some gentle stair climbing.

12. If you want to ride *Space Mountain* or *Splash Mountain*, get a FASTPASS if available (consult your Times Guide). Meanwhile. . .

13. Consider an early dinner. Either honor your advance reservations or enjoy counter-service food at Tomorrowland Terrace Noodle Station. The Liberty Tree Tavern has an entertaining character dinner.

14. Depending on when the park closes, you may be able to enjoy more attractions after dinner. During the two hours before closing, check out

Pirates of the Caribbean, Monsters, Inc. Laugh Floor, The Magic Carpets of Aladdin, the *Country Bear Jamboree*, and/or *Stitch's Great Escape!* (use FASTPASS if it's available; consult your Times Guide). Do not wait in any long lines. Check the Tip Board across from Casey's Corner for approximate attraction wait times (it's not always accurate). If the park is crowded and the lines seem long, check out the following attractions (which usually don't have long waits): *The Enchanted Tiki Room, "it's a small world," Walt Disney's Carousel of Progress* (this attraction may close early), and *Tomorrowland Transit Authority*.

15. Visit the virtual games at the Main Street Cinema (if available).

16. Check your Times Guide for any evening parades and fireworks. Line up at the ropes in Frontierland or along Main Street 20 to 30 minutes before parade time. Have someone fetch some refreshments while you wait. If two evening parades are scheduled, the later one is less crowded and you can stake out your position 10 to 15 minutes before parade time.

Adults and Teens Day Two Plan for Extra Magic Hours' Early Entry Days

(WDW property guests only)

Note: During evening Extra Magic Hours, the crowds are sometimes lighter. You can use the non Early Entry day touring plan for attractions that are open or simply tour at leisure with your own itinerary.

1. If you're up for more roller coasters, ride *Space Mountain* again (see "The Race to Space," page 90, for the fastest way to get there). When you exit, make an about face and ride it yet again!

2. Exit straight ahead and ride *Buzz Lightyear's Space Ranger Spin*.

3. Take the route to Fantasyland past *Tomorrowland Indy Speedway*. Ride *The Many Adventures of Winnie the Pooh* and then check out *Snow White's Scary Adventures* if open and the line isn't too long.

4. If you still have more than 25 minutes before the official opening time, ride *Peter Pan's Flight* again if the wait is five minutes or so.

5. 15 minutes before the official opening time, line up at the rope between Fantasyland and Liberty Square. Ask the Disney rope attendant if the speaker is working so you can hear the park opening spiel. If there's any doubt, walk back through Fantasyland, turn right just before Cinderella Castle, pass by the Cinderella fountain, and line up at the rope on the small walkway to Liberty Square. If you have a few minutes, buy some

coffee or refreshments to enjoy while you wait at the rope.

6. When the rope drops, hurry through Liberty Square to Frontierland. Or, if you're at the second rope by Cinderella Castle, go down the Liberty Square path and turn right at the Sleepy Hollow eatery, then left before the Liberty Tree to enter Frontierland. Hustle to the end of the Frontierland path and ride *Splash Mountain*.

7. Ride *Big Thunder Mountain Railroad*.

8. Pick up the following plan at step 3. Skip any steps you've already done.

Adults and Teens Day Two Plan for Non Early Entry Days

1. Ride *Splash Mountain* (see "The Dash to Splash," page 91, for the fastest way to get there).
   Tip: The entry queue may split into two sides. If both lines seem about equally long, choose the left side; it's shorter at the loading dock.

2. Exit *Splash Mountain* and walk away from the *Walt Disney World Railroad* station. Turn left to the nearby entrance to *Big Thunder Mountain Railroad* (BTMR) and ride.

3. Exit and walk straight ahead past *Splash Mountain* to Adventureland. Ride *Pirates of the Caribbean*. Choose the left queue if it's open; it's often shorter.

4. Ride *Jungle Cruise*. The queue may be getting long by now at *Jungle Cruise*, but unfortunately there's not another predictably good time of day to enjoy this popular attraction. Nevertheless, skip it if the wait is longer than 15 minutes; a long wait in this line is energy-sapping (use FASTPASS if it's available; consult your Times Guide).
   Alternative: Try *Jungle Cruise* 30 minutes before park closing. Just be aware that the line still may be too long!

5. If you haven't experienced *Country Bear Jamboree* yet, turn right past *The Enchanted Tiki Room*, then left through the passageway to Frontierland. Just to your left is *Country Bear Jamboree*. Enjoy it!

6. Eat an early lunch. Try Pecos Bill Café in Frontierland or Columbia Harbour House in Liberty Square for fast food (sit upstairs in the latter for less congestion). You can get seated quickly if you show up at the Plaza Restaurant on Main Street near its 11:00 a.m. usual opening time. Also consider the character lunch at The Crystal Palace buffet restaurant if you can get there before its 11:30 a.m. opening time. While eating, review your Times Guide and note any live shows or parades you want

to see. Work them into the touring plan.

7. Go to the closest *Walt Disney World Railroad* station (Main Street or Frontierland) and ride the train to Mickey's Toontown Fair. Once there, visit *Mickey's Country House* and *Minnie's Country House*, too. Be sure to give yourself time to wander around and explore all the interesting details of Mickey's neighborhood.

8. Re-board the *WDW Railroad* train and make a complete circuit of the Magic Kingdom.

9. Consider disembarking at Main Street Station and returning to your hotel for a rest or swim if you are staying on property. Keep any parking receipts for free re-entry to the parking lot.

   Alternative: If you don't want to leave the park or you are staying off property, which makes leaving for a rest impractical, seek a shady place to relax for a while with refreshment. Among your options: the small alcove to the right of the entrance to *Pirates of the Caribbean* or the shed at the edge of the rose garden between the two bridges to Tomorrowland.

   Note: If the MK is too crowded for your comfort and your ticket allows, switch to a non Early Entry Disney park at this point and start with the afternoon section of the appropriate touring plan.

10. In mid or late afternoon, after your rest, alternate FASTPASSes for *The Many Adventures of Winnie the Pooh* and *Buzz Lightyear's Space Ranger Spin*. Go to Liberty Square to ride the *Liberty Square Riverboat* (it sometimes closes at dusk) if you haven't enjoyed it already. On the riverboat, listen to the overhead spiel for some humorous Mark Twain aphorisms.

11. Go to any of the following attractions that you would enjoy and haven't yet experienced: *The Enchanted Tiki Room*, *"it's a small world,"* *Monsters, Inc. Laugh Floor*, *Walt Disney's Carousel of Progress* (open seasonally), *Stitch's Great Escape!*, and the *Tomorrowland Transit Authority*. Check the Tip Board across from Casey's Corner for approximate attraction wait times (it's not always accurate).

12. Eat dinner or honor your reservations when the time comes.

13. If you want to ride *Space Mountain* or *Splash Mountain* again, get a FAST-PASS if available. Meanwhile, consult your Times Guide and head for any attractions that you still want to ride before the park closes, especially if you haven't yet visited *Mad Tea Party*, *Astro Orbiter*, or *The Magic Carpets of Aladdin*. Try these three attractions (in the order listed) during the evening parade. Remember that lines for popular attractions can remain long even at park closing time, especially during busy seasons.

14. Plan to see one of the evening parades and the fireworks if you haven't

already done so. Check your Guidemap for any other entertainment options that appeal to you.

15. Shop on Main Street in the late afternoon or on your way out. Visit the virtual games at the Main Street Cinema (if available) and enjoy the Disney window scenes at the Emporium shop.

Two-Day Touring Plans for Families with Young Children

Tip: Some children do better if they visit Magic Kingdom last. If they experience it first, they may not enjoy the other parks quite as much because they may expect all of WDW to be just like the MK.

This plan assumes you will arrive at opening time on both days. If you want to sleep in, just pick up the non Early Entry plan around step 4 or 5. If the park is crowded and you arrive late, consider skipping the afternoon break and use the time to visit attractions that usually have minimal waits (see page 83) ; or consult your Times Guide for stage shows. For crowded attractions, use FASTPASS or the singles line option (if you and your children are comfortable with it) when available.

Note: I consider a wait of more than 15 to 20 minutes "too long."

Note, too, that because families generally take advantage of the Extra Magic Hours' Early Entry privilege only once at each park, the Early Entry tour plan is similar for Day One and Day Two. I include it under both days so that you don't have to flip back and forth in your book.

Tip: Consider buying a Pal Mickey interactive doll at an MK shop to entertain your kids.

Families Day One Plan for Extra Magic Hours' Early Entry Days

(WDW property guests only)

Note: During evening Extra Magic Hours, the crowds are sometimes lighter. You can use the non Early Entry day touring plan for attractions that are open or simply tour at leisure with your own itinerary.

1. Rent strollers if necessary. You'll find them past the entrance turnstiles and under *Walt Disney World Railroad*.

2. Line up at the rope nearest Cinderella Castle. When it drops, or if the rope is not up, head up either walkway and through Cinderella Castle to Fantasyland. Ride *Dumbo the Flying Elephant*. Hey, this is Walt Disney World! Get back in line and soar on *Dumbo* again!

3. Exit and walk left to ride *The Many Adventures of Winnie the Pooh*.

4. Turn left at the exit and ride **Peter Pan's Flight** (entrance photo below). Or get a FASTPASS to ride later if the wait is too long.

5. Turn right at the exit, cross to the right of *Cinderella's Golden Carrousel* and ride *Snow White's Scary Adventures* if it has opened.
    Caution: Be aware that this ride can frighten children age 6 and younger. If your child is the squeamish type, skip the ride.

6. Across from *Peter Pan's Flight* is *"it's a small world."* If you have 15 minutes or more before the official opening time, enjoy the ride.

7. After *"it's a small world,"* take some refreshment from one of the Fantasyland vendors.

8. When the park officially opens to the general public, ride *Cinderella's Golden Carrousel.*

9. Next, get in line for *Mickey's PhilharMagic*.

10. Now ride *Snow White's Scary Adventures* and *Mad Tea Party* if you have not yet done so.

11. If your kids want more autographs (and what kids don't), exit and walk to the right of *Dumbo* and line up to meet Ariel at *Ariel's Grotto* at the rear of Fantasyland on the lagoon. The queue passes by an interactive fountain. If you don't mind your kids getting wet, strip them down to

their bathing suits or other essentials (hopefully you brought along dry clothes for them) and let them go crazy! If the line for *Ariel's Grotto* is short, get Ariel's autograph before loosing your kids in the fountain.

12. After 10 minutes or so in the fountain, dry the kids off. Then go to the following plan and skip any steps you've already done today.

Families with Young Children
Day One Plan for Non Early Entry Days

1. Rent strollers if necessary past the entrance turnstiles and under the *Walt Disney World Railroad*.
2. Line up at the rope nearest Cinderella Castle. When it drops, or if the rope is not up, head up either walkway and through Cinderella Castle to Fantasyland and ride *Dumbo the Flying Elephant*.
3. Exit and walk left to ride *The Many Adventures of Winnie the Pooh*.
4. Turn left at the exit and ride *Peter Pan's Flight*. Or get a FASTPASS and ride later if the wait is too long.
5. Turn right and line up for *Mickey's PhilharMagic* next door. Ask the attendant how long the wait is for the next show. Someone in your party can get refreshments if the wait's long enough.
6. Line up to meet Ariel at *Ariel's Grotto* at the rear of Fantasyland on the lagoon. The queue passes by an interactive fountain. If you don't mind your kids getting wet, strip them down to their bathing suits or other essentials (hopefully you brought along dry clothes for them) and let them go crazy!
7. Exit right and leave Fantasyland for Liberty Square. Take a right after entering Liberty Square and ride *The Haunted Mansion*. The ride is not all that scary, but the darkness and loud sounds may frighten some squeamish youngsters.
8. If you have 25 minutes or more before your lunch reservations, walk across Liberty Square and into Frontierland. Turn left into the passageway just past the *Frontierland Shootin' Arcade*. Enter Adventureland and turn right to ride *Pirates of the Caribbean*.
   Tip: Choose the left queue if it's open; it's often shorter.
9. If you haven't made plans for lunch, eat after *Pirates* at Pecos Bill Café in Frontierland, or better yet at The Crystal Palace character buffet if the wait isn't too long.
10. If you are staying on property, leave the Magic Kingdom after lunch and return to your hotel for a swim and naps. Keep any parking and stroller

receipts handy for your return, so that you won't have to pay for them twice in the same day.

Alternative: If you're not staying on property or can't bring yourself to leave the park, find a resting spot to park your family for a respite and maybe even naps for the kids, such as the shady park in Liberty Square across from Sleepy Hollow and behind Ye Olde Christmas Shoppe.

Note: If the park is too crowded for your comfort, switch to a non Early Entry park after your rest (if your ticket allows) and start with the afternoon or evening section of the appropriate touring plan.

11. Claim a position for the 3:00 p.m. parade about 20 minutes before it starts. (If you left the MK for a rest, return at around 2:30 p.m. and re-acquire a stroller with your receipt.) Find a shady spot along the rope in Frontierland. One good place: between the columns along the covered walkway next to the Liberty Tree Tavern. Ask a Disney cast member where the parade is starting from. If it begins at Main Street, you have 15 or more minutes after starting time before the parade hits Frontierland. Send someone for refreshments if you wish.

    Warning: People can get a bit pushy at parade time, so protect your viewing spot to prevent any potential irritation.

    While you're waiting, check your Times Guide for any live shows that interest you. Remember you have two days to fit the live shows in. Insert the shows into the touring plan as time permits.

12. After the parade, walk toward *Splash Mountain.* If your kids are tall enough (40" or more) and want to ride, get in line or use "switching off." Use FASTPASS if it's available and the line is long.

13. Walk to the first bridge to the *Tom Sawyer Island* raft loading dock. Ride the raft to *Tom Sawyer Island* and spend 45 minutes or so exploring the caves, trails, bridges, and other interactive playthings.

14. The Magic Kingdom may close early or late. If you have time before dinner, take in **Storytime at Fairytale Garden** in Fantasyland or a live show at either the Castle Forecourt Stage or in Tomorrowland at the Galaxy Palace Theater (check your Times Guide). To get decent seats, arrive at the theater about 20 minutes before showtime.

15. Ride *Buzz Lightyear's Space Ranger Spin* (get a FASTPASS if available to ride later if the wait's too long).

16. Whenever it's appropriate, honor any dinner reservations you may have made. Or check out the counter-service food at Cosmic Ray's Starlight Café (entertainment included!).

17. Leave Tomorrowland and go left around the central hub to Adventureland. Check the Tip Board across from Casey's Corner for approxi-

mate attraction wait times (it's not always accurate) and then see if *The Enchanted Tiki Room* and *Country Bear Jamboree* are still open. If so, enjoy *The Enchanted Tiki Room* show first.

Caution: The Tiki Goddess can scare little ones!

18. Exit left and go through the passageway to Frontierland. Turn left and see the *Country Bear Jamboree* if the wait is 15 minutes or less).

19. If your kids are intrigued by the loud car noises, check out the line for the *Tomorrowland Indy Speedway*. If it's not too long (a 10-minute wait or less), go ahead and ride. While in the car, a parent can work the foot pedal while the child steers.

   Tip: The right queue to the first loading area is a shorter distance and thus may have a shorter wait.

   Height alert: You must be at least 52" tall to ride alone.

20. Leave time to see the evening parade. Stake a spot 20 minutes before parade time along the ropes in Frontierland or on Main Street. Get some refreshments to enjoy while you wait and watch. Meanwhile . . .

21. In Tomorrowland, see *Monsters, Inc. Laugh Floor*, then walk around *Astro Orbiter* and relax aboard the *Tomorrowland Transit Authority*.

22. Wander over to Fantasyland and ride *Cinderella's Golden Carrousel* if the wait is 10 minutes or less. The *Carrousel* is especially beautiful at night.

23. Ride *"it's a small world"* if you haven't already.

24. Get some refreshments and relax until time for the *Wishes* fireworks. Walk to the middle of the main bridge to Tomorrowland. Just as the fireworks begin, Tinker Bell floats down from near the top of Cinderella Castle to a rooftop in Tomorrowland (weather and wind permitting). After the fireworks, leave the park with everyone else or shop on Main Street until the crowds thin out. If you dawdle, be sure to enjoy the Disney window scenes at the Emporium shop.

Families Day Two Plan
for Extra Magic Hours' Early Entry Days

(WDW property guests only)

Note: During evening Extra Magic Hours, the crowds are sometimes lighter. You can use the non Early Entry day touring plan for attractions that are open or simply tour at leisure with your own itinerary.

1. Rent strollers if necessary. Look for them past the entrance turnstiles and under the *Walt Disney World Railroad*.

2. Line up at the rope nearest Cinderella Castle. When it drops, or if the

rope is not up, head up either walkway and through Cinderella Castle to Fantasyland. Ride *Dumbo the Flying Elephant*. If your kids want to ride it again, get in line for another go!

3.   Exit and walk left to ride *The Many Adventures of Winnie the Pooh*.

4.   Turn left at the exit and ride *Peter Pan's Flight*. Or get a FASTPASS and ride later if the wait is too long.

5.   Next ride *Buzz Lightyear's Space Ranger Spin*, *Snow White's Scary Adventures* (if open), or *"it's a small world."*

   Caution: *Snow White's Scary Adventures* can frighten children ages 6 and under. If your child is the squeamish type, skip the ride.

6.   Now get some refreshment from one of the Fantasyland vendors.

7.   Check your Times Guide to see if Mickey's Toontown Fair opens with the rest of the park. If it does, 15 minutes or so before official opening time, walk past the *Mad Tea Party* ride and line up at the rope across the path to Mickey's Toontown Fair.

8.   When the rope drops, walk to Mickey's Toontown Fair and pick up the following touring plan at step 4. Skip any attractions you've already enjoyed, or enjoy them again!

   Alternative: If Mickey's Toontown Fair opens later than the rest of the park, ride *The Magic Carpets of Aladdin*, *Astro Orbiter*, and *Mad Tea Party*. Then go to Toontown Fair when it opens.

Families with Young Children
Day Two Plan for Non Early Entry Days

1.   Rent strollers if necessary. You'll find them past the entrance turnstiles and under the *Walt Disney World Railroad*.

2.   Line up at the rope across the second entrance to Tomorrowland near Cinderella Castle. This leads to the most direct route to Mickey's Toontown Fair.

3.   When the rope drops, walk straight past Cosmic Ray's Starlight Café in Tomorrowland and then to the right of the *Mad Tea Party* to Mickey's Toontown Fair. If Mickey's Toontown Fair doesn't open until later in the morning (check your Times Guide), ride *Dumbo the Flying Elephant*, *The Many Adventures of Winnie the Pooh*, *Peter Pan's Flight*, *Mad Tea Party*, and any other attractions in Fantasyland with short lines. Use FASTPASS to your advantage. Enter Mickey's Toontown Fair as soon as it opens.

4.   Go to *The Barnstormer at Goofy's Wiseacre Farm*. This short roller

coaster may be too zippy for some young kids, but other kids 6 and older may like it.

Height alert: You must be at least 35" tall to ride.

5. Next enjoy *Mickey's Country House* (below), then walk through his backyard and line up to meet Mickey for autographs and photos.

6. Now stop at the *Toontown Hall of Fame* between Mickey's and Minnie's houses to meet more characters. Your kids can choose one of three queues, each leading to a different set of characters. Let the kids wait through all three lines if they're up for it.

7. Next meander through *Minnie's Country House*.

8. The final stop in Mickey's Toontown Fair is *Donald's Boat*. Kids go wild in this interactive fountain, and they can get drenched. Hopefully, you're prepared for wet munchkins.

9. Eat an early lunch. If you don't have plans, pick up some fast food at Cosmic Ray's Starlight Café or Casey's Corner (and watch cartoons!).

10. If you're staying on property, leave the Magic Kingdom after lunch and return to your hotel for a swim and naps. Keep any parking and stroller receipts; so long as you have them, you won't have to pay again when you return.

   Alternative: If you're staying off property, or if you can't bring yourself to leave the park, find a resting spot to park your family for a respite and maybe even naps for the kids. The small alcove with benches to the right of the entrance to *Pirates of the Caribbean* in Adventureland makes a good resting place.

   Note: If the Magic Kingdom is too crowded for your comfort, switch to a non Early Entry Disney park after your rest break (if your ticket allows) and start with the afternoon or evening section of the appropriate touring plan.

11. If you've left the MK for a rest, return at around 2:30 or 2:40 p.m. and reclaim your stroller(s) with your receipt. If your kids want to meet more characters, now's a good time to do it. Check your Times Guide for "Character Greeting" areas. Board the *Walt Disney World Railroad* train at the Main Street station to ride to the appropriate land.

   To meet Peter Pan and other characters, get off at the Frontierland station and go to the *Pirates of the Caribbean* attraction building, where you will usually find them outside, on the *Splash Mountain* side of the building. Alternatively, disembark at Mickey's Toontown Fair and meet the characters there or walk on to Fantasyland to the *Mad Tea Party* ride area where still more characters may await you.

   Note: Character areas may change. The Times Guide and the separate

"Character Greeting Location Guide" (if available) will provide current information.

Note, too: Only collapsible strollers are allowed on the train; leave a non-collapsible stroller at the station and retrieve it later. Or get a replacement stroller with your rental receipt at your destination.

12. Catch a show circa 4:00 p.m. – at the Castle Forecourt Stage, the Galaxy Palace Theater, or the Fairytale Garden. Claim your seats about 15 to 20 minutes before showtime.

13. Go to Tomorrowland and see *Walt Disney's Carousel of Progress*.

14. Then check out *Monsters, Inc. Laugh Floor* or *Stitch's Great Escape!* if you want to.

    Warning: *Stitch's Great Escape!* is frightening to children of all ages, especially those 6 and under.

15. The Magic Kingdom may close early or late. Plan to ride *Jungle Cruise* and *The Magic Carpets of Aladdin* during the hour before closing or during the evening parade (during the early parade if there are two scheduled). Alternatively, use the FASTPASS option for *Jungle Cruise* if it's available.

16. Whenever it's appropriate, honor any dinner reservations you may have made. The character dinner at Liberty Tree Tavern is worthwhile.

17. See *The Enchanted Tiki Room* and/or *Country Bear Jamboree* if you missed them before.

18. Ride the "Liberty Belle" around *Tom Sawyer Island* if it is still running (the riverboat attraction sometimes shuts down at dusk).

19. Play a while in *Pooh's Playful Spot*, and plan to see any attractions you haven't yet visited or want to see again. For approximate wait times, consult the Tip Board on Main Street. It's across from Casey's Corner and not always accurate.

    Also, schedule any last-minute shopping you may want to do. (And don't forget to partake of periodic refreshments.)

    Tip: Lines for attractions tend to be shortest during evening parades.

20. In the hour before park closing, ride *Jungle Cruise* or *The Magic Carpets of Aladdin* or any other attraction you wish. If your kids have been asking about *Splash Mountain* and if they're tall enough (40" or more), go get in line or use "switching off." But be aware that the wait will be long. Use FASTPASS (if available).

21. Enjoy the *Swiss Family Treehouse* if time permits.

22. Watch the evening fireworks, *Wishes*, from the main bridge to Tomorrowland or from the end of Main Street near the central hub. Or leave before the fireworks if you want to beat the exit crowds.

Two-Day Touring Plans for Seniors

This plan includes no fast, scary, or spinning attractions. If you enjoy such rides, follow the touring plans for adults and teens.

This plan assumes you will arrive at opening time on both days. If you want to sleep in, just pick up the non Early Entry plan around step 5. If the park is crowded and you arrive late, you might consider skipping the after-lunch break and using the time to visit attractions that usually have minimal waits; or consult your Times Guide for stage shows you would enjoy. Use FASTPASS or the singles line option (when available) to minimize your waits for crowded attractions.

Note: Because visitors generally take advantage of the Extra Magic Hours' Early Entry privilege only once at each Disney park they visit, the Early Entry tour plan is virtually the same for Day One and Day Two. I include it under both days so that you don't have to flip back and forth in your guidebook. Moreover, because this Two-Day plan for mature visitors anticipates that the young-at-heart may want to spend the early morning hours elsewhere on at least one of their two Magic Kingdom days, steps 1 through 5 of the Day One and Day Two non Early Entry plans are also virtual duplicates.

Note: I consider a wait of more than 15 to 20 minutes too long. Don't wait; go on to the next step and come back later. Pick up a FASTPASS (if available) for the attraction you are skipping.

Seniors Day One Plan for Extra Magic Hours' Early Entry Days

(WDW property guests only)

Note: During evening Extra Magic Hours, the crowds are sometimes lighter. You can use the non Early Entry day touring plan for attractions that are open or simply tour at leisure with your own itinerary.

1. Line up at the rope nearest Cinderella Castle. When it drops, or if it is not up, head up either walkway and through Cinderella Castle to Fantasyland. Walk past *Snow White's Scary Adventures*, turn right and ride *The Many Adventures of Winnie the Pooh*.

2. Turn left at the exit. Cross to the other side of Fantasyland and ride *Peter Pan's Flight*.

3. Turn right at the exit and ride *Snow White's Scary Adventures* if it's open (it may not be open yet).

4. Walk back towards *Peter Pan's Flight* and ride *"it's a small world"* or *Cinderella's Golden Carrousel*.

5. 15 minutes before the official opening time, line up at the rope between Fantasyland and Liberty Square. If you have a few minutes, buy some coffee or refreshments to enjoy while you wait for the rope to drop (or wait and take a break after step 6).

6. When the rope drops, take your time walking into Liberty Square. Walk under the overpass and then turn right to ride *The Haunted Mansion*.

7. Pick up the following plan at step 6. Skip any steps you've already done today.

Seniors Day One Plan
for Non EMH Early Entry Days

1. Line up at the rope nearest Cinderella Castle. When the rope drops or if the rope is not up, head up either walkway and through Cinderella Castle to Fantasyland. Walk past *Snow White's Scary Adventures*, turn right and ride *The Many Adventures of Winnie the Pooh*.

2. Turn left at the exit. Cross to the other side of Fantasyland and ride *Peter Pan's Flight*.

3. Turn right at the exit and ride *Snow White's Scary Adventures*.

4. Cross into Liberty Square. Grab some refreshment in Liberty Square or Frontierland and take a break.

5. When you're hydrated and rested, visit *The Haunted Mansion* in Liberty Square.

6. Walk across Frontierland to the *Country Bear Jamboree* on your left and enjoy the show.

7. Turn right at the exit. Walk to the *Liberty Square Riverboat* and board at the next departure. On the riverboat, listen to the overhead spiel for some humorous Mark Twain aphorisms.

8. Consider an early lunch. The Plaza Restaurant on Main Street usually opens at 11:00 a.m. and is a good place to lunch.

9. Cross to Adventureland and ride *Pirates of the Caribbean*.
   Tip: Choose the left queue if it's open; it's often shorter.

10. Exit *Pirates of the Caribbean* and turn left. Pass by *Splash Mountain* and

then turn left again to board the *Walt Disney World Railroad*. Ride it around the entire park and exit at Mickey's Toontown Fair on your second pass.

11. Visit **Mickey's Country House** (right) and *Minnie's Country House* and enjoy the details of Mickey's neighborhood.

12. If you're staying on Disney property and you start feeling tired, consider leaving the park (via the train to Main Street) to refresh yourself at your hotel for a while. Keep any parking receipts for free same-day parking at any WDW theme-park lot. Return to the park when you feel re-energized and pick up the touring plan where you left off. If the timing is right, eat an early dinner in your hotel or at the park and resume the touring plan after dinner if the park is open late.

Alternative: If you are staying off property or just don't feel like leaving the park, rest in a shady spot for a while in mid-afternoon (like the park across from the Sleepy Hollow eatery behind Ye Olde Christmas Shoppe in Liberty Square).

Note: If the Magic Kingdom is too crowded for your comfort and your ticket allows, switch to a non Early Entry Disney park after your rest and start with the afternoon or evening section of the appropriate touring plan.

13. Walk to Tomorrowland. Enjoy the show at *Walt Disney's Carousel of Progress*.

14. See *Monsters, Inc. Laugh Floor*, across from *Stitch's Great Escape!*

15. Leave Tomorrowland and walk through or around the central hub on the right. Enter Liberty Square and catch the next show at *The Hall of Presidents*.

16. Turn right at the exit and walk past Columbia Harbour House eatery to Fantasyland. Walk to *Mickey's PhilharMagic* on your right. Enjoy the show if the line is not too long. Use FASTPASS (if available) if the wait is long.

17. Ride *"it's a small world"* across from *Peter Pan's Flight*. The wait for *"it's a small world"* is usually not too long.

18. Leave Fantasyland through Cinderella Castle and enjoy the elaborate mosaic mural inside on the Castle wall. Turn left and walk to the second entrance to Tomorrowland. Walk past *Monsters, Inc. Laugh Floor*

and *Astro Orbiter* on your left to *Tomorrowland Transit Authority*. While you're enjoying it, consider your dinner options if you don't already have advance dining reservations. The Crystal Palace buffet is a good bet (Disney characters visit your table), as is Cinderella's Royal Table in Cinderella Castle if you can get there early. Otherwise try good counter-service food at Tomorrowland Terrace Noodle Station.

19. See the show at *The Enchanted Tiki Room* in Adventureland.

20. Ride *Jungle Cruise* in Adventureland. If the wait is long, use a FASTPASS if available. Or if two evening parades are scheduled, get in line during the early evening parade.

21. Plan to see one of the evening parades and the fireworks show. Find a viewing spot in Frontierland 20 to 30 minutes before parade time. Ask a Disney cast member where the parade is starting from. If it begins at Main Street, you have 15 or more minutes after starting time before the parade hits Frontierland. Send someone for refreshments if you wish. If you have time before the parade, relax with some ice cream or coffee from the Plaza Ice Cream Parlor. Find a chair near the Plaza Restaurant or in the small side street off Main Street.

Later, watch the fireworks from the middle of the main bridge to Tomorrowland. Look up as the fireworks start; Tinker Bell floats down from near the top of Cinderella Castle to a rooftop in Tomorrowland (weather and wind permitting).

22. Close down the park with any last-minute attractions you want to see, and shop on Main Street on your way out. Enjoy the Disney window scenes at the Emporium shop.

Seniors Day Two Plan for Extra Magic Hours' Early Entry Days

(WDW property guests only)

Note: During evening Extra Magic Hours, the crowds are sometimes lighter. You can use the non Early Entry day touring plan for attractions that are open or simply tour at leisure with your own itinerary.

1. Line up at the rope nearest Cinderella Castle. When it drops, or if it is not up, head up either walkway and through Cinderella Castle to Fantasyland. Walk past *Snow White's Scary Adventures*, turn right and ride *The Many Adventures of Winnie the Pooh*.

2. Turn left at the exit. Cross to the other side of Fantasyland and ride *Peter Pan's Flight*.

3. Turn right at the exit and ride *Snow White's Scary Adventures* if you can (it may not be open yet).
4. Ride *Cinderella's Golden Carrousel*.
5. Relax for a while at a table near *Ariel's Grotto*. Then 15 minutes before the official opening time, line up at the rope between Fantasyland and Liberty Square. Buy some coffee or refreshments to enjoy while you wait at the rope.
6. When the rope drops, walk at a leisurely pace into Liberty Square. Go under the overpass and turn right to ride *The Haunted Mansion*.
7. Pick up the following plan at step 6. Skip any steps you've already done today or yesterday (or enjoy doing them again).

Seniors Day Two Plan for Non Early Entry Days

1. Line up at the rope nearest Cinderella Castle. When the rope drops, or if it is not up, head up either walkway and through Cinderella Castle to Fantasyland. Walk past *Snow White's Scary Adventures*. Turn right and ride *The Many Adventures of Winnie the Pooh*.
2. Turn left at the exit. Cross to the other side of Fantasyland and ride *Peter Pan's Flight*.
3. Turn right at the exit and ride *Snow White's Scary Adventures*, then enjoy *Mickey's PhilharMagic* if you haven't yet seen it.
4. Cross into Liberty Square. Grab some refreshment in Liberty Square or Frontierland and take a break.
5. When you're hydrated and rested, visit *The Haunted Mansion* in Liberty Square.
6. Go to the raft to *Tom Sawyer Island*. Ride the raft to the island and enjoy a sandwich and lemonade for lunch on the riverside porch at Aunt Polly's Dockside Inn (operates seasonally). Explore *Tom Sawyer Island* all the way back to Fort Sam Clemens.
7. If you're staying on Disney property and feel tired, consider leaving the park (via the train from Frontierland station to Main Street) to refresh yourself at your hotel for a while. Keep any parking receipts for free re-entry to the parking lot. Return to the park when you feel re-energized. Pick up the touring plan where you left off.
   Alternative: If you are staying off property or don't want to take the time to leave and return, an alternative is to rest in a shady spot for a while in mid-afternoon (like the benches in the small alcove to the right

of the entrance to *Pirates of the Caribbean*).

Note: If the Magic Kingdom is too crowded for your comfort, switch to a non Early Entry Disney park after your rest (if your ticket allows) and start with the afternoon or evening section of the appropriate touring plan.

8. Return to the Magic Kingdom at about 2:30 p.m. to get a viewing spot along Main Street or in Frontierland for the 3:00 p.m. afternoon parade. Enjoy the parade.

9. Walk through one of the passageways to Adventureland and ride *Jungle Cruise* if you didn't ride it yesterday (or if you want to ride it again). If the line for *Jungle Cruise* is long, get a FASTPASS if available and return later to enjoy the boat ride.

10. Check the Times Guide for the next available shows at the Castle Forecourt Stage (in front of Cinderella Castle) and/or the Galaxy Palace Theatre in Tomorrowland.

11. Ride *Snow White's Scary Adventure* if you haven't already and if the wait isn't too long.

12. Try to see the Flag Retreat in Town Square (usually around 5 p.m.).

13. If you don't have reservations for dinner, consider an early dinner at Liberty Tree Tavern, Tony's Town Square Restaurant, or The Plaza Restaurant. Disney characters visit your table at the Liberty Tree Tavern.

14. Revisit any of your favorite attractions where the waiting lines aren't too long. Check the Tip Board next to Casey's Corner on Main Street for approximate current waiting times (it's not always accurate). Check your Guidemap for any other entertainment options that appeal to you.

15. Browse through the shops on Main Street.

Caution: Avoid Main Street if a parade has just ended.

16. If you're up for more fun, enjoy the evening parade and the fireworks show.

Tip: If two parades are scheduled, the second one is less crowded. Try a popular attraction (such as *Pirates of the Caribbean*) during the early parade. Or take a look at *Cinderella's Golden Carrousel*. It's especially attractive at night.

17. When you exit the park, relax for a while on benches along the lakefront path below the monorail station. If the timing is right, you can enjoy the Electrical Water Pageant on the lake. It sometimes passes the Magic Kingdom around 10:15 to 10:20 p.m.

The view from the ride is a large part of the fun of Astro Orbiter, *a futuristic* Dumbo *ride in Tomorrowland featuring steerable rockets that fly in a circle.*

Walt Disney World Railroad *circles the Magic Kingdom in about 20 minutes, stopping at Main Street, Frontierland, and Mickey's Toontown Fair.*

Travel from the present to ancient Mexico in minutes by walking from Spaceship Earth in Future World (above) to the Mexico Pavilion in World Showcase.

Chapter 3

Epcot

Walt Disney's "experimental prototype community of tomorrow," or "Epcot" for short, never materialized into the grand self-sustaining city of the future he had envisioned. Instead, since his death, it has become one of the most unusual entertainment parks anywhere in the world. Epcot is a more adult-oriented park than the Magic Kingdom and is more than twice as large as either the Magic Kingdom or Disney's Hollywood Studios – giving you room to spread out even on busy days.

Epcot shelters two "Worlds," Future World and World Showcase. Future World is a collection of pavilions that house rides and attractions showcasing technology and progress. World Showcase offers visitors a glimpse of the cultures of eleven different countries, including the U.S.A. and our near neighbors Canada and Mexico, with samples of their characteristic foods, goods (many for sale), and attractions. Each "country" in World Showcase is housed in its own pavilion, and the pavilions are set along a wide, 1.3-mile promenade surrounding a lagoon. Bridges connect the two worlds and wind around the Odyssey Center, a large facility used for special events.

Note that in addition to the attractions described below, Epcot occasionally stages parades and regularly presents a number of performing artists at various spots around Future World and World Showcase.

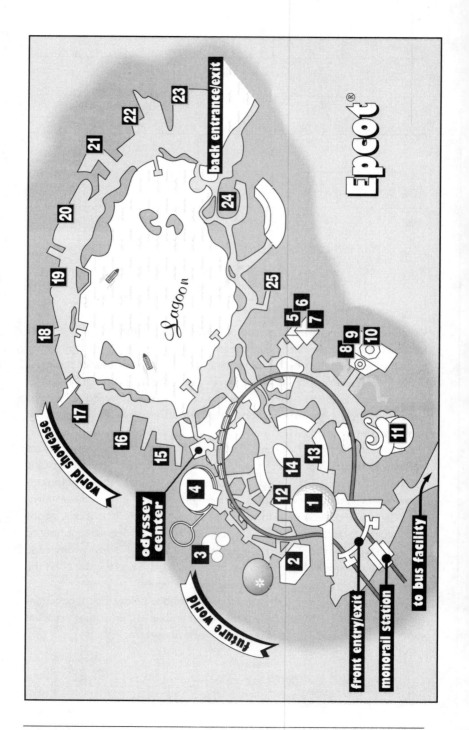

Epcot®

world showcase

future world

Lagoon

odyssey center

back entrance/exit

front entry/exit

monorail station

to bus facility

FUTURE WORLD

1. Spaceship Earth Pavilion
2. Universe of Energy Pavilion
3. Mission: SPACE Pavilion
4. Test Track Pavilion

Imagination! Pavilion
5. Honey, I Shrunk the Audience
6. Journey Into Imagination with Figment
7. ImageWorks

The Land Pavilion
8. Living with the Land
9. The Circle of Life
10. Soarin'

11. The Seas with Nemo & Friends Pavilion
12. Innoventions East Side
13. Innoventions West Side
14. Innoventions Plaza

WORLD SHOWCASE

15. Mexico: Gran Fiesta Tour
16. Norway: Maelstrom
17. China: Reflections of China
18. Germany
19. Italy
20. The American Adventure: The American Adventure Show
21. Japan
22. Morocco
23. France: Impressions de France
24. United Kingdom
25. Canada: O Canada!

Future World

You enter Future World after passing through the main (front) entrance turnstiles to Epcot. Directly in front of you is the awesome Spaceship Earth geosphere, the first of nine pavilions you'll find in this world of gleaming silver, futuristic designs, and bright colors.

Spaceship Earth

Rating: ❤❤❤❤
Type: Educational "dark ride"
Time: 16 - 17 minutes
Steve says: History can be fun! Visually stunning

This huge aluminum geodesic sphere houses a ride that carries you past Audio-Animatronics scenes depicting the evolution of communications. Your car begins at the dawn of language and alphabets and takes you forward through the centuries – past the Age of Rome, Gutenberg's printing press, the invention of movies and television, the first personal computer (in the inventor's garage!), and other landmark achievements – to the current age of virtual reality and the Internet. Smile as your photo is snapped at the beginning. During the last part of the ride, when you interact with the video touch screen in front of you to create your own personal future, your photo is inserted on the screen as your future unfolds!

At the exit of the ride you'll find **Project Tomorrow**, a large area with interactive technology exhibits. You can email your photo from your *Spaceship Earth* ride using computers here. Skip the exhibits in the morning. Return and have fun here in the early evening when you're visiting Innoventions nearby.

Tip: Project Tomorrow sometimes stays open during *IllumiNations,* the evening fireworks show. You can access it without taking the ride by walking in a side door below the geosphere.

Universe of Energy

Rating: ❤❤❤❤
Type: Indoor theater show and "dark ride"
Time: 27 minutes (plus pre-show of up to 8 minutes)
Steve says: A bit ponderous but the dinosaur segment is fun

While you're waiting to enter the theater, a pre-show prepares you for the *Jeopardy* adventure to come. Once inside, huge theater cars travel slowly between large rooms for a series of entertaining presentations about energy.

Bill Nye, the Science Guy, preps Ellen DeGeneres for a *Jeopardy* game show competition with Jamie Lee Curtis. In the middle of the show, your car accompanies Ellen and Bill back in time to a prehistoric forest for some relatively close encounters with convincing Audio-Animatronics allosauruses, pteranodons, velociraptors, a tyrannosaurus rex, and other reptilian cousins.

Mission: SPACE

Rating:	♥♥♥♥♥
Type:	Simulator ride
Time:	About 4 minutes for the ride; up to 15 minutes including two pre-boarding videos
Steve says:	Another Disney first, unique and thrilling

Wonder what it would be like to experience weightlessness? *Mission: SPACE* lets you simulate that experience, along with the "liftoff" from planet Earth. The sustained G-forces of the "launch" are like nothing you've ever experienced! Each guest in the 4-person X-2 rockets has a specific task to perform to ensure a successful group mission to Mars. (Don't worry, your group will succeed regardless.) A post-show area contains several interactive space game experiences, a **space-themed playground** for the kids, and an **email station** where you can send video mug shots of yourself "from space" to friends and family. Outside in the entrance plaza, walk past Mars, the Earth, and the Moon (with marked sites of all lunar landings).

Tip: Be alert; the landing on Mars is a bit bumpy!

Height restriction: You must be 44" or taller to ride. Switching off is available.

Strong Caution: People prone to vertigo or claustrophobia may have problems with this intense experience. If you have chronic heart or blood pressure problems, I recommend that you skip this attraction or, at most, choose the "toned down" noncentrifuge option. Several riders have died in recent years after experiencing the regular *Mission: SPACE*.

Test Track

Rating:	♥♥♥♥♥
Type:	Combination roller coaster and flight simulator
Time:	4 - 5 minutes
Steve says:	Unique track ride with a high-speed section

This fast-moving ride simulates an automobile test track. As you approach it, your queue winds past displays on automobile testing – the brake test, corrosion test, and even the "seat squirm test" among others. These displays feature the testing equipment complete with convincing video and sound effects. You end up in a briefing room where you are prepared for your ride in a six-seater test vehicle. Then it's on to the "proving grounds" for high-speed tests on straightaways and curves, over bumpy terrain, and through hot and cold temperatures and near-collisions. Two sudden braking sequences test the difference between regular and antilock brakes. More displays of automotive technology await you at the ride exit. You'll walk away with a visceral appreciation of the extensive testing to which car components are subjected along with firsthand knowledge of the benefits of antilock brakes and other safety features.

Height restriction: You must be 40" or taller to ride. Switching off is available.

Imagination! Pavilion

Outside this pavilion is an **"upside-down waterfall,"** which is especially colorful at night. Inside are two attractions, *Honey, I Shrunk the Audience* and *Journey Into Imagination with Figment.* You'll find a series of **unusual fountains** with jumping and leaping water effects at the exit of *Honey, I Shrunk the Audience.* It's fun to spend a few minutes here.

Honey, I Shrunk the Audience

Rating: ♥♥♥♥♥

Type: 3-D movie in a sit-down theater

Time: 17 - 18 minutes

Steve says: The audience squeals with delight through this one

This 3-D film has some of the best special effects anywhere. Rick Moranis and company are back to introduce some of the Professor's new inventions, including a duplicator machine that copies a mouse and inadvertently releases hundreds of mice into the audience! You also get to meet a cat, a lion, and a snake up close and personal. The new deluxe model shrinking machine accidentally miniaturizes the entire theater audience, and the result is quite believable. In the final big scene, imagine a face-to-face encounter with a snotty-nosed dog who lets loose with a huge sneeze.

Tip: Avoid the first few rows; the 3-D effects may be diluted.

Journey Into Imagination with Figment

Rating: ♥♥♥

Type: "Dark ride"

Time: 8 - 9 minutes

Steve says: Whimsical ride, relaxing, but not worth a long wait

A gently moving vehicle takes you through the sensory testing labs of the Imagination Institute, where you experience some amazing demonstrations of sound, sight, and smell (your nose will get a jolt!). Figment (the small, purple dragon from a previous attraction here) accompanies you through the ride and shows off his upside-down house.

Tip: At one point you'll feel a strong wind, so take off your hat before you ride!

ImageWorks

Rating: ♥♥♥

Type: Interactive exhibit area

Time: As long as you want, but 15 minutes at a minimum

Steve says: These unusual exhibits can be enjoyed by folks of all ages

This interactive playground has stations where you can experiment with photography, colors, and music. You can conduct an orchestra of sounds by raising and lowering your hands, step among splotches of light on the floor to cause a cacophony of animal and other noises, and create a unique photograph of yourself that you can send immediately by email to your home or someone else's computer. And that's just for starters.

Caution: It's easy to lose track of time at *ImageWorks,* and children often don't want to leave.

The Land Pavilion

This pavilion contains several attractions and one of the best food courts in WDW (the veggies are grown in The Land's own greenhouses, which you can tour for a fee (sign up near the entrance to *Soarin'*). This pavilion is also a choice place to get out of the rain.

Living with the Land

Rating: ♥♥♥♥

Type: Indoor, gentle boat ride

Time:	12 - 14 minutes
Steve says:	More proof that education (in this case, science) can be fun

The first part of the *Living with the Land* boat ride takes you past Audio-Animatronics scenes of various ecosystems: rain forest, prairie, desert, and a family farm complete with crops and farm animals. You then float through a series of active greenhouses lush with edible plants (used in meals at WDW restaurants), followed by research areas for aeroponics, fish farming, and even experimental moon-soil gardening. Along the way, a recorded spiel entertains and informs you.

The Circle of Life

Rating:	❤❤❤
Type:	Indoor movie in a sit-down theater
Time:	13 minutes
Steve says:	Entertaining movie about a serious subject

Characters from *The Lion King* (Simba, Timon, and Pumbaa) are the stars in a film about the potential dangers of mankind's mishandling of the environment. Timon and Pumbaa dam a river to create a lake for a new resort. Simba teaches them about the unfortunate consequences their for-profit venture creates in nature. The theater is comfortable and the presentation lighthearted but educational. Television monitors in the pre-show area flash interesting ecological facts about our earth and how we treat (and mistreat) it.

Soarin'

Rating:	❤❤❤❤❤
Type:	Simulator ride
Time:	About 5 minutes for the ride
Steve says:	This gentle "flight" taps into the adventuresome spirit in all of us

You're lifted in a simulated hang glider to soar above projections of such beautiful California scenery as the Golden Gate Bridge, Lake Tahoe skiers, and Los Angeles at night. The scenery is projected inside a gigantic domed screen and offers a feast for the eyes. You feel the wind in your face and smell the pine trees and orange groves below you. Your feet almost "touch" the water as you glide over the ocean.

Tip: If you're concerned about motion sickness, get in row three which leads to the lowest (and least altitude-challenged) row of seats.

Height restriction: You must be 40" or taller to ride.

The Seas with Nemo & Friends

Rating: ♥♥♥♥ (for exhibits); ♥♥♥ (for ride)

Type: Combination ride and gigantic aquarium with exhibits

Time: Ride: about 4 minutes

Exhibits: as long as you want, but a minimum of 15 minutes depending on the crowds

Steve says: An awesome and beautiful oceanic experience

This pavilion houses a huge saltwater aquarium teeming with more than 65 species of marine life and coral reefs. The pavilion's front entrance leads to a winding queue with outdoor beach scenes that lead, in turn, to an "underwater" trail. You then board a "clamobile" to enjoy a gentle ride ("The Seas with Nemo & Friends") past animated scenes of your quest to find Nemo.

After the ride, you enter a large area where you can spend more time gazing into the aquarium (including a section devoted to manatees) and explore exhibits about sea life, marine research, and current ocean exploration techniques. You and your kids will enjoy **"Turtle Talk with Crush,"** in which a computer-animated Crush (the surfer turtle from *Finding Nemo*) talks to and interacts with individual audience members for about 15 minutes in a small theater.

Tip: You can access the exhibit area through the rear doors of the pavilion, bypassing the ride.

Innoventions East Side and West Side

Rating: ♥♥♥♥

Type: Indoor exhibits

Time: As long as you want, but allow a minimum of 10 minutes per building for a walk-through, more if you interact with the exhibits

Steve says: These new, cutting-edge products can occupy you for an afternoon or an entire day

Two large buildings, one on the east side of Future World and one on the west, curve gently away from Spaceship Earth. These buildings house a series of walk-through exhibits that will keep technology buffs happy for hours on end. The Innoventions buildings showcase new and developing consumer products. Companies proudly display their latest technologies in interactive games, Internet and email exhibits, and computers galore. Among the interesting sights you may encounter: a walk-through house of the future (how about voice-control commands for everything in your home and a whirlpool bath with surround sound!), a studio where you can design your own plastic robot to take home (for free!), a fun interactive game that challenges you and your kids to find fire hazards in your home, and large areas filled with video games – many of them free to play.

Tip: Unless you plan to spend at least two days at Epcot, use your day-light hours to experience the park's other attractions and return to Innoventions in the late afternoon or early evening.

Note: Walk to the end of Innoventions West Side to **Club Cool** to enjoy refreshing, **free** soft drinks from foreign countries.

Innoventions Plaza

As you pass by Spaceship Earth, you'll spot a large electronic **Tip Board** in the middle of the square between the two Innoventions buildings. The board gives approximate wait times for Epcot attractions. Further along in the plaza, the large Fountain of Nations comes to life every 15 minutes (on the hour, quarter-hour, and so on) with a beautiful **water ballet**, complete with a rousing musical score. The 4-minute ballet is worth a stop.

Caution: The water shoots high in the air, so consider the wind direction if you want to assure yourself a dry viewing spot.

Past the Innoventions buildings on the right side of the middle path to World Showcase is a small **interactive fountain**. Random spurts of water in different formations emanate from a flat, circular padded area, drawing kids like bees to honey. It's delightful to watch them cavorting carefree.

Note: This fountain proved so popular that similar ones have shown up all over WDW. In fact, your kids may have already spotted the colorful **interactive fountain** outside Innoventions East Side on the walkway to *Mission: SPACE*. Hope you brought dry clothes for them.

World Showcase

Surrounding a large lagoon are eleven areas representing specific countries. Each re-creates some of that country's classic characteristics and landmarks in fascinating detail. The shops, food, architecture, and attractions reflect the particular country, as do the live performers and shows. Adding to the feeling of authenticity, the Disney cast members employed in each country are natives or descendants of natives. The overall effect provides a convincing, cosmopolitan experience for the tourist strolling from one country to the next along the Showcase's wide promenade. Shopping is especially fun in this part of Epcot.

Note: If you're a ham, you can volunteer to participate in the show put on by the strolling **World Showcase Players**.

Note for Kids: Only some countries offer traditional theme park attractions, such as rides or movies, but each one offers a **Kidcot Fun Stop** and a **Passport Center**. Kids can make masks and do other crafts free of charge at the *Fun Stops* under the supervision of a Disney cast member. They can also get their "Passports" stamped by a cast member and endorsed with a handwritten foreign phrase (there's an $11.00 charge for the Passports, none for the stamping and endorsement). Fun Stops open around 11:00 a.m. (sometimes 9:00 a.m. in Future World) and close around 9:00 p.m. (Check your Times Guide for *Fun Stop* times on the day of your visit.)

Mexico

A great pyramid enveloped in lush vegetation greets you at the Mexico Pavilion. Just inside is a collection of valuable **cultural artifacts**. Further along you will find a beautiful shopping plaza.

Walk through the shopping plaza to reach the entrances to both *Gran Fiesta Tour Starring the Three Caballeros* (just after the last shop on the left) and the San Angel Inn restaurant.

Tip: As you leave Mexico and walk away toward Norway, admire the tropical trees and plant life along a short path to your left.

Gran Fiesta Tour Starring the Three Caballeros

Rating: 💛💛
Type: Indoor boat ride
Time: 7 - 8 minutes
Steve says: Pleasant and relaxing, but not worth a long wait

A boat floats you gently past scenes of Mexico past and present, from ancient Mayan culture to current city life, including holiday fireworks, and cliff divers. You're treated to animated scenes of José Carioca (a parrot) and Panchito (a rooster) trying to find the third Caballero: Donald Duck (from the 1944 Disney movie, *The Three Caballeros*). You'll find some of the Audio-Animatronics figures reminiscent of those in the Magic Kingdom's *"it's a small world"* ride.

Norway

The central courtyard is surrounded by replicas of Norway's architectural landmarks: a wooden stave church (which contains a gallery of artifacts), the 14th-century Akershus Castle, and other historic buildings. A statue of legendary marathoner Grete Waitz stands behind the bakery (on the side nearest the Mexico Pavilion). Near the statue is a Viking ship, which makes a decent photo backdrop.

Maelstrom

Rating: ♥♥♥♥

Type: Indoor boat ride

Time: 12 - 14 minutes (5-minute boat ride, 2 - 4 minutes exploring a Norwegian fishing village, 5-minute movie)

Steve says: Ride soon after World Showcase opens or you're in for a long wait (or a FASTPASS)

A Viking longboat takes you along Norwegian waterways past a maelstrom (giant whirlpool), a waterfall, a deep-sea oil rig, and menacing trolls. After the boat journey, you get to explore a seaside Norwegian village and then watch an informative film about Norway. You can skip the film by walking across the theater and out the exit doors on the far side, but the movie is worth watching to give yourself the full Disney-style experience of Norway and its interesting culture.

China

An archway of good fortune welcomes you to a scaled-down replica of Beijing's Temple of Heaven. Beautiful gardens filled with rosebushes and reflecting ponds add to the quiet, relaxing atmosphere of this pavilion. There's usually an interesting exhibit relating to Chinese art or culture on offer.

Note: Various **acrobats** stage appealing shows here; check your Times Guide for performance times.

Reflections of China

Rating: ♥♥♥
Type: Indoor movie in Circle-Vision
Time: About 15 minutes
Steve says: A collage of spectacular scenes

The Temple of Heaven houses this informative movie about the mysterious country of China. Disney filmed scenes in cities such as Beijing, Hong Kong, and Shanghai, as well as other sites such as the Great Wall. The film is in "Circle-Vision 360 degrees": the screens encircle you and you have to stand to watch.

Warning: Wheelchairs are welcome, but there are no seats in the theater. If you can't stand for 15 minutes (and aren't using a wheelchair), you should give this one a skip.

Germany

Architecturally diverse buildings border the courtyard here and are sure to impress visitors. The beer hall at the rear of the square houses a restaurant that comes alive with mealtime entertainment. The shops around the square contain abundant items of interest, including Hummel figurines and a huge assortment of cuckoo clocks. An elaborate **G scale miniature railroad**, complete with farms and villages, is located on the side of the pavilion toward Italy.

Italy

Like Germany, the Italy Pavilion has a courtyard surrounded by examples of diverse Italian architectural styles, including a replica of the fourteenth-century Doge's Palace in Venice. The sea god Neptune watches over the fountain at the rear of the piazza, and Venetian gondolas are moored in the lagoon nearby. The shops here contain popular items such as Armani collectibles and Venetian glass, and the entertainment is unique. Especially notable: **Sergio**, a skilled juggler who interacts with the audience.

The American Adventure

A huge Colonial-style mansion sits at the southernmost part of World Showcase in The American Adventure, the central country pavilion of the Epcot eleven. On the lagoon side of the World Showcase promenade is the **America Gardens Theater**, a large open-air venue for live entertainment.

Flower beds in front of the theater are usually planted in red, white, and blue blossoms.

The American Adventure Show

Rating: ❤❤❤❤❤

Type: Indoor historical theater presentation

Time: About 30 minutes

Steve says: Patriotic for Americans, compelling history experience for others

This show is staged in a theater inside The American Adventure mansion. You get to sit in comfortable seats for the show, which uses Audio-Animatronics, animation, and photo collages to take you on a journey through American history. The experience is much more than a dry history lesson; it's a wonderfully entertaining view of American heritage. Mark Twain and Ben Franklin are the main narrators. They review the uplifting (Thomas Jefferson, Alexander Graham Bell, Susan B. Anthony, John Muir, Jackie Robinson, Will Rogers, and many others) as well as some of the sobering aspects of U.S. history. Some folks will have moist eyes after the Civil War segment.

Between the holding area and the theater is the **Hall of Flags** corridor, which displays 44 historic flags. Try to catch the **Voices of Liberty**, a terrific a cappella group that performs just inside the entrance, usually from late morning through late afternoon (check your Times Guide for performances).

Japan

A five-story pagoda sits at the entrance to this pavilion. Behind it is a garden with walking paths that wind among streams, flowers, and trees. Brightly colored koi fish lounge lazily in the pools. You can enter the garden via a path from the promenade on The American Adventure Pavilion side of the pagoda. As you walk up this path, look to your right and you'll see a monkey puzzle tree, the only tree monkeys can't climb because of the small sharp spines sticking out of the bark (the tree label says "Bunya-Bunya" tree). A gallery in the rear of the pavilion displays interesting cultural items. The large building across from the pagoda on the other side of the pavilion was modeled after the Imperial Palace in Japan's old capital, Kyoto.

Serene is the word for the Japan Pavilion. It's a perfect place to sit and relax. Enjoy one of the **Japanese drumming routines** by the Matsuriza group of drummers; your Times Guide lists performance times.

Morocco

Ocher-colored stuccoed buildings and archways encompass the central court-yard and market area of the Morocco Pavilion. A replica of the prayer tower in Marrakesh stands at its entrance, and beautifully colored tile decorates the indoor walls of the shops and the museum of Moroccan culture. Restaurant Marrakesh offers tasty food, often accompanied by a belly dancer.

France

A model of the Eiffel Tower overlooks the streets and buildings of this pavilion. The architecture of the front part of the pavilion is reminiscent of Parisian architecture in the Belle Epoque ("beautiful age," 1870 to 1914).

On the promenade you'll find kiosks covered with advertisements for artists and museums Parisians might have seen during that era. The shops sell perfume, jewelry, and other luxury items. At the far side of the pavilion, near the waterway to the Epcot resort hotels, is a beautiful and peaceful garden – a perfect spot to relax and get away from the crowds.

The influence of Impressionist French artists is visible both in the rose-colored dresses the hostesses wear and in one of the shops; it sells gift items (such as umbrellas and mugs) covered with scenes from famous paintings.

Impressions de France

Rating: ❤❤❤❤
Type: Indoor movie
Time: 18 minutes
Steve says: Delicious, like fine wine

This beautiful, lyrical film is shown in a theater with comfortable seats. The movie is projected on a wide screen (not 360 degrees) and accompanied by a wonderful classical music score. You visit many French landmarks (including the Eiffel Tower, Versailles, Cannes, and the French Alps), as well as some lesser known scenic areas. Many sites were filmed from the air, including one filmed from a balloon. Like the France Pavilion in general, the film is enchanting and relaxing.

United Kingdom

The variety of historic architectural styles in this pavilion is fascinating to behold. You stroll past a cottage modeled on Anne Hathaway's (William Shakespeare's wife), past a panoply of changing historical architectural styles (including formal Tudor and Victorian) to a quiet, serene park reminiscent of the beautiful parks of London. Behind the facades are shops aplenty, all of them connected but each designed to match the exterior "architecture." Even the pub on the lagoon side of the promenade retains the focus; it's built in a combination of historical pub styles. Behind the shops, you'll find a scenic path that will take you through traditional English flower and herb gardens.

Canada

This pavilion has a refreshing outdoor atmosphere. A giant totem pole greets you at the entrance and a large Rocky Mountain rises up at the rear of the pavilion. Winding paths bring you to a waterfall, a gurgling stream, and an expansive hillside flower garden modeled after the Butchart Gardens in Victoria, British Columbia.

O Canada!

Rating: 🐭🐭🐭
Type: Indoor movie in Circle-Vision
Time: 18 minutes
Steve says: Energetic tribute to our northern neighbor

Host and narrator, Martin Short, introduces us to his home country in this "Circle-Vision 360 degree" film (in other words, you must stand during the movie). Along with the beautiful rivers, mountains, and wildlife of this vast country, the film introduces you to the Royal Canadian Mounted Police, chuck wagon racers at the annual Calgary Stampede, celebrities, hockey players, and an assortment of other people, along with a number of Canadian cities. The theater is inside the pavilion's "Rocky Mountain."

Warning: Give this a skip if standing for 18 minutes is too much for you. There are no seats in the theater. Wheelchairs are welcome.

IllumiNations

Rating: 🐭🐭🐭🐭🐭
Type: Fireworks and laser show
Time: About 15 minutes
Steve says: Not to be missed!

Weather permitting, most evenings end with this spectacular multimedia fireworks show, which takes the theme of global friendship to a new dimension. I suggest optimal viewing spots for you in each of the touring plans to maximize your view and help you leave the park afterward without a hassle.

Note: *IllumiNations* is considered one of the best fireworks shows in U.S.

Attractions with Minimal Waits (Usually)

- *The Circle of Life* in The Land Pavilion. The wait is usually the time until the next show, especially in the afternoon or evening.
- Innoventions buildings. Some exhibits are accessible any time.
- *Gran Fiesta Tour* in Mexico. The wait is usually short, except on very crowded days.
- *Reflections of China* in China. The wait is usually the time until the next show.
- *The American Adventure* in The American Adventure Pavilion. The wait is usually the time until the next show.
- *Impressions de France* in France. The wait is usually the time until the next show, except on very crowded days.
- *O Canada!* in Canada. The wait is usually the time until the next show.

Attractions That May Frighten Children

Remember that switching off is available at some of these attractions (see *Chapter One*, "Good Things to Know About").

- *Universe of Energy.* The realistic dinosaur segment of the dark ride can frighten preschoolers.
- *Mission: SPACE.* The G forces and weightlessness effect may be too scary for some children. Switching off is available.
- *Test Track.* This fast, intense "car ride" (roller coaster and simulator) can frighten anyone. Switching off is available.
- *Honey, I Shrunk the Audience.* The 3-D visual effects and loud noises may frighten young children.
- *Journey Into Imagination with Figment* in the Imagination! Pavilion. Loud noises in the dark may frighten young children.
- *Maelstrom* in Norway. Angry-looking trolls can frighten wee ones.

Least Crowded Restrooms

- The outside restrooms to the right of the Imagination! Pavilion.
- The restrooms at either side of the Odyssey Center, located between Future World and World Showcase.
- The restrooms on the right side of Germany.

Resting Places

- Several benches inside the Innoventions buildings.
- The benches in the small alcove on the side of France to the right of the Plume et Palette shop.
- The benches in the park at the rear of the United Kingdom.

Hidden Mickeys

Here are just a few of the hidden Mickeys you may want to look for in Epcot:

- *Spaceship Earth.* When you pass by the sleeping monk, look back at the document he is working on. You'll find an ink blot in the upper far corner that's shaped like a silhouette of Mickey's head.
- *Living with the Land* ride in The Land Pavilion. When you reach the greenhouses in your boat, begin to look for a large window in front of you that looks into a laboratory. Inside the laboratory room on the right side is a white disc tilted upward with test tubes resting in holes in the disc. The test tubes form a pattern: a silhouette of Mickey Mouse's round head and ears.
- *Maelstrom* at the Norway Pavilion. Stare at the left side of the large wall mural at the loading area where you enter the boats. One of the Vikings on the ship deck has Mickey ears for a helmet.

Balloons in The Land's lobby (left) hang over the food court (one of the best in all of WDW).
An archway of good fortune (below) welcomes you to the China Pavilion, a scaled-down replica of Beijing's Temple of Heaven.

Touring Epcot

Epcot is one of the largest of the WDW theme parks and feels relatively spacious even on busy days. Compared with the Magic Kingdom, it's a cinch to enter and leave. Nonetheless, it pays to know the lay of the land.

Note: The park opens an hour early to Disney property guests for "Extra Magic Hours" (see *Chapter One*) at least one day a week. By the time the park opens to other visitors on Early Entry days, it is already crowded. I strongly advise visiting on another day of the week if you are not eligible for Early Entry or choose not to take advantage of it.

Tip: *Mission: SPACE, Test Track*, and *Soarin'*, all located in Future World, are simulator rides. If you are prone to **motion sickness** but want to give them a try, take an over-the-counter remedy before you enter the park.

If you like to shop, remember that you don't have to carry your purchases with you as you tour the park. Just ask the shops to send them to "package pickup" near the front exit. The service is free. If you are staying on-property, they will deliver right to your room, also at no charge.

Entrances

Epcot has two entrances, the main entrance in front and another in the rear. The front entrance opens into Future World, the rear into World Showcase. The parking lot is at the front and it's here that the WDW monorail and buses stop. The rear entrance opens out onto a walkway to the Epcot resort hotels and a dock for the boat that carries visitors to and from the Epcot hotels and Disney's Hollywood Studios.

If you plan to arrive first thing in the morning (recommended), you'll want to head for the front entrance if possible. World Showcase doesn't open until 11:00 a.m., and visitors who arrive at the rear entrance have to trek first to Future World. By the time they get there, they are usually at the back of the pack of early arrivals who came in the front way.

Getting to and from Epcot

By car. The quickest way to get to Epcot's front entrance is by car, even if you are staying within walking distance at an Epcot resort hotel. Drive in, park in the main parking lot, and head for the entrance turnstiles. Later in the day, if you decide to leave to spend the afternoon in the Magic Kingdom, you can take the monorail from Epcot (about a 30-minute trip one way) and then return by monorail in the evening to retrieve your car. If you want to go anywhere else, you can drive there.

Insider Tip 1: If you plan to spend the entire day at Epcot, consider moving your car in the afternoon to an Epcot resort hotel (especially if you're staying in one; if not, tell the guard you want to visit or eat at the hotel). You'll avoid the mass exodus through the front gates when Epcot closes. Simply stroll out the rear exit toward the hotel parking lot and your car.

Insider Tip 2: If you arrive by car in the afternoon, try to wend your way to the front of the parking lot to cut your distance to the entrance turnstiles.

Without a car. You can walk from any of the Epcot resort hotels in five to ten minutes (see *Chapter One*, "WDW Lodging"), but you have to enter through the rear entrance. That's a major disadvantage in the early morning, as noted above. Don't be dismayed if it's your only choice, however. Epcot is a large park and the touring plans below will give you an advantage over most visitors. Car-less guests at other WDW properties can take the monorail or bus to the front entrance (check your Transportation Guide). Off-property visitors without cars will have to depend on cabs (expensive), hotel shuttles (if available), and public transportation (also if available). All three tend to be inconvenient. Ask at your hotel Guest Services how long it will take you to get to the Epcot front entrance.

Note: If you don't have a car and decide to switch from Epcot to another Disney theme park in the afternoon, take a WDW bus or monorail (or a 25- to 35-minute boat ride or 30- to 40-minute walk) to Disney's Hollywood Studios. Consult your WDW Transportation Guide for schedules or ask a Disney attendant at one of the Epcot exits.

When to Arrive

Come early in the day, preferably before opening time, so that you can experience some of the major attractions with minimal waits. Be at the front entrance turnstiles about 35 to 40 minutes before the official opening time (or at least 75 minutes ahead of the official opening time if you're an Extra Magic Hours' Early Entry guest). Add 10 minutes if you have to buy your admission tickets. Pick up a Guidemap and Times Guide as you enter (at the turnstiles or just inside at a map stand).

Note 1: Walkers from Epcot resort hotels should be at the rear entrance turnstiles 15 minutes earlier than the above times. Then walk to Future World as quickly as you can without straining yourself.

If the morning lines are long at all entrance turnstiles, line up in an outside queue. Sometimes, an attendant will open up a nearby turnstile at the last minute, and you may be positioned to move with other excited guests to the new and shorter queue.

Note 2: All the touring plans below assume you will arrive at or before opening time. If you want to sleep in, simply pick up the appropriate non Early Entry plan later in the day. Use FASTPASS or the singles line option (if available) to minimize your wait at crowded attractions.

I consider a wait of more than 15 to 20 minutes too long.

Start with Advance Dining Reservations

Unless you plan to eat fast food all day, or to leave the park to eat, be sure you make dining reservations for lunch and dinner. The food in Epcot is good and the restaurants tend to fill up fast. So if you don't already have advance reservations, make them as soon as you clear the entrance turnstiles. Walk quickly around the left side of Spaceship Earth to Guest Relations. Among your options: lunch at San Angel Inn Restaurant in Mexico or great seafood at Akershus Royal Banquet Hall in Norway (character meals with various Disney Princesses); dinner at Coral Reef restaurant at The Seas with Nemo & Friends Pavilion or The Garden Grill Restaurant's Disney character meal in The Land Pavilion. If you come back for a second day, consider lunch at Rose & Crown Dining Room in the United Kingdom or a bit more exotic fare at Restaurant Marrakesh in Morocco. For dinner, try Biergarten in Germany or Tutto Italia in Italy.

Tip: Try for lunch at around 11:30 a.m. and dinner around 5:30 p.m. to minimize your waiting time and get the best possible tables. *Exception:* If most of Future World closes at 7:00 p.m. (check your Times Guide), make dinner reservations for 7:00 to allow for optimal touring.

G scale miniature railroad in Germany, Biergarten in background.

Mission: SPACE entrance plaza in Future World

*Colorful koi swim
in Japan's
serene garden
in World Showcase.*

One-Day Touring Plans for Adults, Teens and Seniors

Be sure to check the entrance, arrival, reservations, and other important recommendations above before you start your tour.

You won't be able to experience every attraction in Epcot in a day, but following this plan will ensure that you experience the best Epcot has to offer adults, teens, and seniors.

Note: These plans do not include an afternoon break. If you're flagging after lunch, return to your hotel for a swim and rest (or rest awhile at the small alcove in France behind the shops). Return to the park in mid-afternoon and take up the touring plan in Japan or France.

Adults, Teens and Seniors One-Day Plan for Extra Magic Hours' Early Entry Days

(WDW property guests only)

Note: During evening Extra Magic Hours, the crowds are sometimes lighter. You can use the non Early Entry day touring plan for attractions that are open or simply tour at leisure with your own itinerary.

Most of the attractions in Future World lie east (to your left from the front entrance) and west of Spaceship Earth and Innoventions Plaza.

1. Ask a Disney attendant what attractions are open for Early Entry guests (this list changes periodically) and then make your advance dining reservations at Guest Relations if you haven't already done so (see page 147).

2. Walk into Innoventions Plaza and through Innoventions West Side (to your right). Then walk to The Land Pavilion and experience *Soarin'* if it has opened.

3. Go through Innoventions East Side and get a FASTPASS (if available) for *Test Track*, and then ride *Mission: SPACE*. (If *Mission: SPACE* is crowded, try the singles line if it's open.)

    Note: Seniors may want to avoid the jerky simulator experiences of *Test Track* and *Mission: SPACE*.

    Caution: Anyone with chronic cardiovascular problems should avoid the *Mission: SPACE* centrifuge (see "Caution," page 131).

4. Ride *Spaceship Earth*. Don't dally at the exhibits at the exit unless you

want to email your ride photo to someone.

5. Enjoy the *Living with the Land* ride and *Test Track* at your FASTPASS time.

6. Get some light refreshments at a snack cart or at the Food Court in The Land Pavilion. At or after the official opening time, proceed to step 4 below. Skip attractions you've already experienced today.

Adults, Teens and Seniors One-Day Plan for Non Early Entry Days

1. On your way in, ask the turnstile attendant if *Soarin'* will open immediately. Before you head for it, go to Guest Relations and make reservations for lunch and dinner if you haven't already done so (see page 147).

2. Go to the walkway through Innoventions West Side. When the rope drops, continue through to The Land Pavilion and enjoy riding *Soarin'*.

3. Cross back through Innoventions West Side and East to get a FAST-PASS for *Test Track*. Then ride *Mission: SPACE*. (Use the singles line, if open, at *Mission: SPACE* if it is crowded.) If the two aren't yet open, come back for your FASTPASS and ride after step 4. In either case, ride *Test Track* during your FASTPASS window.

   Note: Seniors may want to skip the roller coaster-simulator ride, *Test Track,* and the "liftoff" G-forces in the *Mission: SPACE* ride.

   Caution: Anyone with cardiovascular problems should avoid the *Mission: SPACE* centrifuge (see "Caution," page 131).

4. Go to The Seas with Nemo & Friends Pavilion. Enter through the rear doors and enjoy *Turtle Talk with Crush*.

5. Go left to the Imagination! Pavilion. See *Honey, I Shrunk the Audience* (avoid the first few rows).

   Tip: Use FASTPASS if eligible if the wait is too long. Don't dally at the exit; the unusual water effects here can be enjoyed later.

6. Cross back through both Innoventions buildings to the east side of Future World and ride *Spaceship Earth*.

7. Exit left and walk past *Test Track* onto the bridges to World Showcase. These bridges pass around the Odyssey Center building. Once on the bridges, keep left to access the bridge to Mexico. World Showcase usually opens at 11:00 a.m. When the opening rope drops, or if it's already down, walk fast past Mexico to the Norway Pavilion and ride *Maelstrom*. Use FASTPASS if the wait is already too long.

Note: The Norway film is worth watching.

8. Go to your lunch restaurant if you have 11:30 a.m. reservations. If you have no reservations, try fast food at Cantina de San Angel at the Mexico Pavilion or at Kringla Bakeri Og Kafe in Norway. Or try to get seated anyway at Akershus Royal Banquet Hall in Norway (if you like dining with Princess characters) since tables are sometimes available. While there, consult your Times Guide for schedules of any outdoor or stage performances or parades you may want to see.

9. Head for *Gran Fiesta Tour* in the Mexico Pavilion. Walk through the interior plaza to the far left corner to the ride entrance. Enjoy.

10. Exit Mexico and head left to China. Browse the shops and exhibits for a short while.

11. Stroll through Germany. Then spend a few minutes at the elaborate outdoor miniature G scale train on the pavilion's right side.

12. Stroll through the Italy Pavilion.

13. Walk left to The American Adventure Pavilion. Check your Times Guide for the next performance of the singing group *Voices of Liberty*. They sing inside the main building at the entrance to the show, *The American Adventure*. This show is a must (sit toward the front of the auditorium), but try to find time for the singers, too. Grab some refreshments from the outside vendors or at the Liberty Inn on the left side of the pavilion if you have time before or after the show.

14. Head left to Japan. Wander awhile amidst its beautiful gardens and streams.

15. Now go to Morocco and stroll through the shops.

16. Walk left to France and see the movie *Impressions de France*.
    Note: This theater has comfortable seats.

17. Head to the United Kingdom. If you're thirsty for a beer, order one at the Rose & Crown pub. Then wander through the UK's shops and gardens.

18. Walk past the entrance to the conference center and on to Canada. Stroll the pathways along its beautiful streams and gardens.

19. Return to Future World via the first path to your left past the Refreshment Port. Walk to the end of Innoventions West Side to **Club Cool** to enjoy exotic, refreshing soft drinks from foreign countries.
    Note: These drinks are on Epcot; you don't pay a thing for them.

20. Get a FASTPASS for *Living with the Land*, then go left to The Seas with Nemo & Friends Pavilion. Enjoy the Nemo ride and exhibits.

21. Enter the Imagination! Pavilion and ride *Journey Into Imagination with Figment*.

Caution: Take off your hat before the ride!

22. Exit and walk toward Innovations West Side. Before reaching it, turn to your right and enjoy the **"talking drinking fountains"** in front of the nearby restrooms. Walk through Innovations West Side and turn left to ride *Spaceship Earth* (if you haven't already). Check the Tip Board in Innovations Plaza for approximate attraction wait times (it's not always accurate).

23. Check your Times Guide for any additional shows or parades you may want to program into your touring plan (especially after dinner).

24. Walk to the *Universe of Energy*. Enjoy the show.
     Tip: Stand near the left front entry door in the pre-show area. When the doors open, walk to the front row of the front car on your left for the best vantage point.

25. Walk back through the Innovations buildings to The Land Pavilion and enjoy the *Living with the Land* ride if you haven't already. (Or ride it at your FASTPASS time.) Also entertaining is *The Circle of Life* sit-down movie.

26. Keep your reservations for dinner. If you don't have reservations, eat at the Food Court in The Land Pavilion (balloons decorate the lobby). If you have time before dinner, enjoy the **water ballet** at the Fountain of Nations between the Innovations buildings. The water dances to music every 15 minutes.

27. If you have more than 30 minutes before the *IllumiNations* fireworks show, spend some time with the exhibits inside the Innovations buildings. (They may close at 7:00 p.m.; check your Times Guide for details.) Or head toward the *ImageWorks* interactive area at the Imagination! Pavilion (if open) to take in some lighthearted and interesting sensory exhibits. Then enjoy the "jumping fountains" area outside the Imagination! Pavilion, and try out the interactive game area at the exit of *Mission: SPACE*.

28. Claim a viewing spot for the *IllumiNations* fireworks display 20 to 30 minutes before showtime, which is usually 9:00 p.m. If you want to leave quickly through the front entrance after the show, find a viewing spot near the water along the wide promenade between Future World and World Showcase. If you can linger after the show, or if you're leaving Epcot through the rear entrance, seek less congested viewing areas along the waterfront in Italy, between Morocco and France, or on the bridges between France and the United Kingdom.
     Tip: If you feel a steady, strong wind, choose a spot where the wind is not directly in your face to avoid the smoke from the fireworks.

One-Day Touring Plans for Families with Young Children

Be sure to check the entrance, arrival, meal reservations, and other important recommendations on pages 145 to 147 before you start your tour.

You won't be able to experience every attraction in Epcot in a day, but following these plans will ensure that you experience the best Epcot has to offer families with young children.

Families One-Day Plan for Extra Magic Hours' Early Entry Days

(WDW property guests only)

Note: During evening Extra Magic Hours, the crowds are sometimes lighter. You can use the non Early Entry day touring plan for attractions that are open or simply tour at leisure with your own itinerary.

Most of the attractions in Future World lie east (to your left from the front entrance) and west of Spaceship Earth and Innoventions Plaza.

1. Rent strollers if necessary. You'll find them on the left (east) side of the main entrance plaza near Spaceship Earth and on the left side of the rear entrance plaza.

2. Ask a Disney attendant what attractions are open today for Early Entry guests (this list changes periodically) and then go to Guest Relations to make your reservations for lunch and dinner if you need them (see page 147).

3. Walk into Innoventions Plaza and on through Innoventions West Side (to your right from the front entrance). Then walk to The Land Pavilion and see *Soarin'* if it's open. After *Soarin'*, get a FASTPASS for the *Living with the Land* ride or (if available) for *Test Track*; then ride *Mission: SPACE*.

    Height/fright alert: *Test Track* and *Mission: SPACE* are too intense for many small children. Switching off is available. Kids must be 40" or taller to ride *Test Track* and 44" for *Mission: SPACE*.

    Caution: Anyone with cardiovascular problems should avoid the *Mission: SPACE* centrifuge (see "Caution," page 131).

4. Ride *Spaceship Earth*. Don't dally at the exhibits at the exit unless you want to email your ride photo to someone.

5. Enjoy the *Living with the Land* ride or *Test Track* at your FASTPASS time.

6. Get some light refreshments at a snack cart or at the Food Court in The Land Pavilion. At or after the official opening time, proceed to step 4 or 5 below. Skip any attractions you've already experienced today.

Families with Young Children
One-Day Plan for Non Early Entry Days

1. Rent strollers if necessary on the left (east) side of the main entrance plaza near Spaceship Earth, or on the left side of the rear entrance plaza.

2. Ask the turnstile attendant if *Soarin'* will open immediately and then go quickly to Guest Relations (around the left side of Spaceship Earth) to make reservations for lunch and dinner if you don't already have them (see page 147).

3. Go to the walkway through Innoventions West Side. When the rope drops, continue through to The Land Pavilion and enjoy *Soarin'*.

4. Cross back through Innoventions West Side and East to get a FAST-PASS for *Test Track*. Then ride *Mission: SPACE*. If the two aren't yet open, come back and ride one or both of them after step 5. Ride *Test Track* during your FASTPASS window.

   Height/fright alert: Both attractions can be too intense for small children; switching off is available. Kids must be 40" or taller to ride *Test Track* and at least 44" to ride *Mission: SPACE*.

   Caution: Anyone with cardiovascular problems should avoid the *Mission: SPACE* centrifuge (see "Caution," page 131).

5. Go to The Seas with Nemo & Friends Pavilion. Enter through the rear doors and enjoy *Turtle Talk with Crush*.

6. Go to the Imagination! Pavilion. See *Honey, I Shrunk the Audience* (avoid the first few rows). Use FASTPASS if eligible if the wait is too long. Don't dally at the exit; the unusual water effects here can be enjoyed later in the day.

   Caution: This 3-D show has a few loud, convincing special effects that may frighten some young children.

7. Now walk to your left and experience the *Journey Into Imagination with Figment* ride.

   Tip: Take off your hat before the ride!

8. Cross back through the Innoventions buildings to the east side of Future

World and ride *Spaceship Earth*.

9. Exit left from *Spaceship Earth* and walk past *Test Track* onto the bridges to World Showcase. (These bridges pass around the Odyssey Center building.) Once on the bridges, keep left to access the bridge to Mexico. The World Showcase usually opens at 11:00 a.m. When the opening rope drops, or if it's already down, walk fast past Mexico to the Norway Pavilion and ride *Maelstrom*. (Use FASTPASS if the wait is too long.) Then watch the Norway film if your kids are up for a movie. Otherwise, walk through the theater to the exit.

10. Go to your lunch restaurant if you have 11:30 a.m. reservations. If you have no reservations, try fast food at Cantina de San Angel at the Mexico Pavilion or Kringla Bakeri Og Kafe in Norway. Or try to get seated anyway at Akershus Royal Banquet Hall in Norway; it sometimes has seats available and Disney Princesses visit the tables at lunch!

11. Ride *Gran Fiesta Tour* in the Mexico Pavilion. Walk through the interior plaza to the far left corner to the ride entrance. After the ride, check out the *Kidcot Fun Stop* in Mexico (there's one in every country) if your children are interested; it's free!

    Note: The *Fun Stops* may not open until 1:00 p.m. or so. Check your Times Guide.

12. Head back to your hotel for a rest or swim. If you leave World Showcase via the central bridge in front of Showcase Plaza, your kids will pass by an **interactive fountain** on their left. If you're prepared, let the kids go crazy and get soaked! Dry them off, then walk to **Club Cool** at the end of Innoventions West Side and enjoy free exotic soft drinks from foreign countries before you leave the park.

    Keep any parking or stroller receipts so that you won't have to pay again when you return.

    Alternative: If you're not staying on property or if you can't bring yourself to leave the park, find a resting spot (such as the small alcove in France behind the shops) to park your family for a respite and maybe even naps for the kids. Consult your Times Guide for any parades, outdoor performances, or stage shows you may want to see in either World Showcase or Future World.

13. Return to Epcot at about 3:00 p.m. and retrieve strollers if necessary. Get a FASTPASS for *Living with the Land*, then walk to The Seas with Nemo & Friends Pavilion and enjoy the Nemo ride and exhibit area.

14. Exit and walk toward Innoventions West Side. Before reaching Innoventions, turn to your right and enjoy the "talking drinking fountains" in front of the nearby restrooms. Now cross through both Innoventions

buildings and turn left to enter the *Universe of Energy*. Enjoy the show. **Tip:** Stand near the left front entry door in the pre-show area. When the doors open, walk to the front row of the front car on your left for the best vantage point.

15. Cross through the Innoventions buildings and walk to The Land Pavilion. Enjoy the *Living with the Land* ride if you haven't already. Or ride it at your FASTPASS time.

16. See *The Circle of Life* in the sit-down theater on The Land Pavilion's upper floor to the right.

17. Exit The Land Pavilion and turn right to the Imagination! Pavilion. Spend 20 minutes or so in the *ImageWorks* interactive playground. Then enjoy the "jumping fountains" area outside the pavilion. Otherwise, shop awhile or visit a *Kidcot Fun Stop* in Future World (check your Times Guide).

18. If you have more than 30 minutes before your dinner reservations, go back through Innoventions East Side and turn right to ride *Spaceship Earth*. Check the Tip Board in Innoventions Plaza for approximate wait times (it's not always accurate). If you have already been on *Spaceship Earth*, spend some time with the interactive exhibits in the Test Track or Innoventions Pavilions.

19. Keep your reservations for dinner. If you don't have reservations, eat at the Food Court in The Land Pavilion or at one of the restaurants in Innoventions.
    Tip: If you still have time before dinner, enjoy the **water ballet** at the huge Fountain of Nations between the Innoventions buildings. The water dances to music every 15 minutes.

20. After dinner, visit the interactive game area at the exit of *Mission: SPACE*, then a *Kidcot Fun Stop* in a Future World Pavilion or World Showcase country. While the kids are busy, consult your Times Guide for any additional outdoor performances, stage shows, or parades you may want to program into your touring plan. Make more *Kidcot Fun Stops*!

21. If you have more than 40 minutes before the *IllumiNations* fireworks display, spend some time wandering through the Innoventions buildings (if open). Both sides have kid-friendly free interactive games. Alternatively, show your kids more sights in World Showcase, such as the outdoor miniature railroad in Germany or more *Kidcot Fun Stops*.

22. Claim a viewing spot for *IllumiNations* 20 to 30 minutes before showtime, which is usually 9:00 p.m. If you want to leave quickly through the front entrance after the show, find an open spot near the water along the wide promenade between Future World and World Showcase. If

you can linger after the show or if you're leaving Epcot through the rear entrance, seek less congested areas along the waterfront in Italy, between Morocco and France, or on the bridges between France and the United Kingdom.

Tip: If you feel a steady, strong wind, choose a spot where the wind is not directly in your face, to avoid smoke from the fireworks.

Two-Day Touring Plans for Adults and Teens

Be sure to check the entrance, arrival, meal reservations, and other important recommendations on pages 145 to 147 before starting.

These plans assume you will arrive at or before opening time. If you want to sleep in, simply pick up the touring plan several steps down to match your arrival time. Later in the day, use FASTPASS or the singles line option (if available) to minimize waits at crowded attractions. Bear the following in mind:

- I consider a wait of more than 15 to 20 minutes "too long."
- Because guests generally take advantage of the morning Extra Magic Hours privilege (when available) only once at each park (or want to do the same popular rides again if they do two EMH Early Entry days), the Early Entry touring plans are similar for Days One and Two. Similarly, the first three steps of the Non Early Entry plans are the same because most visitors who spend two days in Epcot either choose to arrive later on one of the days or come early both days to experience the same popular rides twice.
- Most of the attractions in Future World lie east (to your left from the front entrance) and west of Spaceship Earth and Innoventions Plaza.

Adults and Teens Day One Plan for Extra Magic Hours' Early Entry Days

(WDW property guests only)

Note: During evening Extra Magic Hours, the crowds are sometimes lighter. You can use the non Early Entry day touring plan for attractions that are open or simply tour at leisure with your own itinerary.

1. Ask a Disney attendant what attractions are open for Early Entry guests this morning (this list changes periodically). Then quickly make your

reservations for meals at Guest Relations if you haven't yet done so.

2. Walk into Innoventions Plaza and through Innoventions West Side on your right. Then head for The Land Pavilion and ride *Soarin'* if it has opened.

3. Get a FASTPASS for *Test Track* (if available). Then ride *Mission: SPACE*. Be sure to use the *Mission: SPACE* singles line, if open, to your advantage if the line is long.
   Caution: Avoid the *Mission: SPACE* centrifuge if you have cardiovascular problems (see "Caution," page 131).

4. Ride *Spaceship Earth*. Don't dally at the exhibits at the exit unless you want to email your ride photo to someone.

5. Enjoy the *Living with the Land* ride in The Land Pavilion and ride *Test Track* at your FASTPASS time.
   Caution: *Test Track* is an exhilarating but rough ride.

6. Get some light refreshments at a snack cart or at the Food Court in The Land Pavilion. At or after the official opening time, proceed to step 4 below. Skip attractions you've already experienced today.

Adults and Teens Day One Plan for Non Early Entry Days

1. Ask the turnstile attendant if *Soarin'* will open immediately. Then quickly make reservations for lunch and dinner at Guest Relations if you don't already have them.

2. Go to the walkway through Innoventions West Side. When the rope drops, continue through to The Land Pavilion to enjoy *Soarin'*.

3. Then get a FASTPASS for *Test Track* and ride *Mission: SPACE*. (Use the singles line if it's open and Mission: SPACE is crowded.) If the two aren't yet open, come back for your FASTPASS and ride after step 4. In either case, ride *Test Track* during your FASTPASS window.
   Caution: Avoid the *Mission: SPACE* centrifuge if you have cardiovascular problems (see "Caution," page 131).

4. Go to The Seas with Nemo & Friends Pavilion. Enter through the rear doors and enjoy *Turtle Talk with Crush* and the exhibits here.

5. Walk through the Innoventions buildings to the east side of Future World and ride *Spaceship Earth*.

6. Exit left and walk past *Test Track* onto the bridges to World Showcase. (These bridges pass around the Odyssey Center building.) Once on the bridges, keep left to access the bridge to Mexico. The World Showcase

usually opens at 11:00 a.m. When the opening rope drops, or if it's already down, walk fast past Mexico to the Norway Pavilion and ride *Maelstrom*. (Use FASTPASS if the wait is already too long.)

Note: The Norway film at the end is worth watching.

7. Exit and head for your lunch restaurant if you have 11:30 a.m. reservations. If you have no reservations, try fast food at Cantina de San Angel at the Mexico Pavilion. Or try to get seated anyway at Akershus Royal Banquet Hall in Norway (if you like dining with Princess characters); this restaurant isn't always booked up.

8. After lunch, ride *Gran Fiesta Tour* in the Mexico Pavilion. (Walk through the pavilion's interior plaza to the far left corner to get to the ride entrance.)

9. Return to your hotel for a rest or swim. If you plan to leave via the front exit, walk to the end of Innoventions West Side to enjoy exotic soft drinks from foreign countries at **Club Cool** on your way out. (They're free!) Keep any parking receipts for free re-entry to the lot on your return.

    Alternative: If you're not staying on property or if you can't bring yourself to leave the park, find a resting spot (such as the small alcove in France behind the shops) and sit down for a respite and maybe a nap.

10. Return to Epcot at about 3:00 p.m. Get a FASTPASS for *Living with the Land*, then walk to The Seas with Nemo & Friends Pavilion and enjoy the Nemo ride and more exhibits.

11. Walk toward Innoventions West Side. Before reaching it, turn to your right and enjoy the **"talking drinking fountains"** in front of the nearby restrooms. Now cross through both Innoventions buildings and turn left to the *Universe of Energy*. Enjoy the show.

    Tip: Stand near the left front entry door in the pre-show area. When the doors open, walk to the front row of the front car on your left for the best vantage point.

12. Cross through the Innoventions buildings and walk to The Land Pavilion. Enjoy the *Living with the Land* ride if you haven't already, or visit it at your FASTPASS time.

13. See *The Circle of Life* in the pavilion's sit-down theater on the upper floor to the right.

14. Exit The Land Pavilion and turn right to the Imagination! Pavilion. Spend 20 minutes or so in the *ImageWorks* interactive playground. It's definitely not just for kids.

15. If you have more than 30 minutes before your dinner reservations, go back through Innoventions East Side and turn right to ride *Spaceship*

Earth if you wish and haven't already done so. Or spend some time with the interactive exhibits inside Test Track or Innoventions. Check the Tip Board in Innoventions Plaza for approximate attraction wait times (it's not always accurate).

16. Keep your reservations for dinner. If you don't have reservations, eat at the Food Court in The Land Pavilion or in one of the restaurants in Innoventions. If you have time before dinner, enjoy the **water ballet** at the huge Fountain of Nations. It's located between the Innoventions buildings. The water dances to music every 15 minutes.

17. Visit Innoventions East Side or West and the interactive game area at the exit of *Mission: SPACE*. (Check your Times Guide for closing times.)

18. Check out any shows in World Showcase that catch your fancy (consult your Times Guide).

19. Claim a viewing spot for the *IllumiNations* fireworks display 30 minutes before showtime, which is usually 9:00 p.m. If you want to leave quickly through the front entrance after the show, find an open spot near the water along the wide promenade between Future World and World Showcase. If you can linger after the show or if you're leaving Epcot through the rear entrance, seek a spot in less congested areas along the waterfront in Italy, between Morocco and France, or on the bridges between France and the United Kingdom.

Tip: If you feel a steady, strong wind, choose a spot where the wind is not directly in your face to avoid smoke from the fireworks.

Adults and Teens Day Two Plan for Extra Magic Hours' Early Entry Days

(WDW property guests only)

Note: During evening Extra Magic Hours, the crowds are sometimes lighter. You can use the non Early Entry day touring plan for attractions that are open or simply tour the park at leisure with your own itinerary.

Consider skipping the afternoon break today (if you have the energy) to spend more time in the countries of World Showcase. Consult your Times Guide early in the day for any parades or outdoor or stage performances that interest you and work them into the touring plan.

1. Ask a Disney attendant what attractions are open for Early Entry guests (this list changes periodically). Then make advance reservations for lunch and dinner at Guest Relations if needed (see page 147).

2. Walk into Innoventions Plaza and through Innoventions West Side on

your right to The Land Pavilion. Ride *Soarin'* if it is open.

3. Get a FASTPASS for *Test Track* and ride *Mission: SPACE*. Then ride *Spaceship Earth*. Be sure to use the *Mission: SPACE* singles line, if open, to your advantage.

    Caution: Avoid the *Mission: SPACE* centrifuge if you have cardiovascular problems (see "Caution," page 131).

4. Ride *Test Track* at your FASTPASS time.

5. Get some light refreshments at a snack cart or at the Food Court in The Land Pavilion. At or after the official opening time, proceed to step 4 below. Skip any attractions you've already experienced today (or enjoy them again!).

Adults and Teens Day Two Plan for Non Early Entry Days

1. Ask the turnstile attendant if *Soarin'* will open immediately, then make lunch and dinner reservations at Guest Relations if you need them (see page 147).

2. Go to the walkway through Innoventions West Side. When the rope drops, continue through to The Land Pavilion to enjoy *Soarin'*.

3. Then get a FASTPASS for *Test Track* and ride *Mission: SPACE*. (Use the singles line if it's open and Mission: SPACE is crowded.) If the two aren't yet open, come back for your FASTPASS and ride after step 4. In either case, ride *Test Track* during your FASTPASS window.

    Caution: Avoid the *Mission: SPACE* centrifuge if you have cardiovascular problems (see "Caution," page 131).

4. Cross back through the Innoventions buildings and bear left to the Imagination! Pavilion. See *Honey, I Shrunk the Audience* (avoid the first few rows). Use FASTPASS if the wait is too long. At the exit, spend 10 minutes or so enjoying the "jumping fountains."

5. Walk to your left and experience the *Journey Into Imagination with Figment* ride. (Take your hat off before the ride!)

6. Check your Times Guide to see if the **JAMMitors** are performing and try to catch a show. If exact showtimes aren't listed, ask a cast member near Innoventions Plaza when they will be entertaining.

7. If you've got some time before World Showcase opens (usually at 11 a.m.) and haven't had a chance to explore the interactive exhibits in the Test Track or Innoventions Pavilions, spend some time exploring one of those areas now.

8. Walk past *Test Track* onto the bridges to World Showcase. When the opening rope drops or if it's already down, walk to Mexico and explore and shop in the pavilion.

9. Go to your lunch restaurant if you have 11:30 a.m. reservations. If you have no reservations, try fast food at Cantina de San Angel in Mexico or the Kringla Bakeri Og Kafe in Norway.

10. Walk to Norway and explore.

11. Go next to China and watch the movie *Reflections of China*. After the film, visit the exhibits.

12. Consider returning to your hotel for a rest or swim. If you leave via the front exit, walk to the end of Innoventions West Side to enjoy exotic refreshment: soft drinks from foreign countries at **Club Cool** (photo below right). They're free! Keep any parking receipts so that you won't have to pay again when you come back.

   Alternative: If you're not staying on property or if you can't bring your-self to leave the park, find a resting spot (such as the small park at the rear of the United Kingdom) to park yourself for a respite and maybe a nap.

   During your break, consult your Times Guide for any performances or parades you may want to see. If they're scheduled, don't miss **Off Kilter** in the Canada Pavilion. It's a rock and roll show with bagpipes.

13. Return to Epcot at around 3:00 p.m. Go to Germany and browse the shops. Spend a few minutes at the elaborate outdoor miniature G scale train on the right side of the pavilion.

14. Next stop is Italy. Enjoy the shops and the decor.

15. Go left to The American Adventure Pavilion. Check your Times Guide for the next performance of the singing group *Voices of Liberty*. They sing inside the main building at the entrance to the show, *The American Adventure*. This show is a must (sit toward the front of the auditorium), but try to find time for the singers, too, if possible. If you have time before the show (or after the show), grab some refreshments from the outside vendors or at the Liberty Inn on the left side of the pavilion.

16. Walk to the Japan Pavilion and wander among the beautiful gardens and streams. Visit the exhibit in the gallery.

17. Honor your reservations for dinner. If you have no reservations, try the Yakitori House fast food in Japan, Tangierine Cafe in Morocco, or fish and chips in the United Kingdom.

18. Go next to Morocco and stroll through the shops and exhibits.

19. Walk left to France and see the movie *Impressions de France*. This the-ater has comfortable seats. Wander around France after the movie, and

enjoy any outdoor or stage performances you can conveniently work in to your touring schedule (check your Times Guide for times).

20. Go next to the United Kingdom. Wander through its shops and gardens. **The British Invasion**, the musical show in the park at the rear of the pavilion, is entertaining (check your Times Guide for times). If you are thirsty for a beer, order one at the Rose & Crown pub.

21. Walk next door to Canada and see the movie *O Canada!* After the show, stroll along the streams and gardens.

22. Check your Times Guide for any additional stage shows, outdoor performances, or parades that you may want to program into your evening touring plan.

23. You have a few more options now: Spend as much time as you like at the exhibits in the Innoventions, Mission: SPACE, or Test Track buildings (if open); explore the Project Tomorrow exhibits at the exit of *Spaceship Earth*; shop in World Showcase or Future World; or revisit any attractions you like that have a short wait. (Check your Times Guide for closing times.)

24. Claim a viewing spot for the *IllumiNations* fireworks display 30 minutes before showtime, which is usually 9:00 p.m. If you want to leave quickly through the front entrance after the show, find an open spot near the water along the wide promenade between Future World and World Showcase. If you can linger after the show or if you're leaving Epcot through the rear entrance, seek less congested areas along the waterfront in Italy, between Morocco and France, or on the bridges between France and the United Kingdom.

Tip: If you feel a steady, strong wind, choose a spot where the wind is not directly in your face to avoid smoke from the fireworks.

Two-Day Touring Plans for Families with Young Children

Note: Be sure to check the entrance, arrival, meal reservations, and other important recommendations on pages 145 to 147 before you start your tour.

These plans assume you will arrive at or before opening time. If you want to sleep in, simply pick up the touring plan several steps down to match your arrival time. Later in the day, use FASTPASS or the singles line option (if available and you and your kids are comfortable with it) to minimize waits at crowded attractions. Bear the following in mind:

- I consider a wait of more than 15 to 20 minutes "too long."
- Because guests generally take advantage of the morning Extra Magic Hours privilege (when available) only once at each park (or want to do the same popular rides again if they do two Extra Magic Hours' Early Entry days), the Early Entry touring plans are similar for Days One and Two. I include them under both days so that you don't have to flip back and forth in your book.
- Most of the attractions in Future World lie east (to your left from the front entrance) and west of Spaceship Earth and Innoventions Plaza.

Tip: Consider buying a Pal Mickey interactive doll at an Epcot shop to entertain your kids.

Families Day One Plan for Extra Magic Hours' Early Entry Days

(WDW property guests only)

Note: During evening Extra Magic Hours, the crowds are sometimes lighter. You can use the non Early Entry day touring plan for attractions that are open or simply tour at leisure with your own itinerary.

1. Rent strollers if necessary. You'll find them on the left (east) side of the main entrance plaza near Spaceship Earth and on the left side of the rear entrance plaza.
2. Ask a Disney attendant what attractions are open for Early Entry guests (this list changes periodically) and then quickly visit Guest Relations to make your reservations for lunch and dinner if you need them (see page 147).
3. Walk into Innoventions Plaza and through Innoventions West Side on your right. Then walk to The Land Pavilion and see *Soarin'* if it has

opened. Afterwards get a FASTPASS for the *Living with the Land* ride or *Test Track*, and then ride *Mission: SPACE* (switching off is available).

Height/fright alert: *Test Track* and *Mission: SPACE* are too intense for many small children. Switching off is available at both rides. Kids have to be 40" or taller to ride *Test Track* and at least 44" tall to ride *Mission: SPACE*.

Caution: Avoid the *Mission: SPACE* centrifuge if you have cardiovascular problems (see "Caution," page 131).

4. Ride *Spaceship Earth*. Don't dally at the exhibits at the exit unless you want to email your ride photo to someone.

5. Enjoy the *Living with the Land* ride in The Land Pavilion or *Test Track* at your FASTPASS time.

6. Get some light refreshments at a snack cart or at the Food Court in The Land Pavilion. At or after the official opening time, proceed to step 4 or 5 below. Skip any attractions you've already experienced today.

Families Day One Plan for Non EMH Early Entry Days

1. Rent strollers if necessary. They are on the left (east) side of the main entrance plaza near Spaceship Earth and on the left side of the rear entrance plaza.

2. Ask the turnstile attendant if *Soarin'* will open immediately, then quickly visit Guest Relations to make your reservations for lunch and dinner if you don't yet have them (see page 147).

3. Go to the walkway through Innoventions West Side. When the rope drops, continue through to The Land Pavilion to enjoy *Soarin'*.

4. Cross back through Innoventions West Side and East to get a FAST-PASS for *Test Track*. Then ride *Mission: SPACE*. Come back and ride *Test Track* at your FASTPASS time. If the two are not yet open, return to ride them after step 5.

Height/fright alert: Kids must be 40" or taller to ride *Test Track* and at least 44" for *Mission: SPACE*. Both rides can be too intense for small children; switching off is available.

Caution: Avoid the *Mission: SPACE* centrifuge if you have cardiovascular problems (see "Caution," page 131).

5. Go to The Seas with Nemo & Friends Pavilion. Enter through the rear doors and enjoy *Turtle Talk with Crush*.

6. Go to the Imagination! Pavilion. See *Honey, I Shrunk the Audience* (avoid the first few rows). Use FASTPASS if eligible if the wait is too long. Don't

dally at the exit; these unusual water effects can be enjoyed later.

Caution: This 3-D show has a few loud and convincing special effects that may frighten young children.

7. Walk to your left and experience the *Journey Into Imagination with Figment* ride.

   Tip: Take off your hat before the ride!

8. Cross back through the Innoventions buildings to the east side of Future World and ride *Spaceship Earth*.

9. Exit left and walk past *Test Track* onto the bridges to World Showcase. (These bridges pass around the Odyssey Center building.) Once on the bridges, keep left to access the bridge to Mexico. The World Showcase usually opens at 11:00 a.m. When the opening rope drops, or if it's already down, walk fast past Mexico to the Norway Pavilion and ride *Maelstrom*. (Use FASTPASS if the wait is already too long.) Watch the Norway film at the end if your kids are up for a movie. Otherwise, walk through the theater to the exit.

10. Go to your lunch restaurant if you have 11:30 a.m. reservations. If not, try fast food at Cantina de San Angel at the Mexico Pavilion. Or try to get seated anyway at Akershus Royal Banquet Hall in Norway; it is not always fully booked and Disney Princesses visit the tables at lunch!

11. Exit and head for *Gran Fiesta Tour* in the Mexico Pavilion. The ride entrance is in the far left corner of the interior plaza. Then check out the *Kidcot Fun Stop* in Mexico if your kids are interested.

    Note: There's a *Kidcot Fun Stop* in every country in World Showcase, but they may not open until 1:00 p.m. or so. (Check the schedule in your Times Guide.)

12. Head back to your hotel for a rest or swim. If you leave World Showcase via the central bridge in front of Showcase Plaza, your kids will pass by an **interactive fountain** on their left. If you're prepared, let the kids go crazy and get soaked! Dry them off, then walk to **Club Cool** at the end of Innoventions West Side and enjoy free exotic soft drinks from foreign countries before you leave the park. Keep any parking or stroller receipts handy; they're good all day.

    Alternative: If you're not staying on property or you can't bring yourself to leave the park, find a resting spot (such as the small park in France behind the shops) to park your family for a respite and maybe even naps for the kids.

13. Return to Epcot at about 3:00 p.m. and retrieve strollers if necessary. Get a FASTPASS for *Living with the Land*, then walk to The Seas with Nemo & Friends Pavilion and enjoy the Nemo ride and exhibits.

14. Walk toward Innoventions West Side. Before reaching it, turn to your right and enjoy the **"talking drinking fountains"** in front of the nearby restrooms. Now cross through both Innoventions buildings and turn left to *Universe of Energy*. Enjoy the show.

    Tip: Stand near the left front entry door in the pre-show area. When the doors open, walk to the front row of the front car on your left for the best vantage point.

15. Cross through the Innoventions buildings and walk to The Land Pavilion. Enjoy the *Living with the Land* ride if you haven't already. Or ride it at your FASTPASS time.

16. See *The Circle of Life* in the pavilion's sit-down theater on the upper floor to the right.

17. Exit The Land and turn right to the Imagination! Pavilion. Spend 20 minutes or so in the *ImageWorks* interactive playground, then enjoy the "jumping fountains" area outside the pavilion.

18. If you have more than 30 minutes before your dinner reservations, go back through Innoventions East Side and turn right to ride *Spaceship Earth*. Check the Tip Board in Innoventions Plaza for approximate attraction wait times (it's not always accurate).

    If you've already been on *Spaceship Earth*, spend some time with the interactive exhibits in the Innoventions or Test Track Pavilions. (Check your Times Guide for exhibit closing times.)

19. Keep your reservations for dinner. If you don't have reservations, eat at the Food Court in The Land Pavilion or at one of the restaurants in Innoventions. If you have time before dinner, enjoy the **water ballet** at the huge Fountain of Nations between the Innoventions buildings. The water dances to music every 15 minutes.

20. Next visit Innoventions East Side or West (if open). You'll find video games (no charge!) and other interactive, kid-friendly games in both buildings. And/or enjoy yourselves in the interactive game area at the exit of *Mission: SPACE*. Then visit a *Kidcot Fun Stop* (or several) in a Future World pavilion (or several of them).

21. Claim a viewing spot for the *IllumiNations* fireworks display 30 minutes before showtime, which is usually 9:00 p.m. If you want to leave quickly through the front entrance after the show, find a spot near the water along the wide promenade between Future World and World Showcase. If you can linger after the show, or if you're leaving Epcot through the rear entrance, seek less congested areas along the waterfront in Italy, between Morocco and France, or on the bridges between France and the United Kingdom.

Tip: If you feel a steady, strong wind, choose a spot where the wind is not directly in your face to avoid fireworks smoke.

Families Day Two Plan for Extra Magic Hours' Early Entry Days

(WDW property guests only)

Note: During evening Extra Magic Hours, the crowds are sometimes lighter. You can use the non Early Entry day touring plan for attractions that are open or simply tour at leisure with your own itinerary.

Consider skipping the afternoon break today (or simply resting in the park for a while) so that you can spend more time in the countries of World Showcase and include *Kidcot Fun Stops* and passport signings for the kids (see step 8 of the "Non Early Entry Plan" below). Be sure to consult your Times Guide early in the day for any outdoor shows, stage performances, parades, or character greetings you want to work in.

1. Rent strollers if necessary, on the left (east) side of the main entrance plaza near Spaceship Earth or on the left side of the rear entrance plaza.

2. Ask a cast member what attractions are open today for Early Entry guests (this list changes periodically). Then quickly make any meal reservations you may need at Guest Relations.

3. Walk into Innoventions Plaza and through Innoventions West Side on your right. Enjoy *Soarin'* again.

4. Get a FASTPASS (if available) for *Test Track*, then ride *Mission: SPACE* or have fun with the interactive games at the exit of *Mission: SPACE*.
   Height/fright alert: *Test Track* and *Mission: SPACE* can be too intense for small children. Kids must be at least 40" tall to ride *Test Track* and at least 44" tall for *Mission: SPACE*. Switching off is available at both.
   Caution: Avoid the *Mission: SPACE* centrifuge if you have cardiovascular problems (see "Caution," page 131).

5. Ride *Spaceship Earth*. If your kids are interested, spend a short while with the exhibits at the exit.

6. Get some light refreshments at a snack cart or at the Food Court in The Land Pavilion. At or after the official opening time, proceed to step 5 below. Skip any attractions you've already experienced (or enjoy them again!).

Families with Young Children
Day Two Plan for Non Early Entry Days

Note: The first five steps are nearly identical to yesterday's steps one through five for two reasons: (1) many families come early on only one of the two days and (2) those who do come early both days frequently want to do the same rides both days.

1. Rent strollers if necessary, on the left (east) side of the main entrance plaza near Spaceship Earth or on the left side of the rear entrance plaza.

2. Ask the turnstile attendant if *Soarin'* will open immediately, then quickly make any meal reservations you may need (see page 147) at Guest Relations.

3. Go to the walkway through Innoventions West Side. When the rope is down, continue through to The Land Pavilion and enjoy *Soarin'* (again)!

4. Cross back through Innoventions West Side and East to get a FAST-PASS for *Test Track*. Then ride *Mission: SPACE*. Come back and ride *Test Track* at your FASTPASS time. If the two are not yet open, return to ride them after step 5.

   Height/fright alert: Kids must be 40" or taller to ride *Test Track* and at least 44" for *Mission: SPACE*. Both can be too intense for small children; switching off is available.

   Caution: Avoid the *Mission: SPACE* centrifuge if you have cardiovascular problems (see "Caution," page 131).

5. Go to The Seas with Nemo & Friends Pavilion. Enter through the rear doors and enjoy *Turtle Talk with Crush* again!

6. Cross back through Innoventions East Side and West Side and bear left to the Imagination! Pavilion. See *Honey, I Shrunk the Audience* (avoid the first few rows). Get a FASTPASS if eligible if the wait is too long.

   Caution: This 3-D show has a few loud, convincing special effects that may frighten some young children.

   At the exit, spend 10 minutes or so enjoying the "jumping fountains." If your kids want to see Figment again, take another ride on *Journey Into Imagination with Figment*.

7. Check your Times Guide to see if the **JAMMitors** are performing. If exact showtimes aren't listed, try to find out from a cast member near Innoventions when they'll be playing.

8. If your kids enjoyed the World Showcase on the first day, consider buying them "passports" ($11 each) to add to their fun today. Ask a cast

member where the passports can be purchased or buy them in any World Showcase country.

9. Walk past *Test Track* onto the bridges to World Showcase, which usually opens at 11:00 a.m. When the opening rope drops, or if it's already down, walk to Mexico to get the kids' passports signed and stamped. Then go to Norway and marvel at the ship on the left side of the pavilion. The kids can get their passports signed and stamped again and have some interactive fun at the *Kidcot Fun Stop* in Norway if it's open. (Check your Times Guide.)

10. Go to your lunch restaurant if you have 11:30 a.m. reservations. If you have no reservations, try fast food at Cantina de San Angel in Mexico or the Kringla Bakeri Og Kafe in Norway.

11. Return to your hotel for a rest or swim. On your way out the main entrance, walk to the end of Innoventions West Side to enjoy exotic (free!) soft drinks from foreign countries at **Club Cool**. Keep any parking and stroller receipts to show when you come back so that you won't have to pay twice in the same day.
    Alternative: If you're not staying on property or if you can't bring yourself to leave the park, find a resting spot (such as the small park at the rear of the United Kingdom) to park your family for a respite and maybe even naps for the kids.

12. Return to Epcot at about 3:00 p.m. and retrieve strollers if necessary. Walk to China to begin the passport and *Kidcot Fun Stop* rounds. In Germany, spend a few minutes at the elaborate outdoor miniature G scale train on the right side of the pavilion. Make stops in any or all of the following countries (depending on your and your kids' stamina and interests): Italy, America (The American Adventure), Japan, Morocco, France, the United Kingdom, and Canada. Shop whenever you feel the urge. If your kids are interested, check your Times Guide for character greeting times in these countries.
    Note: The movies in World Showcase are not included in this touring plan because they're not generally popular with children.

13. Consult your Times Guide for any other outdoor performances, stage performances, or parades you may want to see in World Showcase or Future World. The **acrobats** in China are fun, as is **Miyuki** (a candy artist) in Japan.

14. Interrupt the *Fun Stop* tour for any dinner reservations you hold. If you have no reservations, try the Tangierine Cafe in Morocco or fish and chips in the United Kingdom.

15. After dinner, check out the United Kingdom musical show, **The British**

Invasion, in the park at the rear of the UK Pavilion; your Times Guide lists showtimes. Then complete the *Fun Stop* and passport tour of any remaining countries your kids want to visit.

Note: The *Fun Stops* sometimes close at 8:00 p.m.

16. Spend time before the *IllumiNations* fireworks display with the Innoventions exhibits (if open). If you don't want to see *IllumiNations* a second time, visit *Kidcot Fun Stops* in Future World and then finish your stay in Epcot at Innoventions. Some folks can easily spend 30 to 60 minutes or more there. Also check out Project Tomorrow (behind Spaceship Earth) if it is open or the interactive games at the exit of *Mission: SPACE* or *Test Track*.

Two-Day Touring Plans for Seniors

My touring plans for Seniors do not include fast, scary, or spinning rides. If you enjoy such attractions, follow the two-day touring plan for adults and teens.

Be sure to check the entrance, arrival, dining reservations, and other important recommendations on pages 145 to 147 before you start.

These plans assume you will arrive at or before opening time. If you want to sleep in, simply pick up the touring plan several steps down to match your arrival time. Later in the day, use FASTPASS or the singles line option (if available) to minimize waits at crowded attractions. Bear the following in mind:

• I consider a wait of more than 15 to 20 minutes "too long."

• Because guests generally take advantage of their morning Extra Magic Hours privilege (when available) only once at each park (or want to do the same popular rides again if they do two Extra Magic Hours' Early Entry days), the Early Entry touring plans are virtually the same for Days One and Two. I include them under both days so you don't have to flip back and forth in your book.

• I also anticipate that you will probably take a more leisurely pace on one day than the other. So steps 2 through 5 of the non Early Entry plans are similar to allow choices.

• Most of the attractions in Future World lie east (to your left from the front entrance) and west of Spaceship Earth and Innoventions Plaza.

Seniors Day One Plan
for Extra Magic Hours' Early Entry Days

(WDW property guests only)

Note: During evening Extra Magic Hours, the crowds are sometimes lighter. You can use the non Early Entry day touring plan for attractions that are open or simply tour at leisure with your own itinerary.

1. Ask a Disney attendant what attractions are open for Early Entry guests. Then head for Guest Relations to make reservations for lunch and dinner if you don't yet have them (see page 147).
2. Walk into Innoventions Plaza and through Innoventions West Side on your right. Then walk to The Land Pavilion and ride *Soarin'*. After *Soarin'*, get a FASTPASS for the *Living with the Land* ride.
3. Ride *Spaceship Earth*. Don't dally at the exhibits at the exit unless you want to email your ride photo to someone.
4. Enjoy the *Living with the Land* ride at your FASTPASS time.
5. Get some light refreshments at a snack cart or at the Food Court in The Land Pavilion. At or after the official opening time, proceed to step 3 below. Skip any attractions you've already experienced today.

Seniors Day One Plan
for Non Early Entry Days

1. Make your reservations for lunch and dinner if you haven't already done so (see page 147).
2. Walk through Innoventions West Side and enter The Land Pavilion. Enjoy *Soarin'* if it has opened for the day.
3. If you're up for it, ride *Mission: SPACE*. Get a FASTPASS (if available) or use the singles line if the wait is too long.
    Caution: Avoid the *Mission: SPACE* centrifuge if you have cardiovascular problems (see "Caution," page 131).
4. Go to The Seas with Nemo & Friends Pavilion. Enter through the rear doors and enjoy *Turtle Talk with Crush*. Then explore the exhibits here.
5. Ride *Spaceship Earth*. Don't dally at the exhibits at the exit unless you want to email your ride photo to someone – perhaps yourself?
6. Cross back through the Innoventions buildings to the east side of Future World and spend some time with the Innoventions exhibits.
7. Exit left and walk past *Test Track* onto the bridges to World Showcase.

(These bridges pass around the Odyssey Center building.) Once on the bridges, keep left to access the bridge to Mexico. The World Showcase usually opens at 11:00 a.m. When the opening rope drops, or if it's already down, walk past the Mexico Pavilion to the Norway Pavilion and ride *Maelstrom*. Use FASTPASS if the wait is too long. Enjoy the Norway film at the end.

8. Exit and head for your lunch restaurant if you have 11:30 a.m. reservations. If you have no reservations, try fast food at Cantina de San Angel in the Mexico Pavilion. Or try for a table at Akershus Royal Banquet Hall in Norway (if you like Princess characters).

9. After lunch, ride *Gran Fiesta Tour* in the Mexico Pavilion. The ride entrance is at the far left corner of the interior plaza.

10. Return to your hotel for a rest or swim. If you leave via the front exit, walk to the end of Innoventions West Side to enjoy exotic soft drinks from foreign lands at **Club Cool** (the drinks are free!). Keep any parking receipts for free re-entry to the lot when you return.
    Alternative: If you're not staying on property or if you can't bring yourself to leave the park, find a resting spot (such as the small alcove in France behind the shops) for a respite and maybe a nap.

11. Return to Epcot at about 3:00 p.m. Get a FASTPASS for *Living with the Land*, then walk to The Seas with Nemo & Friends Pavilion and enjoy the Nemo ride and more exhibits.

12. Walk toward Innoventions West Side. Before reaching it, turn to your right and enjoy the **"talking drinking fountains"** in front of the nearby restrooms.

13. Next, cross through both of the Innoventions buildings and turn left to the *Universe of Energy*. Enjoy the show.
    Tip: Stand near the left front entry door in the pre-show area. When the doors open, walk to the front row of the front car on your left for the best vantage point.

14. Cross through the Innoventions buildings and walk to The Land Pavilion. Enjoy the *Living with the Land* ride if you haven't already. Or ride it at your FASTPASS time.

15. See *The Circle of Life* in the pavilion's sit-down theater on the upper floor to the right.

16. Exit The Land Pavilion and turn right to the Imagination! Pavilion. Spend 20 minutes or so in the *ImageWorks* interactive playground for adults and kids.

17. If you have more than 30 minutes before your dinner reservations, go back through Innoventions East Side and turn right to ride *Space-*

ship Earth (or to ride it again). Check the Tip Board in Innoventions Plaza for approximate attraction wait times (it's not always accurate). If you've already "done" *Spaceship Earth*, spend time with the interactive exhibits at the *Mission: SPACE* exit.

18. Keep your reservations for dinner. If you don't have reservations, eat at the Food Court in The Land Pavilion (the best in WDW) or at one of the restaurants in Innoventions.

    Note: If you have time before dinner, enjoy the **water ballet** at the huge Fountain of Nations between the Innoventions buildings. The water dances to music every 15 minutes.

19. Visit an Innoventions building (if open); enjoy the exhibits.

20. Check out any shows in World Showcase that catch your fancy (consult your Times Guide for show times).

21. Claim a viewing spot for the *IllumiNations* fireworks display 30 minutes before showtime, which is usually 9:00 p.m. If you want to leave quickly through the front entrance after the show, find an open spot near the water along the wide promenade between Future World and World Showcase. If you can linger after the show or if you're leaving Epcot through the rear entrance, seek a less congested viewing area along the waterfront in Italy, between Morocco and France, or on the bridges between France and the United Kingdom.

    Tip: If you feel a steady, strong wind, choose a spot where the wind isn't blowing directly in your face to avoid the smoke from the fireworks.

Seniors Day Two Plan
for Extra Magic Hours' Early Entry Days

(WDW property guests only)

Note: During evening Extra Magic Hours, the crowds are sometimes lighter. You can use the non Early Entry day touring plan for attractions that are open or simply tour at leisure with your own itinerary.

Consider skipping the afternoon break today (if you have the energy) to spend more time in the countries of World Showcase. Consult your Times Guide for any outdoor performances, stage shows, or parades that interest you and fit them in to the touring plan. Remember, most of the attractions in Future World lie east (to your left from the front entrance) and west of Spaceship Earth and Innoventions Plaza.

1. Ask a Disney attendant what attractions are open for Extra Magic Hours guests this morning. Then make reservations for lunch and dinner

if you have not already done so (see page 147).

2. Next walk into Innoventions Plaza and on through Innoventions West Side on your right to The Land Pavilion to experience *Soarin'*. Afterword, get a FASTPASS for the *Living with the Land* ride.

3. Ride *Spaceship Earth* and then spend a short while with the exhibits at the exit.

4. Enjoy the *Living with the Land* ride at your FASTPASS time.

5. Get some light refreshments at a snack cart or at the Food Court in The Land Pavilion. At or after the official opening time, proceed to step 3 below. Skip any attractions you've already experienced today or yesterday (unless you want to enjoy them again).

Seniors Day Two Plan for Non Early Entry Days

1. Make meal reservations if you need them (see page 147).

2. Ride *Soarin'*.

3. If you're up for it, ride *Mission: SPACE*. Get a FASTPASS (if available) or use the singles line (if open) if the wait is too long.
   Caution: Avoid the *Mission: SPACE* centrifuge if you have cardiovascular problems (see "Caution," page 131).

4. Cross back through the Innoventions buildings and bear left to the Imagination! Pavilion. See *Honey, I Shrunk the Audience* (avoid the first few rows). At the exit, spend 10 minutes or so enjoying the "jumping fountains."

5. Enjoy *Journey Into Imagination with Figment*. Just be sure to take off your hat before the ride!

6. Check your Times Guide to see if the **JAMMitors** are performing. If so, see them now if the schedule works. If exact showtimes aren't listed, try to find out when they'll be playing from a cast member near Innoventions.

7. Spend some time in the Innoventions buildings.

8. Walk onto the bridges to World Showcase, which usually opens at 11:00 a.m. When the opening rope drops, or if it's already down, walk to Mexico and explore the pavilion.

9. Exit and go to your lunch restaurant if you have 11:30 a.m. reservations. If you have no reservations, try fast food at Cantina de San Angel in Mexico or the Kringla Bakeri Og Kafe in Norway.

10. After lunch explore Norway.

11. Go next to China and watch the movie *Reflections of China*. After the film, visit the exhibits.

12. Consider returning to your hotel for a rest or swim. If you leave via the front exit, walk to the end of Innoventions West Side for a round of exotic soft drinks from foreign countries served free at **Club Cool**. Keep any parking receipts for free re-entry when you come back.

    Alternative: If you're not staying on property or if you can't bring yourself to leave the park, find a resting spot (such as the small park at the rear of the United Kingdom) for a respite and maybe a little nap. Check your Times Guide for shows or parades you may still want to see.

13. Return to Epcot at around 3:00 p.m. Go to Germany and browse the shops. Spend a few minutes at the elaborate, outdoor miniature (G scale) train on the right side of the pavilion.

14. Your next stop is Italy. Enjoy the shops and the decor.

15. Exit left to The American Adventure Pavilion. Check your Times Guide for the next performance of the choral group *Voices of Liberty*. They sing inside the main building at the entrance to the show, *The American Adventure*. This show is a must (sit toward the front of the auditorium), but try to find time for the singers, too. If you have time before the shows (or after the shows), grab some refreshments from the outside vendors (or at the Liberty Inn on the left side of the pavilion).

16. Walk to Japan. Wander among the beautiful gardens and streams and visit the exhibit in the gallery.

17. Go on to Morocco and stroll through the shops and exhibits.

18. Honor your reservations for dinner. If you have no reservations, try the Yakitori House fast food in Japan, the Tangierine Cafe in Morocco, or fish and chips in the United Kingdom.

19. Exit left and walk to France. See the movie *Impressions de France*, where you can sink into comfortable theater seats.

20. Wander around France after the movie, and enjoy any outdoor or stage performances you can conveniently catch (check the performance schedules in your Times Guide).

21. Visit the United Kingdom and stroll through its shops and gardens. If you're thirsty for a beer, order one at the **Rose & Crown** pub (photo opposite).

22. Walk next door to Canada and watch the movie *O Canada!* After the show, stroll along the pavilion's streams and gardens.

23. If the timing is right, enjoy any outdoor performances in World Showcase or Future World that catch your interest (check your Times Guide for showtimes). Some worthwhile options are the **acrobats** in China,

the **Fife and Drum Corps** in The American Adventure Pavilion, **Matsuriza** drumming in Japan, and the **musicians** in Canada (*Off Kilter*) and the United Kingdom (*The British Invasion*).

24. After the performance(s), you'll have to make some choices. In the time remaining before the *IllumiNations* fireworks, you can explore the exhibits in the Innoventions buildings (if open), at the exit of *Test Track*, or in Project Tomorrow at the exit of *Spaceship Earth*. Or shop. If you saw the fireworks last night and don't want to see them again, you can leave Epcot during the show to beat the crowds or continue to enjoy the exhibits and shops. Project Tomorrow sometimes remains open during the show.

25. If you haven't yet seen *IllumiNations* (or want to see it again), claim your viewing spot 30 minutes before showtime, which is usually 9:00 p.m. If you want to leave through the front entrance immediately after the show, find an open spot near the water along the wide promenade between Future World and World Showcase. If you can linger after the show or if you're leaving Epcot through the rear entrance, seek a less congested viewing area along the waterfront in Italy, between Morocco and France, or on the bridges between France and the United Kingdom.

   Tip: If you feel a steady, strong wind, choose a spot where the wind is not directly in your face to avoid fireworks smoke.

The Sorcerer Mickey Hat, icon of the Studios, stands 100 feet tall. It was created in 2001 to commemorate Walt Disney's 100th birthday.

Chapter 4

Disney's Hollywood Studios

Disney's Hollywood Studios is a combination theme park and working movie and television production facility. It's filled with exciting rides, stellar shows, and entertaining tours.

As you approach the entry turnstiles, the architecture, overhead music, and Art Deco colors create the illusion that you are walking onto a Hollywood movie set of the past. Perhaps that's one reason why repeat visitors tend to refer to the park as "the Studios."

Attractions Described and Rated

Lights, Motors, Action! Extreme Stunt Show

Rating: 🖤🖤🖤🖤
Type: Stunt show
Time: 30-35 minutes
Steve says: Exciting stunt car action

Learn how action-movie stunts are planned and filmed. Daredevils drive specially designed cars, motorcycles, and jet skis, accompanied by loud, fiery special effects. Cars screech along the streets and leap through the air in a

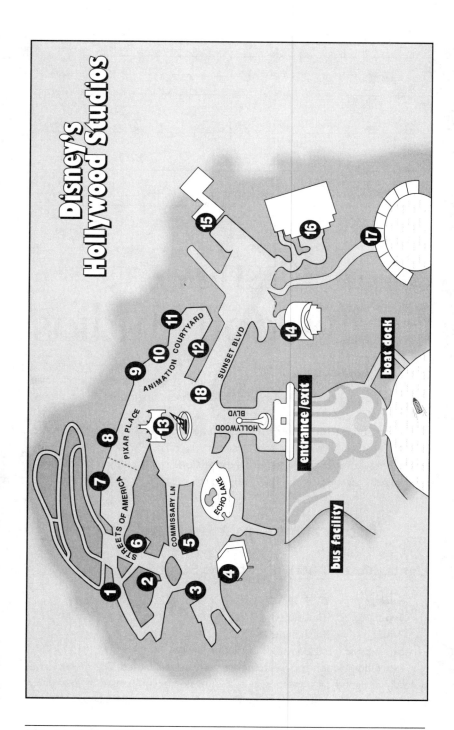

Disney's Hollywood Studios

1. Lights, Motors, Action! Extreme Stunt Show
2. MuppetVision 3-D
3. Star Tours
4. Indiana Jones™ Epic Stunt Spectacular
5. Sounds Dangerous — Starring Drew Carey
6. "Honey, I Shrunk the Kids" Movie Set Adventure
7. Studio Backlot Tour
8. Toy Story Midway Mania
9. Walt Disney: One Man's Dream
10. Voyage of The Little Mermaid
11. The Magic of Disney Animation
12. Playhouse Disney — Live on Stage!
13. The Great Movie Ride
14. "Beauty and the Beast" — Live on Stage
15. Rock 'n' Roller Coaster Starring Aerosmith
16. The Twilight Zone Tower of Terror™
17. Fantasmic!
18. Guest Information Board

carefully choreographed show with plenty of near misses.

Tip: For the best view, sit two-thirds of the way up or higher.

MuppetVision 3-D

Rating: ❤❤❤❤

Type: 3-D movie in a sit-down theater

Time: About 18 minutes

Steve says: A real gas, from start to finish

This show is a convincing 3-D movie with special effects added inside the theater. The comedy stars the Muppets (on-screen and live) and an odd prankster called "The Spirit of 3-D," a creation of the Muppet Labs' Dr. Bunsen Honeydew. Miss Piggy performs a romantic solo, which is turned into a hilarious fiasco by Bean Bunny. The jokes and one-liners are plentiful. Thanks to a short pre-show on TV monitors (mounted in a large room outside the main theater), you'll be laughing even before you sit down.

Note: This attraction is located under the big green and yellow Kermit balloon. To get to the entrance, cross the Streets of America in front of the Empire State Building facade and walk past the Miss Piggy fountain.

Caution: Lines can get long at midday, and cannon shots and fireworks in the theater are loud enough to shock toddlers.

Star Tours

Rating: ❤❤❤❤❤

Type: Flight simulator thrill ride

Time: 7 - 8 minutes

Steve says: A winner that will have you smiling throughout

This flight simulator ride is a perennial favorite at the Studios. The pre-show on overhead TV monitors briefs you on the tour you're about to take to the Moon of Endor. Once on board, however, something goes awry and your rookie robot pilot barely escapes tragedy, over and over again. Your craft flies among ice crystals, through a comet. Then it's suddenly in the midst of a space battle between the good rebels and the evil Empire. Along the way, you meet familiar *Star Wars* movie characters. All ends well, and you finish the trip feeling a lot more cheerful than when you started.

Note: *Star Tours* is past *Sounds Dangerous* on the left side of the park.

Height restriction: Kids must be 40" or taller to ride.

Caution: If you are prone to motion sickness but want to give this flight simulator ride a try, take an over-the-counter motion-sickness remedy before you enter the park (follow the directions on the label) or opt for the "no-motion" version of the ride.

Indiana Jones Epic Stunt Spectacular

Rating: ❤❤❤❤

Type: Stunt show in open-air theater

Time: About 30 minutes

Steve says: Fun to see how some action-movie stunts are done

Professional stunt men and women demonstrate action sequences along the lines of those used in the *Indiana Jones* movies. A stunt man avoids booby traps to find a golden treasure in a temple. Then, he and his woman friend fight bad guys on the streets of Cairo and dodge Nazi bullets in the desert. Volunteers are chosen from the audience to be extras in the show.

Tip: If you want to be picked, sit toward the front of the theater in any of the sections (and near the center), then stand up, wave your arms, and make noise when the casting director is choosing volunteers. You just might get lucky! To stake out these front seats, arrive early: queue up 20 minutes before showtime for the first show and up to 45 minutes before showtime for later shows (especially during busy seasons). Or use FASTPASS.

Note: This stunt demonstration show is staged in a huge open-air, canopied theater at the far side of Echo Lake just past the big green dinosaur (Dinosaur Gertie's Ice Cream of Extinction).

Sounds Dangerous — Starring Drew Carey

Rating: ❤❤❤

Type: Indoor sound effects movie

Time: 12 - 13 minutes

Steve says: Humorous plot and acting

Undercover agent Drew Carey dons a microphone and a small movie camera to track down diamond smugglers in this movie short. You experience the action firsthand as you watch his video transmission and listen through earphones to his broadcast. Then his movie camera fails, the theater turns pitch black, and your earphones become your only link to Mr. Carey's movements. That's when you discover that the realistic sound effects give you all the clues you need to interpret the frantic action even though you can't see a thing.

At the exit, you enter **SoundWorks**, a small, interactive sound-effects area. Here you can dub your voice into short film clips, listen to amazingly realistic sounds through headphones in a soundproofed room, and enjoy other adventures with your ears.

Tip: This small area can get crowded as guests pour into it after the *Sounds Dangerous* show. For a less crowded experience, enter SoundWorks directly from outside and time your visit 10 to 15 minutes before the next sound effects studio show (ask a cast member at the entrance) to give guests from the previous show time to have moved on. Better yet, visit in the evening.

Note: The ABC Sound Studio is across the plaza from *Star Tours*.

"Honey, I Shrunk the Kids" Movie Set Adventure

Rating: ♥♥♥
Type: Imaginative outdoor playground
Time: As long as you want, minimum 15 minutes
Steve says: Great place for energetic kids to let off steam

This creative playground at the end of the Streets of America is filled with oversized blades of grass, ants, toys, and anything else you might find in your backyard if you were shrunk to the size of an ant's antenna. The playground is strewn with slides, tunnels, rope ladders, and things to climb on; most surfaces are padded. One area has an oversized leaky hose that randomly squirts water onto the wet kids below. The blades of grass are as tall as trees and provide some protection from the sun.

Caution: The playground can get crowded by late morning. On summer afternoons, the lack of good ventilation combined with all those little bodies having fun can turn this adventure area into a hot and humid place to play.

Studio Backlot Tour

Rating: ♥♥♥♥
Type: Guided tram and walking tour
Time: 30 - 35 minutes
Steve says: Lets you in on some secrets of movie-making

A large water tank special-effects area is the first stop on this entertaining tour of film production techniques. Several guests are chosen from the tour group to help demonstrate how storms and battles at sea are reproduced for movies and television. Then you board trams for a guided tour past the huge Disney wardrobe department, television and movie sets, and a collection of cars, boats, and other vehicles from well-known movies. Your next stop is the highlight, the aptly named **Catastrophe Canyon**. Here your tram is subjected to an earthquake, an explosion with fire, and a flash flood (folks on the left side of the tram can get wet). Then the tram guide takes you behind the huge canyon set to explain how some of the special effects were created. In the final segment, the tram turns past the Streets of America for a good view of the "forced perspective" of the Empire State and other buildings (in other words, it's an optical illusion: the buildings are constructed and painted to make them seem taller than they really are).

Note: The entrance to the *Studio Backlot Tour* is near the Studio Catering Company.

Toy Story Midway Mania

Rating: ❤❤❤❤❤
Type: 3-D virtual dark ride with interactive elements
Time: About 6 minutes
Steve says: It's the Buzz Lightyear attraction taken to the
          next level.

This ride will surely delight fans of the Pixar movies and their entertaining characters and amazing graphics. You get the chance to test your skills – and compete with other riders for points – by targeting balloons and firing off darts, balls, and other virtual projectiles with a toy cannon as you ride along a virtual midway. The Good Guys (Woody, Buzz Lightyear, and the Green Army Men among others) encourage you on to your best performance.

Note: The intense 3-D experience can cause motion-sickness in susceptible riders.

Walt Disney: One Man's Dream

Rating: ❤❤❤
Type: Walk-through exhibit with a sit-down film
Time: 25 - 30 minutes
Steve says: A stirring tribute to the great man himself

Walk past fascinating memorabilia from Walt Disney's life, including a re-creation of his working office and his models of theme park attractions. Walt tells you about his life and works in audio clips throughout the exhibit and in a 15-minute film at the end.

Note: The entrance is near the *Voyage of The Little Mermaid*.

Voyage of The Little Mermaid

Rating: ❤❤❤❤
Type: Indoor musical stage show
Time: About 15 minutes
Steve says: A feast for the eyes and ears

At the front of the Animation Courtyard, on the left side, is this perennially popular attraction. You sit in a comfortable theater and watch a multimedia show that includes animation, puppetry, and live acting. Ariel, Eric, Flounder, Sebastian, Ursula, and other characters from the animated movie act and sing to tell the dramatic and uplifting story. Special effects in the theater, such as laser lights and falling sheets of water, add to the experience. The rendition of the song "Under the Sea" is truly memorable.

The Magic of Disney Animation

Rating: ♥♥♥

Type: Guided walking tour plus interactive presentations

Time: 15 to 30 minutes, depending on your choices

Steve says: Enriching and amusing, but pared down from previous versions

At the rear of the Animation Courtyard is the "Animation Tour" building. Your tour starts with a short introduction by a Disney artist, who interacts with an animated character to illustrate how such characters are created. You then walk past the area where animators used to work (they're all in California now) to a large room with interactive displays. There, you can (among other things) find out what Disney character you most resemble and insert your own voice into a Disney character. You can then participate in the **Animation Academy**, where you can draw (and keep for free!) your own Disney character with guidance from a Disney artist. The specific interactive activities may change at times.

Note: On busy days, you may have to wait to get into the Animation Academy because attendance is limited. It's worth the wait if you are interested in animation.

Note, too: There's sometimes a greeting area inside with characters from recent Disney movies.

Playhouse Disney - Live on Stage!

Rating: ♥♥

Type: Musical children's theater show

Time: About 22 minutes

Steve says: Especially fun for younger fans of Disney TV characters

Past the Hollywood Brown Derby Restaurant is the archway that leads to the Animation Courtyard. Just inside the archway on the right is the entrance to the *Playhouse Disney* stage show. Characters from "The Book of Pooh," "Little Einsteins," "JoJo's Circus," and other Disney Channel kids' shows sing, dance, and have fun. You sit on a carpeted floor and enjoy the performance with your happy kids, who quickly realize that they're not confined by chairs, lap bars, or anything else! They can join in the dancing at times during the show and usually do.

Tip: Where you sit matters. You may not be able to catch all the action on stage if you sit too close, so choose the middle or rear if you can.

The Great Movie Ride

Rating: ♥♥♥♥
Type: "Dark ride" past movie sets
Time: 20 - 22 minutes
Steve says: Lose yourself in some classic movie scenes

You enter *The Great Movie Ride* through a replica of Hollywood's Chinese Theater and join an inside queue. A montage of short takes from famous movies plays on a large screen in front of you to keep you entertained until you board a tram-like vehicle. Your vehicle takes you for a gentle ride past Audio-Animatronics scenes from – what else? – more movies. *Mary Poppins*, *Alien*, *Casablanca*, *Raiders of the Lost Ark*, *The Wizard of Oz*, and other big-screen classics are given the robotic treatment, along with such stars as Gene Kelly, Clint Eastwood, Harrison Ford, James Cagney, John Wayne, Julie Andrews, Dick Van Dyke, Judy Garland (as Dorothy) and Margaret Hamilton (as Dorothy's nemesis, the Wicked Witch). Your ride ends with a fast-paced series of classic movie clips.

"Beauty and the Beast" — Live on Stage

Rating: ♥♥♥♥
Type: Outdoor live musical show
Time: About 25 minutes
Steve says: Timeless story, terrific show

The first major attraction you approach on Sunset Boulevard is the Theater of the Stars on your right. The *Beauty and the Beast* musical stage show comes to life at this covered open-air theater at the showtimes listed in your Times Guide. Belle, Gaston, Mrs. Potts, the Beast, and the rest of the cast entertain you with the well-known story. The "Be Our Guest" song is especially delightful.

Tip: The show is an uplifting experience, unless you're at the theater on a hot afternoon, when heat and sweat can dampen your mood.

Note: This show isn't always open; consult your Times Guide.

Rock 'n' Roller Coaster Starring Aerosmith

Rating: ♥♥♥♥♥
Type: Indoor roller coaster
Time: 2 - 3 minute pre-show; 1.5-minute ride
Steve says: Join with everyone else: scream from start to finish!

Coaster junkies should love this high speed jaunt (0 to 60 mph in 2.8 seconds) in the dark with twists and turns, two loops, and a corkscrew – all to a background beat of rock-and-roll music. You meet the rock band Aerosmith and their manager during a pre-show. Then your super-stretch limo zips through nighttime Los Angeles streets to get Aerosmith to its concert on time!

Tip: If you want to ride in the front seats, queue up at the very front of the loading area after you pass through the last turnstile.

Height restriction: Riders must be 48" or taller.

The Twilight Zone Tower of Terror

Rating: ❤❤❤❤❤

Type: Indoor ride with more than one drop

Time: 2 - 3 minute pre-show; 3 - 4 minute ride

Steve says: An elevator ride like no other

As you approach the old, out-of-service Hollywood Tower Hotel at the end of Sunset Boulevard, you can hear the screams from the elevator shafts. But intrepidly, you walk through the dusty lobby into the hotel library, where you watch Rod Serling narrate a television reenactment of that terrible night years ago when lightning struck the hotel and the elevator fell 13 stories with 5 helpless people inside. Undeterred, you join the queue through the boiler room to line up for the elevator, which takes you past eerie audiovisual special effects and then up 13 stories for a bird's eye view of the Studios. Suddenly the cable breaks and you drop. In the nick of time, you feel the elevator stabilize, but just when you think you're safe . . .

Note: The precise sequence of elevator ups and downs is computer-programmed by Disney's Imagineers. It changes from time to time to keep the ride fresh for repeat visitors, of which there are legions.

Height restriction: Kids must be 40" or taller to ride.

Fantasmic!

Rating: ❤❤❤❤❤

Type: Outdoor live amphitheater show

Time: 25 minutes

Steve says: A perfect way to wind up your day in the Studios

This multimedia production is performed on an island and a lagoon in front of a huge amphitheater located behind *The Twilight Zone Tower of Terror*. Getting to a seat is cumbersome, but the performance is well worth the effort. Mickey Mouse, as the Sorcerer's Apprentice from *Fantasia*, has a nightmare in which he struggles against classic Disney villains. The scenes are staged with lasers, fireworks, music, live action, flames on the lagoon, and images projected onto a wall of water mist.

Tip 1: Center front seats provide the best view, but you generally have to arrive 60 to 90 minutes before showtime to claim them. That's a long time to sit and wait on hard benches, especially with restless children. So be aware that seats in the outer sections of the amphitheater provide good views of the action and can usually be had if you arrive 30 minutes or so before the first (or only) show of the evening. If two shows are scheduled, the later show is always less crowded. To ease the discomfort of waiting, a comedian often regales the audience before the show.

Tip 2: If you have blow-up seat cushions, bring them along. You'll be a whole lot more comfortable.

Tip 3: You may get damp from the water mist if you sit in the first 13 rows or so.

Tip 4: For a more leisurely entrance and exit, buy a *Fantasmic!* **Dinner Package** (407-WDW-DINE). The package includes reserved seats on the near side of the amphitheater, so you don't have to come early and wait.

Note: This show may be cancelled in bad weather.

Attractions with Minimal Waits (Usually)

- *Studio Backlot Tour.* Except on busy days, the wait is often relatively short for this tram and walking tour.
- *Walt Disney: One Man's Dream.* The wait is usually short.

Attractions That May Frighten Children

Remember that switching off is available at some of these attractions (see *Chapter One*, "Good Things to Know About").

- *Lights, Motors, Action! Extreme Stunt Show.* Loud, fiery special effects may frighten young children.
- *Star Tours.* This intense flight simulator ride may frighten young children and can cause motion sickness in anyone. Switching off is available.
- *Sounds Dangerous – Starring Drew Carey.* The theater goes completely black during part of the show. That and the startling, realistic sound effects may frighten young children.
- *Studio Backlot Tour.* Prepare children for the Catastrophe Canyon segment during which an earthquake, fire, and flash flood are simulated.
- *The Great Movie Ride.* Some of the realistic displays can frighten young children.
- *Rock 'n' Roller Coaster Starring Aerosmith.* Unless your kids (48" or taller) relish fast roller coasters, this one may scare them. Switching off is available.

- *The Twilight Zone Tower of Terror*. The elevator drop can frighten anyone, especially children. Switching off is available.
- *Fantasmic!* Some special effects, such as gunshots and an explosion, may frighten young children.

Least Crowded Restrooms

- To the left of the entrance to The Hollywood Brown Derby is a door that leads to inside restrooms not noted on the Guidemap.
- Walk into the Tune-In Lounge and turn left at the rear to some usually uncrowded restrooms (not noted on the Guidemap).

Resting Places

- The benches in the trees between the Sci-Fi Dine-In Theater Restaurant and *Star Tours*.
- The benches at the edge of Echo Lake across from the 50's Prime Time Café, but there's not much shade.
- The chairs under cover (in the shade) at the Studio Catering Company, but be aware that it's often noisy because of the nearby *"Honey, I Shrunk the Kids" Movie Set Adventure* playground.
- A few benches on a side street across from the entrance to *Beauty and the Beast*.

Hidden Mickeys

Here are just a few of the hidden Mickeys you may want to look for in the Studios:

- *The Great Movie Ride*. As you pass through the *Indiana Jones* movie set, look at the wall to your left near the corner past the last statue. Mickey is etched into the wall design, sitting on a chair facing left. Opposite Mickey is Donald Duck.
- *The Twilight Zone Tower of Terror*. During the pre-show film in the library, the little girl in the elevator holds a plush Mickey Mouse doll.
- Find Mickey in the fountain in front of *MuppetVision 3-D* below the character with the megaphone. Mickey's eyes and snout bulge out.

Touring Disney's Hollywood Studios

The park opens an hour early to Disney property guests for "Extra Magic Hours" (see *Chapter One*) at least one day a week. By the time the park opens to other visitors on these Early Entry days, it's already crowded. I strongly advise visiting on another day of the week if you aren't eligible for Early Entry or choose not to take advantage of it.

Getting there: Whether you are staying on property or off, the fastest way to get to Disney's Hollywood Studios (aka "the Studios") is to drive your car to the main parking lot. Otherwise take a bus or boat (check your Transportation Guide). Buses run from all the WDW properties and some off-property lodgings as well. The boat brings guests from Epcot and the Epcot resort hotels. Bear in mind that taking the bus is not as convenient as driving, and the boat is rather slow-loading and slow-moving (taking up to 35 minutes one way); so you should drive from the Epcot resort hotels to the Studios if you have a car. Or you can walk to the Studios from Epcot (30 to 40 minutes) or from the Epcot resort hotels (15 to 30 minutes). However you choose to travel, ask at your hotel Lobby Concierge how long it will take you to get to the Studios entrance.

Note: If you are prone to motion sickness and want to ride *Star Tours* or *Toy Story Midway Mania*, take an over-the-counter remedy before you leave for the park.

Dining recommendations: Before you come, or shortly after you arrive, you may want to make advance reservations for lunch and/or dinner. Among the possibilities for lunch: Sci-Fi Dine-In for an entertaining meal or Mama Melrose's for Italian food. For dinner consider: The Hollywood Brown Derby for an elegant setting or the 50's Prime Time Café for an entertaining meal. Eat an early lunch to beat the crowds (11:00 to 11:30 a.m.) and plan to eat a later dinner (7:00 p.m.) to allow for early shows and optimal touring.

When to Arrive

Plan to arrive early in the day, preferably before opening time, so that you can experience the major rides and attractions with minimal waits. You'll want to be at the front entrance turnstiles about 30 minutes before the official opening time (or at least 75 minutes ahead of the official opening if you're an Extra Magic Hours' Early Entry guest). Allow an additional 10 minutes to get from the parking lot to the turnstiles plus another 10 minutes if you have to buy your admission tickets.

Tip: If the morning lines are long at all entrance turnstiles, line up in an outside queue. Sometimes, an attendant will open up a nearby turnstile at the last minute, and you may be positioned to move with other excited guests to the new and shorter queue.

One- and Two-Day Touring Plans for All

You probably won't be able to experience every attraction in Disney's Hollywood Studios in one day. If possible, return a second morning to complete the tour, especially if you take an afternoon break on Day One.

Tip 1: I recommend taking a break if the park is open late (7:00 p.m. or later) so that you have the energy to enjoy every minute of your visit. If you want to sleep in, pick up the non Early Entry plan later in the day.

Note: At the end of Hollywood Boulevard near the Starring Rolls Cafe is a chalk Tip Board ("Guest Information Board") which lists approximate wait times for the attractions and start times for the shows. I consider a wait of more than 15 to 20 minutes "too long." If the wait is longer, use FASTPASS or the singles line option (if available) or move on to the next attraction and come back later.

Tip 2: If you arrive by car in the afternoon, try to wend your way to the front of the parking lot to cut your walk to the entrance turnstiles and speed your exit.

Tip 3: Consider buying a Pal Mickey interactive doll at an MGM shop to entertain your kids.

One-Day (or Day One) Plan for Extra Magic Hours' Early Entry Days

(WDW property guests only)

Note: During evening Extra Magic Hours, the crowds are sometimes lighter. You can use the non Early Entry day touring plan for attractions that are open or simply tour at leisure with your own itinerary.

1.   Pick up a Guidemap and Times Guide at the turnstiles or just inside at a

vendor. Check to see if a "Star of the Day" (an entertainment celebrity) is scheduled to appear. If so and you're interested, make time for this special event in the touring plan. Then find out what attractions are open for Early Entry. Plan to skip any you don't want to experience.

2. Rent strollers, if needed, at Oscar's Super Service inside the entrance turnstiles on the right.

3. If *Toy Story Midway Mania* has opened and you're anxious to try your shooting skills, head there first. Walk to the end of Hollywood Boulevard. If a rope is up, line up at the rope with the other guests. When it drops, walk past the right side of Mickey's Sorcerer's Hat, down the steps, and turn left into Pixar Place.

4. When you exit the ride, retrace your steps to Mickey's Sorcerer's Hat and turn left to Sunset Boulevard to ride *Rock 'n' Roller Coaster*.
   Height restriction: Kids must be 48" or taller to ride. Switching off is available (see *Chapter One,* "Good Things to Know About").

5. Turn left at the exit and ride *The Twilight Zone Tower of Terror.*
   Fun Tip: When you're safely seated in the *Tower of Terror* elevator, place a penny in your open palm before the drop. Try to catch the floating penny when your elevator "hits" bottom.
   Height/fright alert: Kids must be 40" or taller to ride *Tower of Terror*, but the elevator drop can frighten even adults. Don't force unwilling members of your party onto this ride. You'll all be unhappy. Again, switching off is available.

6. Walk back down Sunset Boulevard. Visit any other attractions open for Early Entry (for example, *Star Tours* and *MuppetVision 3-D*).

7. Now calm down with some refreshments; a good bet is the Starring Rolls Cafe on Sunset Boulevard just past the Guest Information Tip Board. After your break, continue with step 6 of the following plan. Skip any attractions you've already experienced, or go again if the lines aren't too long!

One-Day (or Day One) Plan for Non EMH Early Entry Days

1. Pick up a Guidemap and Times Guide at the turnstiles or just inside at a vendor. Check to see if a "Star of the Day" (an entertainment celebrity) is scheduled to appear. If so and you're interested, make time for this special event in the touring plan. Skip any attractions you don't want to experience.

2. Rent strollers, if needed. You'll find them at Oscar's Super Service inside the entrance turnstiles on the right.

3. If **Toy Story Midway Mania** has opened, ride it first. Walk to the end of Hollywood Boulevard, then past the right side of Mickey's Sorcerer's Hat, down the steps, and turn left into Pixar Place.

4. On exiting, retrace your steps to Mickey's Sorcerer's Hat and turn left to Sunset Boulevard to ride *Rock 'n' Roller Coaster.*
   Height/fright alert: You must be 48" or taller to ride this coaster. Don't force unwilling kids or seniors to ride the *Rock 'n' Roller Coaster*. Use switching off instead.

5. Ride *The Twilight Zone Tower of Terror*. Use switching off if some members of your party prefer to skip this ride.
   Fun Tip: When you're safely seated in the *Tower of Terror* elevator, place a penny in your open palm before the drop. Try to catch the floating penny when your elevator "hits" bottom.
   Height alert: Kids must be 40" or taller to ride the *Tower of Terror.*

6. If *Voyage of The Little Mermaid* starts its next show in 30 minutes or less (check in your Times Guide for showtimes), walk back down Sunset Boulevard, turn right in front of the Starring Rolls Cafe and right again along the curving sidewalk in front of The Hollywood Brown Derby restaurant. Pass under the arch, turn left, and get in line for the show. Otherwise, return later for the Little Mermaid show. Send someone to bring back coffee or other refreshments if your wait is long enough.
   Tip: When you're admitted to the pre-show area, stand close to the left or middle doors at the side of the room. After the doors open, pick a row in the middle or rear (your left) of the theater, let six to ten folks in before you, and sit toward the far end of the row. This maneuver will give you a good view of the stage and a relatively quick exit.

7. Walk back under the arch and turn right to ride *The Great Movie Ride*. Ask a Disney attendant at the entrance or inside how long the wait is. If it is more than 15 minutes, skip to step 8 and return to *The Great Movie Ride* in the hour before the park closes.

8. Walk across the park with Echo Lake on your left to enter and ride **Star Tours** (entrance photo opposite). If the line is too long, use the

FASTPASS option if it is available to you.

Caution: This is a rough flight simulator ride, maybe too rough for seniors and kids under 7 or 8 years of age. If your kids seem reluctant, ask the Disney attendant inside about switching off.

Height alert: Kids must be 40" or taller to ride.

9.   Catch a show (*Beauty and the Beast, Indiana Jones Epic Stunt Spectacular*, the *Lights, Motors, Action! Extreme Stunt Show,* or any other listed show) before lunch if the timing is right (check your Times Guide).

10. Keep your reservations for lunch. If you don't have reservations, try the Backlot Express for burgers and sandwiches, the Toy Story Pizza Planet for pizza, or the ABC Commissary for salads and stir-fry.

11. After lunch, enjoy *MuppetVision 3-D* if the wait isn't too long.

12. Now it's time to consider your alternatives. If the park is open past 7:00 p.m., I recommend taking a break about now. If the afternoon parade is about to start, find a shady spot near (or on) the steps in front of the ABC-TV Theater (or in the area with statues called The Academy of Arts and Television Hall of Fame) and enjoy the parade. Then consider leaving the park for a couple of hours' rest in your hotel. If the parade is scheduled for later in the afternoon, consider leaving the park now for a nap or swim at your hotel and returning in about two hours.

Alternative: If you don't want to nap or swim, consider boating to the Epcot Resort area: Walk out of the Studios; turn left to the boat dock; embark, and then disembark at the BoardWalk. Wander around the shops and then go to one of the hotel lobbies to rest awhile on the comfortable couches. Return to the Studios in about two hours.

Note: Remember to keep any parking and stroller receipts handy so that you won't have to pay for them twice in the same day.

Tip: If the park is too crowded for your comfort and your ticket allows, switch to a non Early Entry Disney park after your break and start with the afternoon or evening section of the appropriate touring plan.

13. If you stay in the park, head for *Studio Backlot Tour*. Walk down the Streets of America and turn right through the Studio Catering Co. area to the tour entrance.

14. Exit and check your Times Guide for character greeting locations for your kids, then get some refreshment at the Studio Catering Co. or

from an outdoor vendor. Tell your kids you'll return to the nearby *"Honey, I Shrunk the Kids"* playground later in the afternoon.

15. If you have young children, be sure to catch a performance of *Playhouse Disney – Live on Stage!* (or its replacement); check the Times Guide for the performance schedule.

16. See the afternoon parade (if you haven't already) from a shady area near *Sounds Dangerous*.

17. When the parade has passed, get in line to see *Sounds Dangerous*.

18. Now you have some more options. If you haven't already done the *Studio Backlot Tour*, head up the Streets of America. Turn right past *"Honey, I Shrunk the Kids"* playground to get in line at the tour entrance. If you've already been on the *Studio Backlot Tour*, go left and then under the arch to get in line to take *The Magic of Disney Animation* tour. Or if the timing is right, go to *Beauty and the Beast, Indiana Jones, Lights, Motors, Action! Extreme Stunt Show,* or any other listed show that you haven't yet seen (check your Times Guide for showtimes). Try to arrive 20 minutes or more before showtime to get decent seats.

    Tip: If you aren't sure which option to choose, check the Tip Board at the intersection of Hollywood and Sunset Boulevards for approximate attraction waiting times to help you make up your mind. If fireworks are scheduled, work them into your evening plans.

19. Next, let your kids play in the *"Honey, I Shrunk the Kids"* Movie Set Adventure playground for 20 to 30 minutes.

20. At the appropriate time, honor any dinner reservations you made. Again, if you don't have reservations, try the Backlot Express for burgers and sandwiches or Catalina Eddie's for pizza and salads.

21. Visit the *Walt Disney: One Man's Dream* exhibit.

22. Head for the *Fantasmic!* amphitheater 30 to 45 minutes before showtime (consult your Times Guide). Grab some refreshments to enjoy while you wait. If you have a blow-up seat cushion in your tote, get it out now. The benches are hard.

    Note: You can save a space for someone, but only up until about 15 minutes before showtime.

23. Enjoy the show and be prepared to be patient on the way out. It takes a long, long time for this huge crowd to exit.

    Tip 1: Try for seats on the right side of the amphitheater to speed your exit, if ever so slightly.

    Tip 2: If you are on the Dinner Package and the show is shortened or delayed by rain, ask at Guest Relations for a voucher for a future show.

Day Two Plan
for Extra Magic Hours' Early Entry Days

(WDW property guests only)

During evening Extra Magic Hours, the crowds are sometimes lighter. You can use the non Early Entry day touring plan for attractions that are open or simply tour at leisure with your own itinerary.

Note: Because guests generally take advantage of the Extra Magic Hours' Early Entry privilege only once at each park – or want to do the same popular rides again if they do two Early Entry days in the Studios – the Early Entry tour plan today is the same as yesterday's, with the exception of step 6. I include them under both days so that you do not have to flip back and forth in your book.

1. Pick up a Guidemap and Times Guide at the turnstiles or just inside at a vendor. Check to see if a "Star of the Day" (an entertainment celebrity) is scheduled to appear. If so and you're interested, make time for this special event in your touring plan. Ditto if a parade is on and you want to see it (or see it again). Then find out what attractions are open for Early Entry. Plan to skip any attractions that don't appeal to you.

2. Rent strollers, if needed, at Oscar's Super Service inside the entrance turnstiles on the right.

3. If *Toy Story Midway Mania* has opened and you're anxious to try your shooting skills, head there first. Walk to the end of Hollywood Boulevard. If a rope is up, line up at the rope with the other guests. When it drops, walk past the right side of Mickey's Sorcerer's Hat and down the steps, then turn left to Pixar Place.

4. When you exit *Toy Story*, retrace your steps to Mickey's Sorcerer's Hat. Turn left to Sunset Boulevard to ride *Rock 'n' Roller Coaster Starring Aerosmith*. If the waiting line is still short, line up and ride again!
    Height restriction: Kids must be 48" or taller to ride. Switching off is available (see *Chapter One,* "Good Things to Know About").
    Don't force unwilling children or seniors to ride the coaster. You'll all end up unhappy.

5. Turn left at the coaster exit and ride *Tower of Terror*.
    Fun Tip: When you're safely seated in the *Tower of Terror* elevator, place a penny in your open palm before the drop. Try to catch the floating penny when your elevator "hits" bottom.
    Height/fright alert: Riders must be 40" or taller, but the elevator drop can even frighten adults. Please do not force unwilling members of your party onto this ride. Switching off is available.

6. Walk back down Sunset Boulevard and straight across the park, with Echo Lake on your left, to ride *Star Tours*.

   Caution: This is a rough flight simulator ride, too rough for many seniors and children under 7 or 8 years of age. If you have reluctant kids, ask the Disney attendant inside about switching off. Use FAST-PASS if the line is too long to suit you.

   Height alert: Kids must be 40" or taller to ride.

7. Exit and calm down with some refreshments; a good source is the Starring Rolls Cafe on Sunset Boulevard just past the Guest Information Tip Board.

8. After your refreshments, go to step 4 of the following plan. Skip any attractions you've already experienced today.

Day Two Plan for Non Early Entry Days

1. Pick up a Guidemap and Times Guide. If *Toy Story Midway Mania* has opened and you're anxious to try your shooting skills, head there first. Walk to the end of Hollywood Boulevard, then past the right side of Mickey's Sorcerer's Hat and down the steps. Turn left to Pixar Place.

2. When you exit Toy Story, head for *Rock 'n' Roller Coaster Starring Aerosmith* if you like rough coasters. Retrace your steps to Mickey's Sorcerer's Hat and turn left to Sunset Boulevard, then left to the coaster. If the waiting line is still short, line up and ride again!

   Height restriction: Kids must be 48" or taller to ride.

3. Now head for the tall, menacing building to your left (photo opposite above) and ride **The Twilight Zone Tower of Terror**. If you're up for it and the wait is short, jump back in line and ride it again!

   Height/fright alert: Kids must be 40" or taller to ride. Use switching off if needed.

4. Walk back down Sunset Boulevard. Turn right on Hollywood Boulevard and ride *The Great Movie Ride*, especially if you didn't have a chance to ride it on Day One.

5. Exit left, go under the arch, and get in line for *The Magic of Disney Animation* tour if you didn't take it on Day One. If the tour isn't open yet, return at its scheduled opening and take it then (consult your Times Guide or the Tip Board at the intersection of Hollywood and Sunset Boulevards for times).

6. Check your Times Guide for character greeting locations for your kids, and go if the timing is right and you have time before lunch.

7. Honor your 11:30 a.m. lunch reservations (for recommendations, see

page 191). If you don't have reservations, try the Backlot Express for burgers and sandwiches, the Toy Story Pizza Planet for pizza, or the ABC Commissary for salad and stir-fry.

8. If you haven't already done so, enjoy *MuppetVision 3-D* if the wait isn't too long.

9. Plan to see *Beauty and the Beast*; the *Lights, Motors, Action!* show, *Indiana Jones*, and/or any other listed show that interests you. Check your Times Guide for showtimes and put the shows you want to see into your afternoon touring plan.

Tip: Arrive 20 minutes or more before showtime for decent seats.

10. If your children want to see it, catch a performance of *Playhouse Disney – Live on Stage!* Check your Times Guide for showtimes.
If your kids want more autographs, check your Times Guide for more character greeting locations.

Tip: Characters often hang out on the Streets of America, in Pixar Place, and near Mickey's Sorcerer's Hat.

11. Shop in a few of the interesting stores here, such as Sid Cahuenga's One-of-a-Kind (movie memorabilia) and the Animation Gallery (Disney movie cels) at the exit of the Animation Tour.

Note: If you're staying on-property, the shops will deliver to your room at no additional charge.

12. Visit any rides, shows, or parades that you want to enjoy again if the waits aren't too long. Get FASTPASSes when appropriate. If fireworks are scheduled, work them into your evening plans. Visit *Walt Disney: One Man's Dream* (or its replacement attraction) if you haven't yet seen it. Check your Guidemap for any other entertainment options.

13. Check Hollywood and Sunset Boulevards for the **Streetmosphere** performers: starlet wannabes, gossip columnists, and a host of other entertainment-related characters who interact with each other and passersby in short, impromptu scenes. They often appear on the half-hour. (Check at Guest Relations for times.)

14. Explore the Streets of America and San Francisco Street, as well as other famous-city streets.

Over 325 animals are sculpted into The Tree of Life, icon of Disney's Animal Kingdom.

Close-up of the Tree's ram, bison, deer, lion, and tiger sculptures.

Chapter 5

Disney's Animal Kingdom

Walt Disney World Resort's youngest theme park is a grand zoological kingdom (over 200 species of animals) with a mix of Disney shows and attractions similar in scale to those at the other major Disney theme parks. Disney's Animal Kingdom pays tribute to all animals while warning humans to do more to help save our fellow creatures and the plants on which all of us depend. The majority of animals here are out in the open. You see them on "hills" and savannas from the vantage point of safari vehicles and in gardens and small parks as you stroll the kingdom's many walking trails. You have to search far and wide to find any cages or bars.

Note: To protect the animals, no balloons, straws, or cup lids (except for hot drinks) are allowed in the park. Your balloons can be stored at the park entrance.

The Oasis

You enter and exit Disney's Animal Kingdom through The Oasis, a lush garden filled with exotic plants and animals that is located just inside the entrance turnstiles. Here you encounter plants and animals while walking along winding trails. You will either see the animals as you walk or read the explanatory tablets and then try to spot the animals in the sloping gardens, in the trees, or

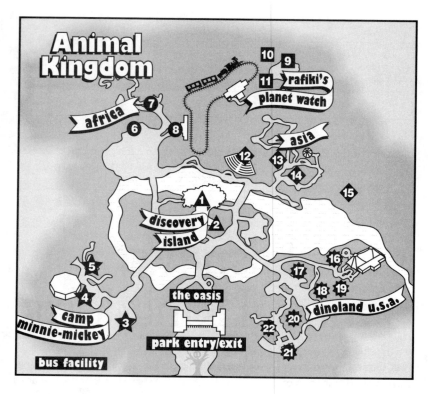

discovery island

△1 The Tree of Life

△2 It's Tough to be a Bug!

camp minnie-mickey

☆3 Outdoor Theater

☆4 Festival of the Lion King

☆5 Character Greeting Trails

africa

⑥ Kilimanjaro Safaris

⑦ Pangani Forest Exploration Trail

⑧ Train to Rafiki's Planet Watch

rafiki's planet watch

9 Conservation Station

10 Affection Section

11 Habitat Habit!

asia

◆12 Flights of Wonder

◆13 Maharajah Jungle Trek

◆14 Kali River Rapids

◆15 Expedition Everest

dinoland u.s.a.

✦16 Finding Nemo – The Musical

✦17 The Boneyard

✦18 TriceraTop Spin

✦19 Primeval Whirl

✦20 Cretaceous Trail

✦21 DINOSAUR

✦22 Dino-Sue T Rex

by the winding streams. The identification tablets are colorful, easy to read, and downright poetic.

Some animals are easy to spot: The lemurs in the vicinity of the Discovery Island Trails are often playing around in plain sight. Others are more difficult to locate in their designated areas. After all, they have their own schedules, and even though they're technically "Disney animals," they aren't particularly interested in how your vacation day is going at their kingdom.

Tip: To expeditiously enter or exit the main park, head straight for one of the walkway trails on either side of The Oasis as you enter through the turnstiles. The walkway on the right side may be a bit shorter and straighter.

Discovery Island

Discovery Island lies in the middle of Disney's Animal Kingdom, connected to its other lands by bridges. Like the Magic Kingdom hub at the end of Main Street, Discovery Island is the central area from which you enter all the other lands in the park. It offers attractions, shops, restaurants, and walking trails. Soaring over the island is the 14-story tall *Tree of Life*, the central symbol and centerpiece of Disney's Animal Kingdom. It is analogous to Cinderella Castle in the MK, Spaceship Earth in Epcot, and Mickey's Sorcerer's Hat in Disney's Hollywood Studios.

The Tree of Life

This amazing structure has over 325 animals sculpted into its roots, trunk, and branches. Walking trails, designed to resemble natural forest trails, snake around the tree and under its roots. These trails offer multiple vantage points for close-up viewing of the tree's beautiful, intricate artistry. *The Tree of Life* is unique and so original it's difficult to stop marvelling at it. Walking paths through gardens, with plants and animals to view, lead you gently away from it and on to the park's other attractions.

Note: The park's **parade** follows a route around *The Tree of Life*.

It's Tough to be a Bug!

Rating: ♥♥♥♥
Type: 3-D movie in a sit-down theater
Time: 8 minutes
Steve says: Insects were never so enjoyable!

This 3-D experience takes place indoors in a theater under the roots of *The Tree of Life*. *It's Tough to be a Bug!* is an eight-minute 3-D film using advanced computer animation techniques. Packed with surprises, the show is nonstop fun. You meet many different bugs up close and personal, including a stink bug who releases a cloud for the benefit of your nose. The special effects are reminiscent of and on a par with Epcot's *Honey, I Shrunk the Audience*.

To find the sign marking the entrance to the show, bear to your right after you walk across the bridge from The Oasis toward *The Tree of Life*. (The entrance site changes from time to time, so consult your Guidemap if you have any difficulty locating it.)

Insider tips: From the holding area, the doors to your extreme left admit you to the back rows of the theater, while the middle two sets of doors admit you to the middle rows. Aim for one or the other, because the middle and back of the theater offer the best vantage points for the show. The long rows are divided into seats by small ridges. The back and bottom of each seat offer the sitter surprises during the show. Just sit comfortably and enjoy the special effects!

And don't worry; the stink bug's not that stinky.

Caution: Younger kids may be terrified by the realistic bugs.

Camp Minnie-Mickey

Camp Minnie-Mickey is a forested area containing character greeting areas and two stage shows. While some characters can be found signing autograph books along the main trails, most characters are located in the rear of the camp at the end of four short trails that snake off to the right of the main thoroughfare (see below). The stage shows are fun-filled live performances.

Festival of The Lion King

Rating: ♥♥♥♥♥
Type: Live musical show in a covered theater
Time: About 30 minutes
Steve says: Superb, one of the best shows at WDW

This theater-in-the-round show is a high-energy musical and dance performance interspersed with audience participation and breathtaking acrobatics. The dancers wear animal costumes, and the fashions, floats, vocals, and choreography are sensational. You'll have a rousing good time.

Tip: If you have children or short adults in your party, sit higher in the bleachers for a better view.

Character Greeting Trails

Rating: ♥♥♥
Type: Outdoor area for meeting characters

Time:	If only a few folks are ahead of you, 5 - 10 minutes per trail; the time lengthens as the lines do
Steve says:	Can be time-consuming

Four trails (named Arbor, Mickey, Forest, and Jungle) with four separate queues lead to different characters. Minnie is usually at the end of the Arbor Trail, while Mickey greets you at his own trail. The Forest Trail leads to several Winnie the Pooh characters, while the Jungle Trail hosts several characters from *The Lion King* and *Jungle Book*.

Note: Trail names and characters may change from time to time.

Africa

The gateway to Africa is Harambe, a re-creation of an East African village. Harambe, like any decent gateway, offers shops, fast food counters, and a cocktail lounge. You must pass through Harambe (which means "coming together" in Swahili) to reach Africa's attractions.

Kilimanjaro Safaris

Rating:	🐭🐭🐭🐭🐭
Type:	Outdoor guided safari ride
Time:	20 - 22 minutes
Steve says:	The animals are nearby, behind camouflaged barriers. There are no cages.

At the end of Harambe's central street is the entrance to the safari ride. Large open-air safari vehicles carry you on a bumpy ride over dirt trails through forests, around hills, and over flat savanna with rocky outcroppings. One short bridge feels especially creaky and unstable (Disney designed it that way for your benefit). Inside your vehicle are pictures of the animals you're likely to spot. Zebras, gazelles, elephants, lions, ostriches, giraffes, cheetahs, and rhinos are visible in open grottos, on hilltops, and by streams on either side of your vehicle. Along the way, your driver entertains you with a humorous and informative spiel. You will help him (or her) chase and trap some evil elephant poachers before the ride ends.

Note: Lines for this one build quickly once the park opens.

Tip: If you have a choice, sit on the left side of the vehicle for the best overall views of the wildlife.

Pangani Forest Exploration Trail

Rating: ♥♥♥♥
Type: Walk-through animal exhibit
Time: About 25 minutes
Steve says: Well-designed zoological nature trail

Next to the exit from *Kilimanjaro Safaris* is the entrance to *Pangani Forest Exploration Trail*. This beautiful walking trail winds by a troop of lowland gorillas, a hippopotamus pool with an underwater viewing area, colorful African birds, agile meerkats, and an interesting glassed display on the naked mole rat.

Rafiki's Planet Watch

This outpost between Africa and Asia will acquaint you with research on the habits and health of animals in the wild. You reach it via train, departing from Africa.

Note: For those who may have missed the movie, *The Lion King*, Rafiki is a wise baboon with a very distinctive voice.

Train to Rafiki's Planet Watch

Rating: ♥♥
Type: Outdoor guided train ride
Time: 4 - 5 minutes one way
Steve says: A means of transportation to Rafiki's Planet Watch

The entrance to this train ride is to the right, at the end of Harambe's central street and across from the entrance to *Kilimanjaro Safaris*. The train itself conjures up images of a real African train, with luggage, boxes, and bicycles roped precariously to the roof of the train cars. All passengers face to one side of the train in tiered seating. During the ride to (past Africa) and from (past Asia) Rafiki's Planet Watch, the conductor gives a short educational spiel on how the Kingdom cares for these creatures. You'll get to see the back of the animal keepers' metal housing for the Kingdom's larger African and Asian inhabitants, such as rhinos and elephants.

Note: You may spot a few animals inside their houses.

Conservation Station

Rating: ❤❤❤

Type: Indoor animal science exhibits

Time: 15 - 20 minutes minimum, longer if your kids stop in the petting zoo

Steve says: Like an interactive science museum

In this building, you'll find a series of walk-through educational exhibits, which change from time to time. An animated cartoon Rafiki talks about various endangered animals. You can experience the sounds of an endangered rain forest (queue up for sound booths in which you don headphones) and watch researchers and veterinarians working with and treating live animals, often ones with injuries. Other imaginative exhibits include computer interactive sessions on conservation.

Tip: Walk into the restrooms near the entrance and take the **"Whiz Quiz."** You'll learn interesting facts about the urination of animals!

Note: Video cameras project close-up shots of the live animals and their caretakers onto overhead monitors, so even the shortest can see what's going on.

Outside the building you'll find **Affection Section**, a large petting zoo, and **Habitat Habit!**, an outdoor animal viewing area.

Note: The hike from the train station to Conservation Station takes three or more minutes (about the same length as the time it takes to walk through The Oasis).

Asia

There are two routes to Asia, a path from Harambe that parallels the river and a bridge from Discovery Island. You will enter this land through the village of Anandapur (which means "place of all delights"). The animals you'll see when you get here are all indigenous to the Asian continent, with roots in such countries as India, Indonesia, and Thailand. Asia has a shop, fast food, and the Yak & Yeti, a moderately priced sit-down restaurant.

Flights of Wonder

Rating: ❤❤❤❤

Type: Outdoor amphitheater bird show

Time: 25 - 30 minutes

Steve says: Sensitive, high-quality avian show

This open-air stage show stars many amazing birds, including a falcon, a hawk, a singing parrot, and other trained avians that perform unusual tricks.

These delightful stunts are not mere tricks, they're enhancements of the birds' natural behaviors.

Maharajah Jungle Trek

Rating: 🐭🐭🐭🐭
Type: Walk-through animal exhibit
Time: About 25 minutes
Steve says: Well-designed zoological nature trail

This nature walk on the left side of Asia brings you close to such animals as Komodo dragons, tigers, antelopes, giant fruit bats, tapirs, gibbons, and many more. The jungle settings are lush, especially the palace ruins.

Kali River Rapids

Rating: 🐭🐭🐭🐭
Type: Raft ride
Time: 5 minutes
Steve says: Not too wild, but definitely wet

A large, circular, free-floating raft takes 12 adventurers twisting and turning down a jungle river past waterfalls, white water rapids, archeological ruins, and a rain forest ravaged by loggers. Your raft drifts perilously close to burning logs and falling lumber. Be prepared to get wet! Some folks will be drenched!

Tip: You must wear shoes on this ride, but consider putting your socks and camera into a plastic bag or the waterproof container at the center of the raft. In fact, you might want to do both. Try to prop your feet up off the floor of the raft to keep your shoes drier. Many folks don ponchos before stepping in.

Height restriction: Kids must be 38" or taller to ride.

Expedition Everest – Legend of the Forbidden Mountain

Rating: 🐭🐭🐭🐭🐭
Type: Roller coaster thrill ride
Time: About 4 minutes
Steve says: Disney theming at its best!

Your "train" will take you through forests, past waterfalls and glaciers, and up into snow-capped peaks. Then things will heat up as the track "ends" and your train speeds both forward and backward through canyons and caverns, only to come face-to-face with a giant abominable snowman!

Height restriction: Kids must be 44" or taller to ride.

DinoLand U.S.A.

A thematically rich land, DinoLand U.S.A. is filled with all manner of dinosaurs and fossils. The animals of this land may be long dead, but DinoLand U.S.A. is really lively! A 50-foot long brachiosaurus forms the entrance gateway. Fossil and excavation exhibits are scattered throughout the area. "Field notes" by paleontology graduate students (with critiques from their professors in red ink) explain some of the exhibits. And if you feel the need to eat or shop, DinoLand U.S.A. has stores and several fast food stops.

Finding Nemo — The Musical (in Theater in the Wild)

Rating: ❤❤❤❤
Type: Live musical show in an enclosed theater
Time: 30 - 35 minutes
Steve says: Vibrant, lively show

Finding Nemo – the Musical is the latest animal-themed show to be featured in Theater in the Wild. This colorful show features original music to accompany our fish friend Nemo and his father on their underwater adventures. It is brought to life by puppets, dancers, acrobats, and animated backdrops. The theater, located on the far left side of DinoLand U.S.A., seats 1,500 in air-conditioned comfort.

The Boneyard

Rating: ❤❤
Type: Imaginative outdoor playground
Time: As long as you want, minimum 10 - 15 minutes
Steve says: Great place for energetic kids to let off steam

A wild and crazy playground, *The Boneyard* swarms with running, crawling, and yelling kids (and smiling adults). You'll find it on the left, just inside the entrance to DinoLand U.S.A. Reminiscent of the *Honey, I Shrunk the Kids* playground at Disney's Hollywood Studios, *The Boneyard* is modeled after a fossil dig site. Budding scientists can dig to uncover dinosaur skeletons embedded in fossil sand pits. (The Disney staff thoughtfully re-conceals them every night.) Unlike real dig sites, *The Boneyard* also has rope ladders and tunnels to climb up and through and plastic tubes to slide down from the rock walls.

TriceraTop Spin

Rating: ❤❤
Type: Flying, steerable dinosaurs

Time: About 2 minutes

Steve says: Circle ride with a prehistoric twist

These four-person dinosaur vehicles (like *Dumbo* with horns!) revolve around a hub, but levers let riders control some of the motion. The two rear riders can make the vehicle go higher and lower, while the two front riders can tilt the beast's nose up and down.

Note: Nearby is **Fossil Fun Games**, a small carnival-style midway area with dinosaur-themed games. Playing them will set you back $2-$3 per game.

Primeval Whirl

Rating: ♥♥♥

Type: Roller coaster with spinning ride vehicles

Time: About 2 minutes

Steve says: The spins add unpredictability to your ride

This relatively mild coaster ride has drops and curves on the way down. The round, four-person ride vehicles spin freely at times until your final descent into the open jaws of a dinosaur fossil.

Height restriction: Kids must be 48" or taller to ride. Switching off is available.

DINOSAUR

Rating: ♥♥♥♥♥

Type: Motion-simulator indoor track ride

Time: 3.5 minutes

Steve says: Realistic, high-energy simulator thrill ride in the dark

This jolting joy ride takes you back in time about 65 million years. You and the rest of your crew board a time vehicle (a motion simulator vehicle that also moves along a track). Your objective is to find a living (vegetarian) dinosaur and bring it back to the present before the species becomes extinct.

Entrance to DINOSAUR ride.

During the mission, you encounter nonstop near-death experiences, confront angry or hungry carnivores, and barely escape the asteroid that collided with earth and (allegedly) blotted out the dinosaurs. This attraction is a magnificent high-tech achievement by Disney's Imagineers.

Tip: As your vehicle nears the exit area, watch the monitor above you for a "real time" view of the dinosaur you just brought back.

Caution: If motion simulators make you queasy, you may want to skip this one. Or prepare for it by taking an over-the-counter motion-sickness remedy an hour or so before you board.

Height restriction: Kids must be 40" or taller to ride.

Cretaceous Trail

Rating: �☺☺

Type: Nature trail

Time: 5 minutes, or as long as you want

Steve says: Relaxing diversion

In the middle of DinoLand U.S.A., the short, winding *Cretaceous Trail* takes you through a lush forest populated with plant and animal species that have survived since dinosaur times. "Field notes" from eager paleontology graduate students introduce you to several changing exhibits, such as soft-shell turtles and small Chinese alligators.

Note: Along the way, you'll find some shade and some places to sit.

Dino-Sue T-Rex

Rating: ☺☺

Type: Outdoor exhibit

Time: 2 minutes

Steve says: Worth a visit and family photo

Billed as the largest and most complete tyrannosaurus rex ever found, Sue is 40 feet long and once weighed 6 to 8 tons. The real Sue is in a Chicago museum, but don't get too close. This replica Sue looks hungry!

Attractions With Minimal Waits (Usually)

- The Oasis. Explore this area anytime.
- *The Tree of Life* Garden and Discovery Island Trails. Explore these trails anytime.
- *The Boneyard.* Especially fun for children; anytime, but bear in mind that the area is exposed to the sun and plan accordingly.
- *Cretaceous Trail.* Explore this area anytime.

Attractions That May Frighten Children

Remember that "switching off" is available at some of these attractions (see *Chapter One*, "Good Things to Know About" and below).

- *It's Tough to be a Bug!* Loud, intense 3-D effects may frighten kids.
- *Kali River Rapids.* The turning raft and rough white water may frighten small children. Switching off is available.
- *Expedition Everest.* Intense; can frighten anyone. Switching off available.
- *Primeval Whirl.* Drops and spins may alarm kids. Switching off available.
- *DINOSAUR.* Intense encounters in the dark with realistic dinosaurs can frighten anyone, especially young children. Switching off is available.

Least Crowded Restrooms

- The restrooms next to Chester and Hester's Dinosaur Treasures in DinoLand U.S.A.
- The restrooms along the trail to the right, before the bridge to Dino-Land U.S.A.
- The restrooms at the rear of Tusker House Restaurant in Africa.

Resting Places

- The shaded chairs in the large sitting area on the waterfront by the Flame Tree Barbecue restaurant.
- The scattered isolated benches along the winding trails (some of them shaded) around *The Tree of Life* in The Oasis.
- The shaded square behind Tamu Tamu Refreshments.

Hidden Mickeys

Here are just a few of the hidden Mickeys you may want to look for in Disney's Animal Kingdom:

- *The Tree of Life.* As you enter Discovery Island from The Oasis, stare at the tree. Partway up the trunk on the right side is a cluster of green algae shaped like Mickey's frontal silhouette.
- *Kilimanjaro Safaris.* More than halfway through the journey, you pass a flamingo pond to your left. An island in the middle of the pond is shaped like Mickey's frontal silhouette.
- Find Mickey's head atop a flagpole that's located just before the second bridge leading into Camp Minnie-Mickey.

Touring
Disney's Animal Kingdom

The park opens an hour early to Disney property guests for "Extra Magic Hours" (see *Chapter One*) at least one day a week. By the time the park opens to other visitors on these days, it is already crowded. I strongly advise visiting on another day of the week if you are not eligible for Early Entry or choose not to take advantage of it.

Note: If you have trouble with motion sickness but want to ride *DINO-SAUR*, take an over-the-counter motion sickness remedy before you leave for the park.

Getting there: The fastest way to get to Disney's Animal Kingdom is to drive your car to the main parking lot. On-property guests can take a Disney transport bus instead (check your Transportation Guide) but it is slower and less convenient. Off-property guests will probably not be satisfied with the bus transportation available, because it tends to run irregularly. Ask at your hotel Guest Services how long it will take you to get to the entrance.

How early should you arrive?

Plan to be at the entrance turnstiles about 30 minutes before the official opening time (or at least 75 minutes ahead of the official opening if you're an Extra Magic Hours' Early Entry guest). Add 10 minutes if you have to buy your admission tickets. Pick up a Guidemap and Times Guide at the turnstiles or just inside at a shop or stand. If you arrive later in the day, plan to use FAST-PASS or the singles line option (if available) at popular crowded attractions.

Tip: If the morning lines are long at all entrance turnstiles, line up in an outside queue. Sometimes, an attendant will open up a nearby turnstile at the last minute, and you may be positioned to move with other excited guests to the new and shorter queue. Or walk through the Rainforest store on your left (if it's open) to the park entrance turnstile outside the back of the store; this turnstile is rarely crowded.

One-Day
Touring Plans for All

If the park is closing early (5 p.m. or 6 p.m.) on the day of your visit, consider staying in the park the entire day, with a short afternoon break (see #15, below), if you want to experience all of the attractions.

Tips for parents: Check your Guidemap for Kids Discovery Club locations. There are areas where your kids can engage in fun, free creative activities (similar to those you'll find at the Kidcot Fun Stops in Epcot). You may also want to consider buying a Pal Mickey interactive doll at a park shop to entertain the kids as you go along.

Notes: I consider a wait of more than 15 to 20 minutes "too long."

One-Day Plan
for Extra Magic Hours' Early Entry Days

(WDW property guests only)

Note: During evening Extra Magic Hours, the crowds are sometimes lighter. You can use the non Early Entry day touring plan below for attractions that are open or simply tour at leisure with your own itinerary.

1. If needed, rent strollers inside the entrance turnstiles on the right at Garden Gate Gifts.

2. Early Entry time at Disney's Animal Kingdom can be used leisurely. Find out from a cast member what areas are open and choose a logical sequence of attractions to enjoy before the park opens to the general public. For example, one workable plan is to first hop on *Kilimanjaro Safaris*, then marvel at *The Tree of Life* (take a few pictures!) and watch *It's Tough to be a Bug!* Then meander along the *Pangani Forest Exploration Trail*. Or, if *Expedition Everest* has opened, ride it first and then enjoy *Kilimanjaro Safaris*, DINOSAUR, *It's Tough to be a Bug!,* and the Pangani trail. Go to any other Early Entry attraction if you have time.

3. Relax with some refreshments at Tusker House Restaurant.

4. When the park opens to the public, go to step 2 of the following plan, and skip any attractions you've already experienced.

One-Day Plan for Non Early Entry Days

1. If needed, rent strollers inside the entrance turnstiles on the right at Garden Gate Gifts.

2. Walk to Asia and enjoy **Expedition Everest** (photo below) if it's opened.

3. Go to *Kilimanjaro Safaris*. Walk at a comfortable pace; there's no need to jog. Enjoy the ride. If the wait is long, get a FASTPASS and return later to ride.

4. After *Kilimanjaro Safaris*, cross Africa and turn left along the river toward Asia. Then cross the bridge to Discovery Island and walk to DinoLand U.S.A. Ride *DINOSAUR* (if you like it, ride it twice!). Then take a picture with *Dino-Sue*, a large T-Rex skeleton near the *DINOSAUR* ride.

   Height/fright alert: DINOSAUR may be too intense and rough for seniors and children under 8 years of age. Kids must be 40" or taller to ride. Switching off is available.

5. See *It's Tough to be a Bug!* in *The Tree of Life*. During your winding walk near the theater, admire the spectacular sculpting on the bark of *The Tree of Life*.

6. Walk to Asia and ride *Kali River Rapids*. If the wait is long (more than 20 minutes), get a FASTPASS for each person in your party. Return to *Kali River Rapids* at your designated FASTPASS ride time for a shorter wait.

   Height alert: Kids must be 38" or taller to ride.

   Caution: you may get wet or even drenched on the *Kali River Rapids*

ride. Be prepared. Many folks don ponchos for *Kali River Rapids*.

7. Get some refreshment in Asia.

8. If you can get to the *Finding Nemo* show in DinoLand U.S.A. 20 minutes before the next show, go ahead and line up for it.

9. Catch **DiVine**, an amazing performance artist dressed as a plant, on the path between Africa and Asia on the hour between 10:00 a.m. and 1:00 p.m. (she's not around every day; ask a cast member.)

10. Eat lunch. You have a number of options here: The Yak & Yeti Restaurant serves Asian food; Rainforest Café at the park entrance offers good food and an interesting ambiance; Tusker House Restaurant in Africa serves salads and sandwiches buffet style. And if you like barbecue, you can't miss at Flame Tree Barbecue.

11. After lunch, work in the *Finding Nemo* show at Theater in the Wild in DinoLand U.S.A. if you haven't yet seen it (check your Times Guide for showtimes). Arrive about 20 minutes before the show. If you have time between lunch and line-up time, do steps 12, 13, and 14 before you line up for the show.

12. Ride **Primeval Whirl** *(photo opposite, below)*. Get a FASTPASS to ride later if the line is long.
    Height alert: Kids must be at least 48" tall to ride this spinning coaster. Switching off is available.

13. Now ride *TriceraTop Spin* if the wait is tolerable. Otherwise, try again in the hour before the park closes.

14. Play some midway games if they appeal to you.

15. Consider returning to your hotel for a nap and swim. Keep any parking and stroller receipts handy so that you won't have to pay for them twice in the same day.
    If you stay in the park, rest awhile in the covered seating area next to the Flame Tree Barbecue restaurant to the right on the lagoon. While resting, study your Times Guide for other theater showtimes. Fit in the steps below as showtimes permit. You may also be able to fit in one of the parades; again check your Times Guide.
    Note: If the park is too crowded for your comfort and your ticket allows, switch to a non Early Entry WDW park at this point and start with the afternoon or evening section of the appropriate touring plan.

16. Walk the *Pangani Forest Trail* in Africa, followed by the *Maharajah Jungle Trek* in Asia.

17. Enjoy the *Flights of Wonder* show circa 3:00 p.m. (check your Times Guide for times). Plan to arrive 15 to 20 minutes before your chosen showtime.

18. If your kids want 'em, get autographs at one of the character greeting trails in Camp Minnie-Mickey. (Lines are sometimes shorter during a *Festival of the Lion King* show.)

19. Watch the afternoon parade (usually 4:00 p.m.) from near Pizzafari Restaurant, then head to the *Festival of The Lion King* show.

20. Enjoy *Festival of The Lion King* at Lion King Theater. Try to arrive about 20 minutes before showtime.

21. Get more autographs, if your kids want them, at the character greeting trails in Camp Minnie-Mickey or elsewhere in the park. Alternatively, explore the gardens and trails around *The Tree of Life,* or enjoy one or more of the **Kids Discovery Clubs** (check your Guidemap).

22. If you have more time in the park, you have several options:
    - Get a quick bite to eat at Pizzafari Restaurant in Discovery Island.
    - If you are visiting with kids, consider meeting more characters in Camp Minnie-Mickey at any of the four different character trails you haven't already visited or at other character greeting locations in the park (check your Guidemap).
    - Otherwise, take the *Train to Rafiki's Planet Watch* from the right rear side of Africa and explore the exhibits in the *Conservation Station* building, along with *Affection Section* and *Habitat Habit!* just outside.
    - Walk along the *Cretaceous Trail* and then let your kids play in *The Bone-yard* playground in DinoLand U.S.A.
    - Play some midway games if they appeal to you.
    - Enjoy another of the **Kids Discovery Club** (locations noted in your Guidemap).
    - Check your Guidemap for any other entertainment options. Try to catch at least one of the ethnic musical groups.

23. In your remaining time before closing, explore the gardens and trails around *The Tree of Life* and The Oasis if you haven't already done so. Keep your eyes open; the animals are often more active in the cooler evening hours.

The high tech games in Downtown Disney's DisneyQuest are a magnet
for young and old alike.

Entrance to Once Upon a Toy, one of the many shops in Downtown Disney.

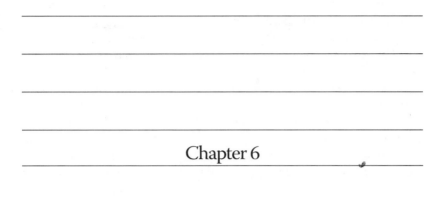

Chapter 6

Downtown Disney & the Water Parks

Located on the shore of one of Walt Disney World's many lagoons, Downtown Disney has three distinct areas, West Side, Pleasure Island, and Marketplace. You'll find shopping, dining, and entertainment in all three, but distinctive pleasures in each one.

Downtown Disney

West Side

West Side offers dining, shopping, and a wide range of entertainment. Adventuresome video game fans will head directly to DisneyQuest. Music fans will gravitate to House of Blues, and dance and theater fans will seek out Cirque du Soleil.

DisneyQuest is an indoor interactive playground in a five-story building. Here you can ride a roller coaster of your own design in a flight simulator-like sphere at *CyberSpace Mountain,* navigate bumper cars that shoot big balls through cannons at your fellow drivers at *Buzz Lightyear's AstroBlasters*, experience innovative interactive and virtual reality games, and even play such classic video games as *PacMan*. One-day tickets cost about $39.00 for adults and about $33.00 for children 3 to 9 years of age.

Height alerts: You must be 51" or taller to ride *CyberSpace Mountain* and *Buzz Lightyear's AstroBlasters*. The *Pirates of the Caribbean* game insists pirates be at least 35" tall.

Admission to DisneyQuest can be covered with a Water Park Fun & More ticket option and is included with the Premium Annual Pass (see *Chapter One*). If you don't have either one and you are staying on Disney property, buy tickets from your hotel Lobby Concierge to save time waiting in line at the DisneyQuest ticket windows. DisneyQuest usually opens at 11:30 a.m., and the first hours after opening (late morning to mid-afternoon) are the least crowded times. (Make *Pirates of the Caribbean* your first stop.)

A New Orleans-style eatery with an attached music hall, the **House of Blues** features Creole and Southern food plus live music in the music hall on most evenings (separate admission charge) and a Sunday gospel brunch. Tickets for the evening shows are available to all comers; the prices range from less than $10 to about $40 or more depending on the performer(s); call 407-934-2583 or visit hob.com for information. If you want a table or bar stool for the evening show, arrive at the music hall an hour or so before showtime. Sunday brunch seatings, which include food and music, are available for 10:30 a.m. and/or 1:00 p.m. Tickets cost about $34 for adults and $17 for children 3 to 9 years of age (including tax and gratuity). Children under 3 are admitted free.

Next door to House of Blues you'll find **Cirque du Soleil**, a unique, 90-minute circus, acrobatics, and modern dance show housed in its own very special "tent" (see below). The show, called "La Nouba," is often described by viewers as "the best show I've ever seen." Tickets cost about $67 to $119

for adults and $53 to $96 for children (9 and younger) depending on the category (there are four) of ticket. I've never met anyone who was disappointed by it. Children 5 years of age and older enjoy it (call 407-939-7600 or visit cirquedusoleil.com for information or tickets; 407-939-7913 for special requests). .

Note: Since some of the show takes place both above the stage and above the audience, seats behind the central horizontal walkway provide viewing that is easier on your neck.

Tip: Make a bathroom stop before the show!

Pleasure Island

Surrounded by a moat and linked to other parts of Downtown Disney by bridges, Pleasure Island (PI), in the middle of Downtown Disney, is in transition. Disney is replacing seven of the nightclubs that were PI's signature attractions with a mix of dining and shopping. Specifics have yet to be announced as we go to press. However, Raglan Road Irish Pub and PI's shops will stay open during the transition.

Marketplace

The Marketplace is a colorful shopping and restaurant area full of visual delights and diversions such as interactive water fountains. The **LEGO Imagination Center** displays some incredible LEGO sculptures, including a sea serpent appropriately rising from the lagoon and an alien family with their spaceship. These sculptures change from time to time, so it's possible you'll see something different. Here, too, you'll find **The World of Disney**, the largest Disney character merchandise shop on earth! Late in the year, Marketplace store windows exhibit Christmas scenes featuring Mickey Mouse and friends. Savor a classic sandwich treat at the Earl of Sandwich eatery. If you enjoy boating, you can rent a variety of watercraft from the Marketplace Marina.

WDW Water Parks

Disney World offers two distinctively themed water parks, **Blizzard Beach** and **Typhoon Lagoon**. Whichever you head for, it's easiest to wear your bathing suit under your street clothes, so you don't have to worry about a dressing room. Bring sunblock and/or suntan lotion, a towel, a cap, money, and your Disney resort I.D. card if you have one. You can drive your car to the park or take a bus. Parking is free.

Note: If you want to use the water slides, wear a bathing suit that has no exposed zippers, buckles, or snaps.

Admission to the water parks is included with certain WDW passes (see

"Admission Tickets," *Chapter One*). Purchased separately, a one-day adult ticket to either Blizzard Beach or Typhoon Lagoon costs about $42 and a child's ticket (for kids 3 to 9) about $35. Children under 3 are admitted free.

Plan to arrive at Blizzard Beach and Typhoon Lagoon 20-30 minutes before the official opening time (45 minutes if you have to buy a ticket) to be among the first in the park. That will give you a chance to stake out your area and enjoy the slides and other attractions without much wait during the first few morning hours. If you want to rent a locker, do so as soon as you enter the park.

Tip: Go during Extra Magic Hours mornings and evenings if you are a water park junkie. Check the disneyworld.com calendar for Extra Magic Hour days.

Blizzard Beach

Blizzard Beach is Disney's wilder water park. The theme is a failed ski resort, which was built (so they tell us) during a freaky, snowy winter in Florida. The park consists of a meandering creek on the outside, two children's areas, a gentle wave pool, and more than 16 water slides. The last include *Summit Plummet*, one of the fastest and tallest freefall speed slides on the planet.

Height restriction: You must be 48" or taller for *Summit Plummet* and two other slides: *Slush Gusher* and *Downhill Double Dipper*, and 32" or taller for the *Chairlift*.

Typhoon Lagoon

Typhoon Lagoon is a "ruin," what was left of a tropical area after a typhoon blew through. The park has one of the world's largest wave pools (in which you can body surf), along with a meandering creek, a salt water snorkeling pool chock-full of fish, a children's area, and 13 water slides. Admission covers the use of snorkeling equipment.

Age and height restrictions: You must be at least 10 years old to snorkel alone, 5 years or older to participate with an adult, and 48" or taller to ride *Crush 'n' Gusher* (a fast "water coaster" tube ride) and *Humunga Kowabunga* (a water slide).

Chapter 7

Lots More to Do at WDW

As if all the attractions and activities we've already covered weren't enough to keep you occupied for days on end, the Walt Disney World Resort offers scores of other fun things to see and do. Some are in the theme parks. Others are on the grounds or in the resort hotels, you don't have to pay theme park admission to enjoy them. In fact, you often don't even have to be a resort hotel guest to participate in the activities it offers.

You'll find over a hundred fun things to do in the pages that follow. Enjoy!

In The Theme Parks

Magic Kingdom:

- When the park opens, **wake up Tinker Bell** at Tinker Bell's Treasure shop in Fantasyland and watch her fly around inside the store. You may get a special certificate from a cast member in the shop.
- Explore Exposition Hall, next to Tony's Town Square Restaurant. Beyond the Camera Center is a long hallway lined with **interactive photo displays**. In the very back they show **vintage Mickey Mouse**

Rent a surrey and go for a spin on the BoardWalk.

Cruise the Seven Seas Lagoon in a pontoon boat. Disney will decorate them for special occasions.

Take a carriage or wagon ride at Fort Wilderness. Or go for a horseback trail ride. Tots 2 to 8 can opt for a pony ride instead.

cartoons continuously. (If they're not running, ask a cast member to start the reel!)

- À la Lady and the Tramp, share a strand of spaghetti with someone you love at Tony's Town Square Restaurant (that's a photo op!).
- **Get a haircut** at the Harmony Barber Shop on the left side of Town Square on Main Street. Currently the shop takes walk-ins only; so step in early in the morning for a minimal wait. The hours are 9:00 a.m. to 5:00 p.m. seven days a week, and prices are about $17 for adults and $14 for children under 13 years of age.

  Note: You can often spot a young boy in the barber chair experiencing his first haircut.
- Get tickets to **Mickey's Pirate and Princess Party** ($51 adult, $45 per child 3-9). Children search the Magic Kingdom for booty, meet characters, and enjoy a pirate-themed parade. Offered on certain evenings during slow seasons.
- Catch a performance of the **Dapper Dans**, a barbershop quartet. They often sing near the top of the hour from 9:00 a.m. until 5:00 p.m. with a break from 3:00 to 4:00 p.m. for the afternoon parade. You will find them at spots along Main Street, such as Exposition Hall, or even on the moving trolley. Ask at the Harmony Barber Shop or at Guest Relations in City Hall for information about the Dapper Dans performance times.
- Enjoy PUSH, the **talking trash can** in Tomorrowland. Most days he appears several times outdoors near Cosmic Ray's Starlight Café. Ask a nearby Disney cast member (especially if he or she is emptying trash cans) where and when PUSH will roll into view.
- Watch the **Flag Retreat**, complete with marching band, at 5:00 p.m. in Town Square on Main Street near the Railroad Station. Check your Times Guide to find out if it's scheduled for the day of your visit.
- Transform your young daughter (age 3 and up) into a Disney princess with hair styling, manicure, makeup, and costume at the **Bibbidi Bobbidi Boutique** inside Cinderella Castle. Boutique packages run $48 to $266 per girl. Boys, meanwhile, can become "Cool Dudes." For $10, the Boutique will spike your son's hair with colored gel and sparkles and add a Mickey Mouse stencil to his hair or cheek. (Call 407-WDW-STYLE for Boutique reservations.)
- Take a special park tour with your kids. **"Disney's Family Magic"** is a 2½-hour **scavenger hunt** through the Magic Kingdom aimed at families with children. The tour guide has families dancing, singing, and searching for clues that will save the Magic Kingdom from evil spells.

In the end, the kids not only save the MK but get to meet a surprise Disney character (costs about $29 per person not including your park admission).

"Keys to the Kingdom" is a 4- to 5-hour, behind-the-scenes look at the Magic Kingdom (costs about $64 per person including lunch, but not including park admission).

"Backstage Magic" offers a 7-hour guided tour to the inner workings of Epcot, Disney's Hollywood Studios, and Magic Kingdom (cost is about $200 per person, which includes lunch; theme park admission is not required).

Note: The "Keys" and "Backstage Magic" tours include a visit to the tunnels under the Magic Kingdom, where you'll see (among other things) characters resting between appearances.

The 3-hour **"Magic Behind Our Steam Trains"** tour shows off the steam locomotives of the WDW railroads. The cost is about $43 per person, not including park admission.

- **"Mickey's Magical Milestones"** tour is a 2-hour stroll through the Magic Kingdom that highlights the creation and career of Mickey Mouse. The cost is about $27 per person and does not include park admission.

Call 407-939-8687 for up-to-the-minute ticket prices, additional information, and reservations for any or all of these tours.

Age restrictions: You must be 16 or older to take the "Keys" and "Backstage Magic" tours and 10 or older for the "Steam Trains" and "Magical Milestones."

- **Cruise the Seven Seas Lagoon and Bay Lake** aboard a yacht or pontoon boat and **watch the evening fireworks** over the Magic Kingdom. For around $480 per hour or $720 for 90 minutes, you and up to 17 other guests can **cruise on the Grand 1 Yacht**. Or rent a pontoon boat to cruise more economically: about $240 per hour for a Pontoon Basic (up to 8 people) or about $293 for a Pontoon Premium (up to 10 people). The Pontoon Premium includes piped in music from the fireworks show. Food and drink are usually extra and can be ordered through yacht catering. However, some price quotes include food and drink; so be sure to ask. You can also **get a pontoon boat that's all "decked out" for a birthday celebration** or other special occasion. They even offer a Pirates-themed pontoon boat.

Call 407-824-2682 to reserve the 52-foot Grand 1 Yacht; 407-939-7529 for a pontoon boat, and 407-824-2473 (private dining) for yacht catering. Or, if you are staying on-property, contact Lobby Concierge at the resort you are departing from for catering information. You can also **rent the boats during the day**.

Tip: These boats are popular, so reserve them 90 days in advance. Or if you will be visiting during high season, reserve your boat when you make your hotel reservations.

- Enjoy any **special seasonal events**, such as "Mickey's Not So Scary Halloween Party" in the fall, "Mickey's Very Merry Christmas Party" in November and December (see "When to Go" in *Chapter One*), and "Night of Joy," a Christian music celebration that's performed for several evenings in early September in one of the theme parks. Single-night tickets for the last cost about $48 and two-night tickets about $81 when purchased in advance.

Epcot:

- Quench your thirst *free* at **Club Cool** (a refreshment center that serves soft drinks popular in countries such as Japan, Mexico, and Italy). You'll find it at the end of Innoventions West Side.
- Buy a same-day ticket (near the entrance to *Soarin'*) or reserve in advance for the 1-hour **"Behind The Seeds"** guided tour of the greenhouses at The Land Pavilion (cost is about $14 for adults and $10 for children ages 3 to 9; booking usually starts at 10:00 a.m.).
- Take a longer tour of Epcot. Visit backstage in some of the Future World pavilions in the 4½-hour **"Undiscovered Future World"** tour ($49 per person not including park admission). Ride **"Around the World at Epcot on a Segway,"** a unique transportation device that responds to your own movements (2-hour tour, $95 per person not including park admission). A 1-hour Segway experience called **Simply Segway** is available for about $35 per person, not including park admission. Find out more about how the park works on **"Backstage Magic,"** a 7-hour guided tour behind the scenes of Epcot, Disney's Hollywood Studios, and Magic Kingdom (costs about $200 per person and includes lunch; theme park admission is not required).

  Call 407-939-8687 for information, ticket prices, and reservations for Epcot tours.

  Weight restriction: 250 pound maximum for Segway.

  Age restriction: Guests must be 16 or older for the longer tours and the Segway tours.
- At The Seas with Nemo & Friends Pavilion: You can **Scuba dive at DiveQuest** if you're scuba certified (daily, about $150 per person

including all necessary gear for a 3-hour session that includes a 40-minute "dive adventure"). **Learn about dolphins** in depth (weekdays, about $150 per person for a 3-hour program; bring your swim suit). Or **take an "Aqua Tour"** of the huge aquarium (daily, about $115 per person for a 2½ -hour experience; bring your swim suit). Park admission is neither included nor required for the above three tours. Call 407-939-8687 for information and reservations for these adventures. Those under 18 must be accompanied by a participating parent or guardian, or bring a signed waiver, for most of these programs.

Age restrictions: Participants must be at least 8 years old for the "Aqua Tour," 10 for scuba diving, and 13 for the dolphin program.

- **Visit the exhibits** in Mexico, Norway, China, The American Adventure, Japan, and Morocco.
- Watch the evening *IllumiNations* from a boat under the bridge between France and the United Kingdom. Very relaxing and romantic! You can **rent a pontoon boat or the Breathless II** (a sleek motor boat) by calling ahead to 407-939-7529. You'll pay about $275 (with tax) to cruise for an hour in either craft – with up to 9 other people in a pontoon or up to 6 others on the Breathless II. Food and drink are not included but can be ordered (contact Lobby Concierge at the resort from which you are departing, or call 407-934-3160). You do not have to be a Disney property guest to rent a boat or order food.

  Tip: IllumiNations **cruises** are very popular. Start calling 2 to 3 minutes before 7:00 a.m. 90 days (even try 91 or 92 days!) in advance of the date you want. That's 7:00 a.m. Florida time! After you dial the number and get the recorded message, the menu number for boat rental is usually "1," so punch "1" right away. Provide a credit card to hold the reservation.

  Note: If you haven't booked ahead but would really like to take an *IllumiNations* cruise, try calling. You can sometimes book on short notice due to a cancellation. Don't give up if there's nothing available the first time you call. Call back daily before the cruise date you're hoping to book and then every couple of hours on the day of the cruise. You may get lucky.

  Note, too: These boats can also be rented during the day. The Breathless costs about $95 for 30 minutes for up to 7 guests.
- Enjoy any special **seasonal festivals** or events at Epcot, such as the International Flower & Garden Festival in the spring and the International Food & Wine Festival in the fall.

Disney's Hollywood Studios:

- **Dine with a Disney Imagineer.** Schedule a lunch chat with an Imagineer at the Hollywood Brown Derby Restaurant on selected days of the week. Call 407-WDW-DINE up to 60 days in advance to check available days and book this unforgettable experience. You can lunch with an Imagineer for about $64 (ages 10 and over) or $37 for children 3 to 9. Dinner with an Imagineer is sometimes available. Ask if you're interested.
- **Go behind the scenes.** "Backstage Magic," a 7-hour guided tour, takes you backstage in Disney's Hollywood Studios, Magic Kingdom, and Epcot. The cost is about $200 per person, including lunch, and theme park admission is not required. Participates must be at least 16 years of age.

Disney's Animal Kingdom:

- Enjoy the 3-hour **"Backstage Safari"** tour and meet some of the animal keepers! Cost is about $70 per person (not including park admission). Or learn about this amazing park's creation in the 3-hour, inside the park **"Wild by Design"** tour. Cost is about $60 per person and, again, does not include park admission. Call 407-939-8687 for information, ticket prices, and reservations.

  Age restrictions: You must be at least 16 to participate in "Backstage Safari" and 14 for "Wild by Design."
- Take your kids to an **educational outdoor class** in Africa near the Harambe Fruit Market. You'll sit on a bench under the trees and hear a cast member talk about African animals or some other aspect of Africa. The talks are mainly aimed at kids. Check the Tip Board nearby or ask a cast member for class times.
- Ask a cast member about the **kite-making class** in Asia.

Fun Outside the Theme Parks

At the Disney Resort Hotels

Staying off-property? You don't have to be a WDW Resort hotel guest to enjoy many of the activities described below. All the golf courses and some tennis courts are open to you, as are a number of other activities.

- **Reserve Suite 1501** at the Beach Club Resort. This suite is the closest hotel room to any of the theme parks in WDW. Suite 1501 is near the bridge to the rear entrance to Epcot. You can recline in the front room and gaze at the Eiffel Tower in France from a side window.
- Enjoy **swimming** in your hotel pool. Some of them are elaborate attractions.
- **Play golf**. WDW has 5 golf courses. Greens fees for 18 holes vary with the course and season from about $89 to $180 per person. Twilight golf rates (after 2:00 or 3:00 p.m., depending on the season) range from about $53 to $80. The 9-hole Oak Trail Course (a walking course) costs about $40 for adults and $20 for juniors 17 and under. Call 407-939-4653 to reserve tee times or golf lessons (about $75 for 45 minutes for adults, $50 for juniors). WDW Resort guests can arrange for a **free taxi ride** to and from the golf course and their WDW hotel.
- Play **tennis**. WDW has 22 tennis courts. Most are free on a first-come first-served basis, but the Grand Floridian usually charges about $11 per hour (with tax) for its courts. Tennis lessons (when available) cost $15 (plus tax) per person for a group clinic and $75 per hour for a private session. You can also **play the professional** for $75 per hour. Call 407-939-7529 for information, or 407-621-1991 for lessons.
- Go for a **walk or jog** near your hotel. Jogging trails are available at many hotels. Ask for information at your hotel Lobby Concierge.
- Ride a **bike**. Bikes can be rented at Fort Wilderness, Wilderness Lodge, Old Key West, Saratoga Springs, BoardWalk, Port Orleans–French Quarter, Port Orleans–Riverside, Caribbean Beach, and Coronado Springs Resorts for about $8 an hour or $22 per day.
- Rent a **boat** at a marina if your hotel is on a lake, river, or lagoon. Several types are available, including canopy boats, pontoon boats, Boston Whalers, pedal boats, canoes, kayaks, sailboats, and the 2-person little white **Water Mouse Sea Raycer speedboats**. Rental rates depend on the size of the boat and range from about $7 to $45 per half hour. *Age/height restrictions:* You must be at least 12 years old and 5 feet tall to pilot a Water Mouse speedboat, and all pilots under 18 must

bring a release signed by a parent or legal guardian. In addition, at the Magic Kingdom resort marinas, at least one person in the speedboat must have a valid driver's license.

- Take a **cruise** on the **Grand I Yacht** from the Grand Floridian Resort. Cost is about $480 per hour ($720 for 90 minutes) for up to 18 guests. Reserve a late cruise to enjoy the evening fireworks over Cinderella Castle (407-824-2682). Food and drink are usually extra (some packages include them) and can be ordered by calling yacht catering at 407-824-2473 (ask for private dining).
- Take a cruise on the **Breathless II** motor boat from the Yacht Club, Beach Club, or BoardWalk Resorts ($275 for up to 7 guests without food or drink). You do not have to be a Disney property guest to rent the Breathless II (call 407-939-7529) or to order provisions from Lobby Concierge (at 407-934-3160).
- Visit a **health club** (at Animal Kingdom Lodge, BoardWalk, Contemporary, Coronado Springs, Dolphin, Grand Floridian, Old Key West, Saratoga Springs, Swan, Wilderness Lodge, Yacht Club, or Beach Club) or **spa** (in the Grand Floridian, Saratoga Springs, Dolphin, or Buena Vista Palace). Health clubs are free to their own hotel guests. They charge about $12 a day up to a flat rate of about $50 for a family length-of-stay for guests of other WDW resorts. **Spa services** such as massages, facials, manicures, and pedicures cost extra (in the $50 to $150 and up range).

  Note: Health and fitness centers' admission policies change from time to time. Check with Lobby Concierge.
- Stroll along the BoardWalk; check out the clubs and shops or **rent a surrey** to pedal along the promenade. Surreys rent for about $19 per half hour for a 3-seater; $20 per half hour for a 6-seater, and $25 per half hour for a 9-seater.
- Sign up kids (ages 4 to 10) for an **"Albatross Treasure Cruise."** It embarks from the Yacht Club Resort and sails around Crescent Lake and the Epcot Lagoon for 2 hours on certain mornings (about $30 per child including lunch). Call 407-WDW-DINE to reserve. (Similar cruises are available at the Grand Floridian, Caribbean Beach, and Port Orleans – Riverside Resorts; 407-WDW-PLAY.)
- In the evening, **dance** to older music or contemporary tunes at Atlantic Dance on the BoardWalk. There's usually no cover charge.

  Age restriction: Guests must be 21 or older. Call 407-939-2444 for hours.
- **Sing along** with the piano players at Jellyrolls on the BoardWalk – a

raucous good time! Hours are 7:00 p.m. to 2:00 a.m. The cover charge is $10 or more per person. Write your song requests on a cocktail napkin and slide it onto one of the pianos. (A tip with the request will improve your chances!)

Note: Smoking will likely still be allowed when you visit. If it is, be aware that it can get smoky inside.

Age restriction: Guests must be 21 or older.

- Relax with **afternoon tea** (2:00 to 4:30 p.m., hours vary) at the Garden View Lounge on the first floor of the Grand Floridian Resort. The cost is about $6 per person for tea only and $11 to $27 per person for various food packages. Children ages 3 through 10 can enjoy apple "tea," lunch, and cupcakes with Alice and her friends from Wonderland at 1900 Park Fare Monday through Friday afternoons from 1:30 to 2:30 p.m., (cost is about $30 per child for the **Wonderland Tea Party**). Tea times are popular; reservations are recommended. (Call 407-939-3463 up to 180 days in advance.)

  For a more in-depth (and expensive) princess experience at the Grand Floridian, check out **My Disney Girl's Perfectly Princess Tea Party** (costs $240 for one adult and one child 3 to 11, plus $80 for each additional person 12 and older and $160 for each additional child). In addition to "tea" and edibles, the child meets Sleeping Beauty and takes home a doll, tiara, scrapbook, and other goodies. (Call 407-939-3463 up to 180 days in advance for reservations.)

- **Learn to dance the hula** for free in the Polynesian Resort lobby. Lessons for kids are Monday through Friday at 3:45 p.m. Adults are welcome to join in Saturday mornings at 10:00 a.m. (The times may change; check ahead.)

- Enjoy a **rest** – with or without a good book – in the lobby of the Grand Floridian Resort. The **Grand Floridian Society Orchestra** alternates with the Grand Pianist to provide soothing music from 3:00 p.m. to near 10:00 p.m. daily in the lobby.

- **Watch fireworks from a resort beach.** Enjoy the Magic Kingdom's nightly *Wishes* fireworks from the Polynesian or Grand Floridian beach. You don't have to be a resort guest to view fireworks from a hotel beach except on major holiday evenings when non-resort guests may not be admitted.

- Take the monorail to the Contemporary Resort's monorail lobby and **look for a five-legged goat** in the colorful mural of scenes from the Native American southwest. You'll spot it up above eye level on the wall facing the entrance walkway to the monorail.

- Kids ages 4 to 10 can sign up for a 2-hour **Disney's Pirate Adventure** to find treasure along the lakes behind the Grand Floridian. The cost is about $30 per child and includes lunch. Call 407-939-3463 for reservations. Also, ask about other current children's programs that may be available when you're visiting the hotel.

- Watch the Grand Floridian service staff do the **Parasol Parade** in the courtyard outside the main building on certain mornings of the week. Inquire at Lobby Concierge.

- Schedule a (free!) art tour of Animal Kingdom Lodge (AKL) and/or a (free!) **culinary tour** of the Lodge's restaurants. In the evening, listen to **stories about African culture** outside next to the AKL's firepit. Then top off the evening by **viewing the Savanna animals through night-vision goggles!** Special children's activities are also available.

- If you are a guest of the AKL, you can sign up for special **Animal Kingdom Lodge Safaris**. The "Sunrise Safari," exclusively for club-level (concierge) guests and about $59 per adult and $29 for children 3 to 9 (not including park admission) takes you on a special tour of Disney's Animal Kingdom savanna and includes breakfast in the Tusker House Restaurant after the tour. The "Wanyama Safari" (about $150 per adult and $75 per child age 8 to 9) will take any AKL guest around the Animal Kingdom Lodge savannas in the early evening and includes dinner at Jiko after the tour.

  Age restriction: You must be 8 years of age or older to take the "Wanyama Safari."

- Find out if the **Lunch with Walt Disney World Animal Specialists** experience is available. It's a 2-hour program offered on certain days at Animal Kingdom Lodge for guests 12 and over. The cost is $65 per person (407-939-8687), and you don't have to be a guest of any of the WDW hotels to participate.

- **Children 6 to 14 can experience Bush Camp** at Animal Kingdom Lodge on Saturdays. Campers learn about African culture and explore the Lodge's animal savannas during the 3-hour experience. (About $75 per child; call 407-WDW-PLAY to sign up.) Bush Camp is open to all; children needn't be WDW Resort guests to participate.

- Any club-level guest at any WDW Resort can book a **Wildlife Discovery Excursion** at Disney's Animal Kingdom. It's a 1-hour van tour through the savanna in Africa and costs about $48 per guest.

- Ask to be **"Flag Family of the Day"** if you're staying at Wilderness Lodge. You get to climb up to the roof and help raise the flags. Then schedule a (free!) tour of this scenic resort.

- From mid-May to mid-June, **sample the Copper River Salmon** (the king of salmons) at Artist Point Restaurant in the Wilderness Lodge. It is also usually available in season at Flying Fish on the BoardWalk, Victoria & Albert's in the Grand Floridian, and Fulton's Crab House at Pleasure Island in Downtown Disney.
- **Enjoy dinner with an Imagineer** at Artist Point on selected days. Book up to 60 days in advance. Cost for adults is about $116 (including tax). Call 407-WDW-DINE.
  Note: Not recommended for children under 14.
- Take a romantic (or family) **carriage ride** in the evening at Fort Wilderness or the Port Orleans or Sarasota Springs Resorts (up to 4 or 5 people, about $35 for a 30-minute ride). For reservations, telephone 407-939-7529.
- Explore Fort Wilderness and the Wilderness Lodge grounds on a Segway in the **Wilderness Back Trail Adventure Segway Tour**. The tour lasts 2 hours, includes a short training session, and costs about $90 per person. You must be at least 16 years of age (and be accompanied by an adult if under 18) and weigh between 100 and 250 pounds. Call 407-WDW-TOUR for reservations.
- Ask about the 2-hour **Bayou Pirate Adventure** for kids at Port Orleans Resort–Riverside or the **Caribbean Pirate Adventure** at the Caribbean Beach Resort. Both take kids ages 4 to 10 on a pirate cruise for about $30 per child. Call 407-939-PLAY for reservations for one of these cruise adventures.
- Eat a dinner buffet while unraveling a mystery and vying for prizes at **MurderWatch Mystery Theater** every Saturday night at the LakeView Restaurant in the Regal Sun Resort in Downtown Disney (407-828-4444 for reservations). About $50 for adults and $15 for children under 10.
- Check your hotel brochure for other activities you might enjoy.

Elsewhere around the World:

The following activities are open to all, whether you are staying on property or off:

- **Ride in the nose of the monorail** with the driver. When you line up for the monorail, ask the gate attendant if you can ride in the nose (usually a maximum of 4 riders). The attendant will check with the next monorail driver to find out if the nose seats are available.
- Explore the **activities at Fort Wilderness**. Rent a canoe, kayak, or

pedal boat (about $7 per half hour). Go **fishing** (on your own or book a 2-hour bass fishing excursion (407-WDW-BASS) for about $225 to $250 for up to 5 people; about $100 for an additional hour or $435 for 4 hours). Visit the horse barn, then meet the blacksmith who shoes the horses that pull the trolleys on Main Street in Magic Kingdom. Go on a 45-minute **wagon ride** (about $8 for adults and $5 for children ages 3 to 9; children 11 and younger must be accompanied by an adult) or a 25-minute **carriage ride** (about $35 for up to 4 adults or 2 adults and 3 kids ages 9 and under). Ask about watching the Magic Kingdom fireworks from your wagon or carriage.

Give your little ones (ages 2 to 8) **a pony ride** ($4). Or take a tame **horseback trail ride** (about $42 per person for 45 minutes).

Age/height/weight restrictions: You must be at least 9, 48" tall, and weigh no more than 250 pounds to take the horseback trail ride. Pony riders can't weigh more than 80 pounds.

Take a swim in either of Fort Wilderness's two pools.

Have fun at the (free!) nightly (7:00 or 8:00 p.m. weather permitting) outdoor **campfire**, which includes live musical entertainment, a marshmallow roast, meeting Chip 'n' Dale, and a Disney movie. Call 407-939-7529 for information and reservations for the above activities.

- If you are 18 or over and have a driver's license, you can **explore Fort Wilderness by electric golf cart** for about $13 per hour. A day's rental runs about $50 (for 24 hours). Call 407-824-2742.

- Enjoy music by a country band, line dancing with Disney characters, and a barbecue picnic at **Mickey's Backyard BBQ** at Fort Wilderness. It's offered on certain days in the spring, summer, and fall. Call 407-939-3463 for specifics. The cost is about $60 for adults and $36 for children 3 to 9, including tax and tip.

- Get rustic! **Spend a night in a tent** at Fort Wilderness (about $42 - $85 per night). The Disney folks will set up the tent before you arrive. Call 407-934-7639 for reservations. Then take a leisurely **hike** on the three-quarter-mile long **Wilderness Swamp Trail**, which starts behind the Settlement Trading Post. Find the lawn mower overgrown by a tree along a sidewalk to the marina.

- **Go fishing**. Arrange an adult or kid excursion at most hotels on a lake or lagoon. You can fish on your own or book a 2-hour **fishing excursion** for about $225 to $250 for up to 5 people; $435 for 4 hours. A **1-hour kid's excursion** (for ages 6 to 12) costs about $10 per child. Call 407-939-7529 or 407-939-BASS for information and reservations.

- **Play miniature golf** at Fantasia Gardens across from the Swan hotel or at **Winter Summerland** (entrance below) next to Blizzard Beach. Cost is about $13 for adults (with tax) and $10 for kids ages 3 to 9. Be aware that Disney's Fairways, one of the courses at Fantasia Gardens, is one of the most difficult miniature golf courses on earth. (No kidding!)

- Ride in or drive a fast stock car along the 1-mile oval WDW Speedway (near the Magic Kingdom) in the **Richard Petty Driving Experience.** The "Riding Experience" (ride-along) costs about $116 with tax; the 3-hour "Rookie Experience" costs about $425 for instruction and driving 8 fast laps; the "King's Experience" (around $851) for 2 sessions, one 8-lap and one 10-lap; the "Experience of a Lifetime" costs around $1,330 and lets you drive 30 laps over 3 sessions. Call 800-237-3889 for information or reservations. Bring your driver's license and limber up your arm for the stick shift!

  Age restrictions: You must be 16 or older to enjoy the "Riding Experience" and 18 or older for the other three experiences.

- Play volleyball or basketball. Many hotels have courts.

- Go **waterskiing,** wakeboarding, or tubing at the Contemporary Resort. Or take a **jet ski tour**. Call 407-939-0754 for information and reservations. Cost is about $85 for 30 minutes or about $165 for an hour. Children under 14 must be accompanied by a paying adult.

  Restriction: Those under 18 must have a parent or legal guardian present to sign a release form.

- Learn to surf at Typhoon Lagoon. **Craig Carroll's Surfing School** offers lessons on selected mornings, 6:45 a.m. to 10:00 a.m. (5:45 a.m. to 9:00 a.m. on Extra Magic Hour mornings). The $140 per person fee covers the lesson, use of equipment, and admission to the park for the lesson only (you have to pay regular park admission if you want to spend

the rest of the day there). Call 407-WDW-PLAY for information or to register.

Restrictions: You must be 8 or older and a good swimmer to take surfing lessons.

- If you're really brave, go **parasailing** over Bay Lake from the Contemporary Resort marina. Call 407-939-0754; cost depends on the time aloft and runs about $101 for 1 person and $170 for 2 to ride tandem. Children under 14 must be accompanied by a paying adult. Flyers under 18 years old must have a parent or legal guardian present to sign a release form.

Weight restriction: Solo flyers must weigh 100 pounds or more.

- At Disney's Wide World of Sports Complex (WWS), **watch the Tampa Bay Buccaneers** during their late summer training camp, the Atlanta Braves during baseball's spring training season, or various amateur events. Call 407-939-4263 for information. Ticket cost, including access to most amateur events scheduled during your visit, runs about $12 for adults and $9 for kids ages 3 to 9. When **Atlanta Braves** games are on, you can purchase a premium ticket to the pro game that includes general admission to the WWS. When available, you can get these tickets on site, via 407-939-GAME, or through TicketMaster (407-839-3900). For additional information and pricing, visit www.disneyworldsports.com. As we go to press, you can watch the Buccaneers train for *free*: no ticket of any kind is needed to watch the team practice!

- Immerse yourself in virtual reality and other interactive fare at **DisneyQuest** at Downtown Disney West Side. One-day tickets are about $39 for adults and about $33 for children 3 to 9 years of age. (Admission is included with the Water Park Fun & More ticket option as well as the Premium Annual Pass; see *Chapter One*, "Admission tickets.")

- Catch a **Sunday Gospel Brunch** buffet with live music entertainment at the House of Blues at Disney's West Side in Downtown Disney. For information or reservations, call the House of Blues Box Office (407-934-2583) or TicketMaster (407-839-3900). Brunch seatings are available for 10:30 a.m. and/or 1:00 p.m., and tickets cost about $34 for adults and $17 for children 3 to 9 years of age including tax and gratuity. Children under 3 are admitted free.

- Also at Downtown Disney West Side, see "La Nouba," the amazing, 90-minute acrobatic and dance show, **Cirque du Soleil**. Tickets cost about $67 - $119 for adults and $53 - $96 for children (9 and younger), depending on the ticket category (there are four). Children 5 years of age and older enjoy it. Call 407-939-7600 for information or tickets and 407-939-7913 for special requests.

Note: Since some of the show happens above the stage and above the audience, seats behind the central horizontal walkway provide viewing that is easier on your neck.

Tip: Make a bathroom stop before the show!

- At The World of Disney store in Downtown Disney marketplace, **transform your young daughter into a Disney princess** (or Hannah Montana!) with hair styling, manicure, makeup, and costume at the Bibbidi Bobbidi Boutique. Boutique packages run $48 to $266 per girl ages 3 and up. Meanwhile, **your son can become a "Cool Dude."** For a flat fee of $10, the Boutique will spike his hair with colored gel and sparkles and add a Mickey Mouse stencil to his cheek or the back of his head. (Call 407-WDW-STYLE for boutique reservations.) In the nearby **Adventure Room**, your child can explore pirate, cowboy, superhero, or space hero gear and games. Girls can pursue their princess dreams in the store's **Princess Room**, where they'll find tiaras, wands, jewelry, and so on.

- **Rent a boat** (several types are available, including canopy boats and the smaller Water Mouse Sea Raycer speedboats) at the Downtown Disney Marketplace marina. Rental rates depend on the size of the boat and average about $20 to $45 per half hour.

  Age/height restrictions: You must be at least 12 years old and 5 feet tall to pilot a Water Mouse speedboat. All drivers under 18 must have a release signed by a parent or legal guardian.

- Watch the **Electrical Water Pageant**, which floats through the waters of Bay Lake and Seven Seas Lagoon. A string of illuminated creatures moves gently to music as it passes by the Polynesian Resort at 9:00 p.m., the Grand Floridian at 9:15 p.m., the Wilderness Lodge at 9:35 p.m., the Fort Wilderness beach at 9:45 p.m., the Contemporary at 10:05 p.m., and sometimes the Magic Kingdom at 10:20 p.m. Times are approximate; check with Lobby Concierge at your hotel for current information.

  Note: The Pageant may be delayed a short while if the Magic Kingdom fireworks are scheduled for 9:00 p.m.

- Eat dinner at the California Grill. If the timing is right, listen to the music inside and **watch the *Wishes* fireworks show** over the Magic Kingdom. Then walk outside to the rear walkway and watch the Electrical Water Pageant on Bay Lake.

- Consider visiting one of the WDW water parks in the evening (if open).

They're beautiful at night and usually less crowded.

- If you happen to get change in **Disney Dollars** (Cinderella or Ariel on the $1 bill, Goofy or Aurora on the $5, Minnie Mouse or Cinderella on the $10, and Mickey Mouse on the $50), you can keep them for souvenirs or exchange them for U.S. currency at any of the WDW parks or hotels or at any Disney Store. The characters on the bills change from time to time. You can order Disney Dollars by writing WDW Ticketing, P.O. Box 10140, Lake Buena Vista, FL 32830. Add $10 for shipping to the total you are requesting in Disney Dollars.

- Take a **VIP Tour** of WDW with your own WDW tour guide. The cost is $125 per hour per group of 1 to 10 guests. The fee does not include park admissions and you must pay for a minimum of 6 hours. The guide tailors the tour to your group's wishes and will take you to any WDW attractions you want (so long as you are willing to pay the admission). VIP Tour groups do not get front-of-the-line privileges, which means they may have to wait in line (or use a FASTPASS when available) like anyone else. Call 407-560-4033 for information and reservations. Ask for discounts on the tour! (WDW offers a wide variety of **discounts** – Passholder, AAA, Florida resident, active military, etc. – on a wide range of tickets and activities. The discounts come and go, but it always pays to ask. You may be pleasantly surprised.)

- If you visit WDW during the Christmas season (Thanksgiving to New Year's Day), enjoy the **Yuletide Fantasy Tour**, a 3- to 3½-hour journey through theme parks and resort hotels that highlights how WDW is transformed into a winter wonderland. The cost is about $73 per person and theme park admission is not required. You must be 16 or older to take the tour. Call 407-WDW-TOUR for reservations.

- Want to join the **pin trading** craze? You can get a starter lanyard and starter pins (for keeping or trading) at many WDW park and resort stores for about $25. Just walk up to any WDW cast member with a lanyard around his or her neck and ask about pin trading. To check into the times for pin trading meets, go to dizpins.com or Google "Disney pin trading" and follow the links.

- Another popular hobby is **collecting pressed coins**. Ask at your resort hotel or any theme park Guest Relations (or go online at www.allearsnet.com and search for "pressed pennies") for a list of WDW machines. For 50 cents per penny-pressing machine (or four quarters for a machine that presses quarters), you can impress a penny or a quarter with various characters. You can store your collection in a pressed coin book (which you'll find in many WDW shops).

Afterword

Orlando, Florida has become one of the premier vacation destinations in the world. WDW addicts abound; I know, I'm one. We keep coming back for our periodic infusion of Disney magic. Many folks who can only rarely accomplish the trek to Orlando have recurrent dreams about returning. Some keep countdown clocks as constant reminders of the pleasures to come! Each day, theme park skeptics are converted into Disney aficionados, especially if they come prepared or with a seasoned tour guide.

What do people complain about after a WDW vacation? The cost, the crowds, the heat. But all of these irritants can be rendered inconsequential with advance planning and smart decision-making while you are in the parks.

Yes, you can drop big bucks at the Walt Disney World Resort, and you can feel crowded and hot. However, the cost of theme park admission is recouped many times over in the course of a day, and you can minimize the cost of hotel, food, souvenirs, and incidentals if you plan well. As for the crowds and the heat, follow the touring plans in this book and you will minimize their irritation.

Your visit to Walt Disney World can and should be as magical as any vacation you've ever taken.

See you there! (I'm the short smiling guy in the Disney floppy hat.)

How well do you know WDW?

Walt Disney World Resort is nothing if not enormous – and filled with interesting sights of all kinds. Can you identify the places and attractions pictured on the following pages and tell exactly where you'll find them in WDW (theme park and land, for example, or specific area within a resort)? You'll find the answers on page 248.

1. Where will you find this shack?

2. Where is this huge dinosaur skeleton and what attraction is nearest to it?

3. (Above) Where can you spot this shop?

4. Do you know where to find Casey?

5. Where can you sit in this chair?

6. Where will you stumble on the notice below?

7. Where can you find this horse for a photo op?

8. Where might you spot this crate?

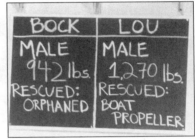

9. Do you know where this sign is?

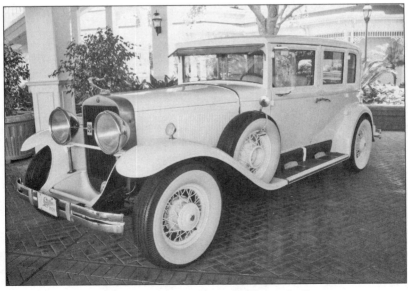

10. Where is this classic Cadillac parked?

11. Where is the Torture Lab?

12. Where can you check this train schedule?

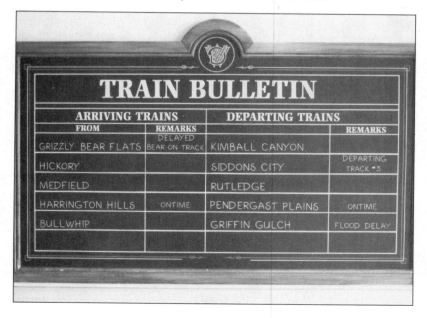

TRAIN BULLETIN

ARRIVING TRAINS		DEPARTING TRAINS	
FROM	REMARKS		REMARKS
GRIZZLY BEAR FLATS	DELAYED BEAR ON TRACK	KIMBALL CANYON	
HICKORY		SIDDONS CITY	DEPARTING TRACK #5
MEDFIELD		RUTLEDGE	
HARRINGTON HILLS	ONTIME	PENDERGAST PLAINS	ONTIME
BULLWHIP		GRIFFIN GULCH	FLOOD DELAY

SAFARI:	DEPARTS:
Kilimanjaro Safari Photo-tour	Daily
Gorilla Sanctuary Walking Safaris	Daily
Masai Mara Game Tour	7:00 AM Mon-Wed-Fri-Sat
Mzima Springs Hippo Watching	Sat. Morning
Samburu Riding Safari	1st THURSDAY - Monthly Enquire for Times
Amboseli Elephant Safari	Fri-Sat-Sun - 8:00 AM
Upcountry Bushwalk	Weekends Only - 6:00 AM
Serengeti Hot Air Balloon Trips	WHEN AVAILABLE - 4:30 AM
Captain Bob's Super Safaris	Daily - 9:00 Am
Ngorogoro Crater Tour	WED & FRI 6:30 AM

13. If you're searching for safari schedules, where will you find this board?

14. Where is this "Missing Persons" sign?

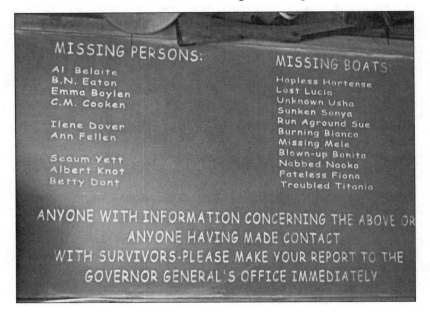

MISSING PERSONS:

Al Belaite
B.N. Eaton
Emma Boylen
C.M. Cooken

Ilene Dover
Ann Fellen

Seaum Yett
Albert Knot
Betty Dont

MISSING BOATS:

Hopless Hortense
Lost Lucia
Unknown Usha
Sunken Sonya
Run Aground Sue
Burning Bianca
Missing Mele
Blown-up Bonita
Nabbed Naoko
Fateless Fiona
Troubled Titania

ANYONE WITH INFORMATION CONCERNING THE ABOVE OR
ANYONE HAVING MADE CONTACT
WITH SURVIVORS-PLEASE MAKE YOUR REPORT TO THE
GOVERNOR GENERAL'S OFFICE IMMEDIATELY

15. Who are these folks and where can you find them?

16. Where are these guys making music?

17. Where does the Irvine sail and what are the other boats in the fleet called?

18. What are you looking at and from where?

Cotton-Top Tamarin
Saguinus oedipus

Cotton-top tamarins are small monkeys found only in the tropical forests of Colombia in South America. They feed on fruit and insects and spend their entire lives on tree branches and vines. That's why saving their natural forest habitat is so critical to their survival.

To learn more about how we are working to save cotton-tops, take a look behind you.

19. Top: Where will you see this sign?

20. Bottom: Where is "Elfstream"?

21. Where is this shop located?

How well do you know WDW? ANSWERS

1. Jungle Cruise, Adventureland, Magic Kingdom (MK). 2. Near The Boneyard, Dino-Land U.S.A., Disney's Animal Kingdom (DAK). 3. Just inside the entrance to Disney's Hollywood Studios (DHS). 4. Outside Casey's Corner, Main Street, U.S.A., MK. 5. In the Harmony Barber Shop, Main Street, U.S.A., MK. 6. On a wall outside the Meadow Trading Post in the center of Disney's Fort Wilderness. 7. On Hollywood Boulevard in DHS. 8. Near Min and Bill's Dockside Diner, Echo Lake, DHS. 9. In the Manatee tank area of The Seas with Nemo & Friends Pavilion, Future World (FW), Epcot. 10. At the front entrance to Disney's Grand Floridian Resort & Spa. 11. Inside Innovations East, FW, Epcot. 12. In the lower level of the WDW Railroad's Main Street Station, MK. 13. Inside the Tusker House Restaurant, DAK. 14. At the Jungle Cruise exit, Adventureland, MK. 15. Munchkins in the "Wizard of Oz" segment of The Great Movie Ride, DHS. 16. Discovery Island, DAK. 17. The Seven Seas Lagoon between the Transportation and Ticket Center and the MK. Its sister ferries are the Admiral Joe Fowler and the General Joe Potter. 18. Disney's Grand Floridian Resort & Spa from inside the California Grill res-taurant in Disney's Contemporary Resort. 19. In Habitat Habit! along the walking trail to Conservation Station, Rafiki's Planet Watch, DAK. 20. Along the Winter Summerland Miniature Golf Course. 21. Hollywood Boulevard, DHS.

Index

The following abbreviations appear in this Index

AK	- Disney's Animal Kingdom	FW	- Fort Wilderness
DD	- Downtown Disney	H	- WDW Resort Hotel(s)
DH	- Disney's Hollywood Studios	MK	- Magic Kingdom
E	- Epcot	WP	- WDW Water Parks
SC	- Disney's Wide World of Sports Complex		

Page numbers in boldface italic indicate a photo.

Note: You do not necessarily have to be a WDW hotel guest to participate in hotel-based activities such as playing golf or tennis or touring the resort. Call the contact numbers listed in this book to inquire.

A

Acrobats (E) 138
Activities, outdoor. *See* Outdoor activities
Activities for kids
  Albatross Treasure Cruise (H) 231
  Bayou Pirate Adventure (H) 234
  Bush Camp (H) 233
  Caribbean Pirate Adventure (H) 234
  daytime 37
  Disney's Pirate Adventure (H) 233
  educational outdoor class (AK) 229
  evening 36
  fishing (FW, H) 235
  hula lessons (H) 232

Activities for kids, cont'd.
  Kidcot Fun Stops (E) 137
  Kids Discovery Clubs (AK) 217
  Mickey's Pirate and Princess Party
    (MK) 225
  My Disney Girl's Perfectly Princess Tea
    Party (H) 232
  Passport program (E) 137
  pony ride (FW) 235
  Wonderland Tea Party (H) 232
Activities with age restrictions
  Albatross Treasure Cruise (H) 231
  Atlantic Dance (H) 231
  Bayou Pirate Adventure (H) 234
  Bush Camp (H) 233

Activities with age restrictions, cont'd.
C. Carroll's Surfing School (WP) 236
Caribbean Pirate Adventure (H) 234
dine with a Disney Imagineer (DH, H)
229
Disney's Pirate Adventure (H) 233
dolphin program (E) 228
guided tours
Aqua Tour (E) 228
Around the World at Epcot on a
Segway (E) 227
Backstage Magic (E, DH, MK) 226,
227, 229
Backstage Safari (AK) 229
Keys to the Kingdom (MK) 226
Magic Behind Our Steam Trains (MK)
226
Mickey's Magical Milestones (MK)
226
Simply Segway (E) 227
Undiscovered Future World (E) 227
Wanyama Safari (H) 233
Wild by Design (AK) 229
Wilderness Back Trail Adventure (H)
234
Yuletide Fantasy Tour 239
horseback trail ride (FW) 235
in Fort Wilderness 234, 235
Jellyrolls (H) 231–232
jet ski tour (H) 236
kid's fishing excursion (H) 235
lunch with animal specialists (H) 233
parasailing (H) 237
pony ride (FW) 235
Richard Petty Driving Experience 236
scuba diving (E) 227–228
snorkeling (WP) 222
speedboat piloting (H) 230, 238
surfing (WP) 237
tubing (H) 236
wakeboarding (H) 236
Wanyama Safari (H) 233
Water Mouse speedboat piloting (H)
230, 238
waterskiing (H) 236
Wonderland Tea Party (H) 232

Activities with height restrictions. See also
Height restrictions, attractions with
horseback trail ride (FW) 235
speedboat piloting (H) 230, 238
Activities with weight restrictions
horseback trail ride (FW) 235
parasailing (H) 237
pony ride (FW) 235
Segway tour of Fort Wilderness and
Wilderness Lodge grounds 234
Segway tours of Epcot 227
Admission tickets 27–34
add-on options 28–29
No Expiration 29
ParkHopper 28
Water Park Fun & More 28–29
advance-purchase discounts 27
buying 33–34
choosing 30–32
passes for Florida residents 30
Advance dining reservations (ADR) 47
Adventureland (MK) 68
Affection Section (AK) 207
Africa (AK) 205–206
Afternoon tea (H) 232
Airlines, charter, to Sanford from the UK 25
Airlines to Orlando 24–25
from Canada 25
from the U.S. 24–25
from the UK 25
Albatross Treasure Cruise (H) 231
All-Star Movies (H) 22
All-Star Music (H) 22
All-Star Sports (H) 22
America Gardens Theater (E) 139
American Adventure Pavilion (E) 139–140
American Adventure Show (E) 140
Animal Kingdom. See Disney's Animal
Kingdom
Animal Kingdom Lodge (H) 20–21
Animal viewing at night (H) 233
Animation Academy (DH) 186
Annual passes
specialty 30
types & benefits 29–30
when they make sense 33
Aquarium (E) 135

Aqua Tour (E) 228
Ariel's Grotto (MK) 76
Around the World at Epcot on a Segway
    227
Arrival day, what to do on 43
Art tour of Animal Kingdom Lodge 233
Asia (AK) 207–208
Astro Orbiter (MK) 82, *125*
Atlanta Braves, spring training (SC) 237
Atlantic Dance (H) 231
Attraction closings 61
Attraction ratings explained 60
Attractions beyond WDW, visiting 41
Attractions that may frighten children
    Disney's Animal Kingdom 212
    Disney's Hollywood Studios 189–190
    Epcot 143
    Magic Kingdom 84
Attractions with minimal waits
    Disney's Animal Kingdom 211
    Disney's Hollywood Studios 189
    Epcot 143
    Magic Kingdom 83

B

Backstage Magic (E, DH, MK) 226, 227, 229
Backstage Safari (AK) 229
Barbecue picnic (FW) 235
Barnstormer at Goofy's Wiseacre Farm,
    The (MK) 79–80
Base (admission) tickets 28
Baseball spring training (SC) 237
Basketball (FW, H) 236
Bayou Pirate Adventure (H) 234
Beach Club (H) 20
Beauty and the Beast - Live (DH) 187
Behind The Seeds (E) 227
Bibbidi Bobbidi Boutique (DD, MK) 225,
    238
Bicycle rentals (FW, H) 230
Big Thunder Mountain Railroad (MK) 72
Biking (FW, H) 230
Blacksmith (FW) 235
Blizzard Beach (WP) 18, 221, *222*
BoardWalk Inn and Villas (H) 20
Boat rentals (DD, FW, H) 221, 230–231,
    235, 238

Boneyard, The (AK) 209
Braves, Atlanta, spring training (SC) 237
Breathless II, motor boat (H) 228, 231
British Invasion, The (E) 163, 170–171, 177
Buccaneers, Tampa Bay, summer training
    (SC) 237
Budgeting for your vacation 35–36
Bush Camp (H) 233
Buzz Lightyear's AstroBlaster (DD) 219
Buzz Lightyear's Space Ranger Spin (MK) 81

C

Cameras, tips on 61–62
Campfire, nightly (FW) 235
Camping (FW) 22, 235
Camp Minnie-Mickey (AK) 204–205
Canada Pavilion (E) 142
Candlelight Processional (E) 16
Canoe rentals (FW, H) 230, 234
Caribbean Beach (H) 21
Caribbean Pirate Adventure (H) 234
Carousel of Progress (MK) 81
Car rentals 36
Carriage rides (FW, H) 234, 235
Carrousel, Cinderella's Golden (MK) 75
Casey statue (MK) *242*
Catastrophe Canyon (DH) 184
Centra Care 42
Character Greeting Trails (AK) 204–205
Character meals 36, 47, 54–56
    at-a-glance 54–56
    by character 54–56
    by location 56
    in Disney's Animal Kingdom 50
    in Disney's Hollywood Studios 49
    in Epcot 49
    in Magic Kingdom 48
    Magic Kingdom 48
Characters, where to meet. See also
        Character meals
    Ariel's Grotto (MK) 76
    Character Greeting Trails (AK) 204–205
    Disney's Family Magic Tour (MK)
        225–226
    Fort Wilderness campfire 235
    Magic of Disney Animation (DH) 186
    Mickey's Backyard BBQ (FW) 235

Characters, where to meet, cont'd.
    Mickey's Christmas Party (MK) 16–17
    Mickey's Country House (MK) 79
    Mickey's Judge's Tent (MK) 79
    Mickey's Pirate and Princess Party (MK)
        225
    Mickey's Toontown Fair (MK) 78–80
    My Disney Girl's Tea Party (H) 232
    near Mickey's Sorcerer's Hat (DH) 199
    Pixar Place (DH) 199
    Streets of America (DH) 199
    Toontown Hall of Fame (MK) 78–79
    Wonderland Tea Party (H) 232
Child's meal 48
Child care 36–37
Children's activities. See Activities for kids
Children's clubs (for resort guests) 36
China Pavilion (E) 138–139, *144*
Christmas decorations 16
Christmas events 16–17, 227, 239
Cinderella Castle (MK) *64*, 74
Cinderella's Golden Carrousel (MK) 75
Circle of Life, The (E) 134
Cirque du Soleil (DD) *220*, 237
Closings, attraction 61
Club Cool (E) 136, *163*, 227
Conservation Station (AK) 207
Contemporary (H) 20
    mural in monorail station 232
Cool Dudes (DD, MK) 225, 238
Coronado Springs (H) 21
Costumes for kids (DD, MK) 225, 238
Country Bear Jamboree (MK) 70–71
Craig Carroll's Surfing School (WP)
    236–237
Cretaceous Trail (AK) 211
Crowded days, what to do on 43–44
Cruises for kids (H) 37, 231, 233, 234. See
    also by name of cruise
Cruising (adult) at WDW (H) 226, 228, 231
Culinary tour of Animal Kingdom Lodge
    restaurants 233
CyberSpace Mountain (DD) 219

D

Dancing, line
    with Disney characters (FW) 235

Dancing, social (H) 231
Dapper Dans (MK) 225
Dash to Splash (MK) 91–92
Deluxe WDW resorts 20–21
Departure day, what to do on 43
Dine with a Disney Imagineer (DH, H) 229,
    234
Dining at WDW. See Where to eat
Dining plans 35
    for Florida residents 30
Dinner packages
    Candlelight Processional (E) 16
    Fantasmic! (DH) 189
Dinner shows 50
    Hoop-Dee-Doo Musical Revue (FW) 50
    MurderWatch Mystery Theatre (DD
        area) 234
    Spirit of Aloha (H) 50
Dino-Sue T-Rex (AK) 211
DinoLand U.S.A. (AK) 209–211
DINOSAUR (AK) *210*, 210–211
Dinosaur skeleton (AK) *241*
Directions to WDW. See *also* Exits from I-4
    to WDW
    for drivers 26
    from the airport 26
Disabilities, guests with 38
    WDW guidebook for 38
Discounts 18, 239
    for Florida residents 30
    on admission tickets 27
Discovery Island (AK) 203–204
Discovery Island Trails (AK) 203
Disney Dollars 239
Disney terminology 39
DisneyQuest (DD) *218*, 219–220, 237
Disney's Animal Kingdom 201–217
    attractions described & rated 201,
        203–211
    getting to 213
    map of 202
    special activities at 229
    touring 213–217
Disney's Family Magic (MK) 225
Disney's Hollywood Studios 179–199
    attractions described & rated 179,
        182–189

Disney's Hollywood Studios, cont'd.
  getting to 191
  map of 180–181
  special activities at 229
  touring 191–199
Disney's Pirate Adventure (H) 233
DiveQuest (E) 227–228
DiVine (AK) 216
Dolphin program (E) 228
Donald's Boat (MK) 79
Downtown Disney 219–221
  Hotel Plaza lodgings 22
  Marketplace 221
  Pleasure Island 221
  West Side 219–221
Driving to WDW 26. See also Exits from I-4
  to WDW
Dumbo the Flying Elephant (MK) 76, **99**

E

Electrical Water Pageant 238
EMH. See Extra Magic Hours program
Enchanted Tiki Room, The (MK) 69
Epcot 127–177
  attractions described & rated 130–143
  getting to 145–146
  hotels 20, 21
  map of 128–129
  special activities at 227–228
  touring 145–177
Exits from I-4 to WDW. See also Driving to
  WDW
  to Disney's Animal Kingdom 26
  to Disney's Hollywood Studios 26
  to Downtown Disney 26
  to Epcot 26
  to Magic Kingdom 26
  to Wide World of Sports 26
Expedition Everest (AK) 208, **215**
Extra Magic Hours program 18–19, 37, 40

F

Family suites, WDW (H) 22
Fantasia Gardens miniature golf course 235
Fantasmic! (DH) 188–189
Fantasyland (MK) 74–78
FASTPASS 37–38

Festival of The Lion King (AK) 204
Fife and Drum Corps (E) 177
Finding Nemo – The Musical (AK) 209
Fireworks, special ways to watch
  IllumiNations (E) 228
  Wishes (MK) 226, 231, 232, 235, 238
Fireworks cruises 226, 228, 231
Fireworks shows
  IllumiNations (E) 142
  Wishes (MK) 83
Fishing (FW, H) 235, 235–236
  bass fishing excursions 235
  1-hour kid's excursion 235
Fitness centers (H) 231
Flag Family of the Day (H) 233
Flag Retreat (MK) 225
Flights of Wonder (AK) 207
Florida residents, special tickets for 30
Fort Wilderness 22
  activities in 22, 234–235
  signs in **224**, **242**
Fossil Fun Games (AK) 210
Fountain of Nations (E) 136
Fountains. See also Interactive fountains
  Disney's Hollywood Studios 182
  Epcot 132, 136, 139
France Pavilion (E) 141
Frontierland (MK) 70–72
Frontierland Shootin' Arcade (MK) 71
Future World (E) 130–139

G

Gardens
  Canada (E) 142
  China (E) 138
  France (E) 141
  Japan (E) 140
  The Oasis (AK) 201, 203
  United Kingdom (E) 142–141
Gay Pride days 17
Germany Pavilion (E) 139, **147**
Getting to the 'Mountains' (MK) 89–92
Golf (H) 28, 29, 230
Golf, miniature 235
Good things to know about 35–45
Gospel Brunch (DD) 220, 237
Grand 1 Yacht cruise 226, 231

Grand Floridian (H) 19, 20, *243*, *247*
Gran Fiesta Tour Starring the Three
	Caballeros (E) 137–138
Gratuities, restaurant 48
Great Movie Ride, The (DH) 187, *246*
G scale miniature railroad (E) 139, *147*
Guided tours
	art tour of Animal Kingdom Lodge 233
	culinary of Animal Kingdom Lodge res-
		taurants 233
	for Animal Kingdom Lodge club-level
		guests
		Sunrise Safari 233
		Wanyama Safari 233
	for on-property club-level guests
		Wildlife Discovery Excursion 233
	in Disney's Animal Kingdom
		Backstage Safari 229
		Sunrise Safari 233
		Wild by Design 229
		Wildlife Discovery Excursion 233
	in Disney's Hollywood Studios
		Backstage Magic 229
	in Epcot
		Aqua Tour 228
		Around the World on a Segway 227
		Backstage Magic 227
		Behind The Seeds 227
		Simply Segway 227
		The Land greenhouses 133
		Undiscovered Future World 227
	in Magic Kingdom
		Backstage Magic 226
		Children's tours 37
		Disney's Family Magic 225
		Keys to the Kingdom 226
		Magic Behind Our Steam Trains 226
		Mickey's Magical Milestones 226
	of Animal Kingdom Lodge 233
	of Fort Wilderness and Wilderness Lodge
		grounds 234
	on a Segway 227, 234
	VIP Tour of WDW 239
	Yuletide Fantasy Tour 239

H

Habitat Habit! (AK) 207, *248*

Hall of Flags (E) 140
Hall of Presidents (MK) 73
Harmony Barber Shop (MK) 225, *242*
Haunted Mansion, The (MK) 74
Health clubs (H) 231
Height restrictions, attractions with
	Barnstormer at Goofy's Wiseacre Farm,
		The (MK) 80
	Big Thunder Mountain Railroad (MK) 72
	Buzz Lightyear's AstroBlaster (DD) 220
	Chairlift (WP) 222
	Crush 'n' Gusher (WP) 222
	CyberSpace Mountain (DD) 220
	DINOSAUR (AK) 210–211
	Downhill Double Dipper (WP) 222
	Expedition Everest (AK) 208
	Humunga Kowabunga (WP) 222
	Kali River Rapids (AK) 208
	Mission: SPACE (E) 131
	Pirates of the Caribbean game (DD) 220
	Primeval Whirl (AK) 210
	Rock 'n' Roller Coaster (DH) 187–188
	Slush Gusher (WP) 222
	Soarin' (E) 134
	Space Mountain (MK) 83
	Splash Mountain (MK) 72
	Star Tours (DH) 182
	Stitch's Great Escape! (MK) 80
	Summit Plummet (WP) 222
	Test Track (E) 132
	Tomorrowland Indy Speedway (MK) 80
	Twilight Zone Tower of Terror, The (DH)
		188
Hidden Mickeys
	general notes on 59
	in Disney's Animal Kingdom 212
	in Disney's Hollywood Studios 190
	in Epcot 144
	in Magic Kingdom 85
Hiking (FW) 235
Hollywood Boulevard photo op (DH) *243*
Honey, I Shrunk the Audience (E) 132
Honey, I Shrunk the Kids Movie Set Adven-
	ture (DH) 184
Hoop-Dee-Doo Musical Revue (FW) 50
Horseback trail ride (FW) 235
Hotels, WDW Resort 19–22

Hotels, WDW Resort, cont'd.
  activities at 230–234
House of Blues (DD) 220, 237
Hula lessons (H) 232

I

IllumiNations (E) 142–143. See also
    Fireworks, special ways to watch
    viewing spots for 142
IllumiNations cruises (H) 228
ImageWorks (E) 133
Imagination! Pavilion (E) 132–133
Imagineer, dine with (DH, H) 229, 234
Impressions de France (E) 141
Indiana Jones Epic Stunt Spectacular (DH)
    183
Innoventions East/West Sides (E) 135–136,
    244
Innoventions Plaza (E) 136
Interactive exhibit areas
    Conservation Station (AK) 207
    Exposition Hall (MK) 68, 223
    ImageWorks (E) 133
    Innoventions (E) 135
    Magic of Disney Animation (DH) 186
    Mission: SPACE post show (E) 131
    Project Tomorrow (E) 130
    SoundWorks (DH) 183
Interactive fountains. See also Water
    playgrounds
    Epcot **136**, 155, 166
    Magic Kingdom 76
    Marketplace (DD) 221
International Flower & Garden Festival (E)
    228
International Food & Wine Festival (E) 228
it's a small world (MK) 74–75
It's Tough to be a Bug! (AK) 203–204
Italy Pavilion (E) 139

J

JAMMitors (E) 161, 169, 175
Japanese drumming routines (E) 140
Japan Pavilion (E) 140, **148**
Jellyrolls (H) 231–232
Jet ski tour (H) 236
Jogging trails (H) 230

Journey Into Imagination with Figment (E)
    133
Judge's Tent, Mickey's (MK) 79
Jungle Cruise (MK) 69, **241**, **245**

K

Kali River Rapids (AK) 208
Kayak rentals (FW, H) 230, 234
Keys to the Kingdom (MK) 226
Kidcot Fun Stops (E) 137
Kids Discovery Clubs (AK) 217
Kilimanjaro Safaris (AK) 205–206
Kites, making (AK) 229

L

Land Pavilion, The (E) 133–134, **144**
La Nouba (DD) 220, 237
Least crowded restrooms
    Disney's Animal Kingdom 212
    Disney's Hollywood Studios 190
    Epcot 143
    Magic Kingdom 84
LEGO Imagination Center (DD) 221
Liberty Belle, The (MK) 73
Liberty Square (MK) 72–74
Liberty Square Riverboat (MK) 73
Living with the Land (E) 133–134
Lodging. See Where to stay
Lunch with WDW animal specialists (H) 233

M

Mad Tea Party (MK) 77
Maelstrom (E) 138
Magical Express airport shuttle service 24
Magical Gatherings 35
Magic Behind Our Steam Trains (MK) 226
Magic Carpets of Aladdin, The (MK) 69
Magic Kingdom 65–125
    attractions described & rated 65, 68–83
    getting to 86–87
    map of 66–67
    monorail resort hotels 20
    special activities at 223–227
    touring 86–124
Magic of Disney Animation (DH) 186
Magic Your Way Plus Dining package 35
Maharajah Jungle Trek (AK) 208

Main Street, U.S.A. (MK) 65, 68

Many Adventures of Winnie the Pooh, The
(MK) 77

Marketplace (DD) 221

Medical services (Centra Care) 42

Mexico Pavilion (E) *126*, 137–138

Mickey Mouse, where to meet 16, 79, 235

Mickey Mouse cartoons, vintage (MK) 223

Mickey's Backyard BBQ (FW) 235

Mickey's Country House (MK) 79, *121*

Mickey's Magical Milestones (MK) 226

Mickey's Not So Scary Halloween Party
(MK) 227

Mickey's PhilharMagic (MK) 75

Mickey's Pirate and Princess Party (MK)
225

Mickey's Toontown Fair (MK) 78–80

Mickey's Very Merry Christmas Party (MK)
16–17, 227

Mickeys, hidden. See Hidden Mickeys

Military personnel, resort for. See Shades of
Green

Miniature golf 235–236
Fantasia Gardens 235
Winter Summerland 236

Minnie's Country House (MK) 78

Mission: SPACE (E) 131, *148*
noncentrifuge ride option 131

Miyuki (E) 170

Moderate WDW resorts 21–22

Monorail
riding in the nose 234

Monsters, Inc. Laugh Floor (MK) 81

Morocco Pavilion (E) 141

Motion-simulator rides. See Simulator rides

Motion sickness 39. See also Simulator rides

Mouse talk (Disney terminology) 39

Movie Ride, The Great (DH) 187

Movies
Circle of Life, The (E) 134
Impressions de France (E) 141

Movies, 3-D
Honey, I Shrunk the Audience (E) 132
It's Tough to be a Bug! (AK) 203

Movies, Circle-Vision 360
O Canada! (E) 142
Reflections of China (E) 139

MuppetVision 3-D (DH) 182

MurderWatch Mystery Theatre (H) 234

My Disney Girl's Perfectly Princess Tea Party
(H) 232

N

Nature trails (AK) 201, 203, 206, 211

Nemo musical (AK) 209

Night of Joy 227

No Expiration ticket option 29
when it makes sense 33

Norway Pavilion (E) 138

O

O Canada! (E) 142

Oak Trail Golf Course (H) 28, 29, 230

Oasis, The (AK) 201, 203

Off Kilter (E) 162, 177

Old Key West (H) 20

Once Upon a Toy (DD) *218*

"Orlando Visitors Guide" 23

Orlando, getting to 24–26

Osborne Family Spectacle of Lights (DH)
16

Outdoor activities
basketball (FW, H) 22, 236
biking (FW, H) 230
boating (DD, FW, H) 230, 234, 238
campfire (FW) 235
camping (FW) 235
canoe rentals (FW, H) 230, 234
carriage rides (FW, H) 234, 235
cruising (H) 226–227, 228, 231
fishing (FW, H) 235
bass 235
1-hour kid's excursion 235
golf (H) 230
hiking (FW) 235
horseback trail ride (FW) 235
jet ski tour (H) 236
jogging (H) 230
kayaking (FW, H) 230, 234
miniature golf 235
parasailing (H) 237
surfing lessons (WP) 236
surrey rentals (H) 231
swimming (FW, H) 230, 235

Outdoor activities, cont'd.
  tennis (FW, H) 230
  tetherball (FW) 22
  tubing (H) 236
  volleyball (FW, H) 22, 236
  wagon ride (FW) 235
  wakeboarding (H) 236
  walking (FW, H) 230, 235
  waterskiing (H) 236

P

Package deals 34–35. See also Admission
    tickets, Magic Your Way Plus Dining
Packing, suggestions for 45–46
Pangani Forest Exploration Trail (AK) 206
Parades
  Disney's Animal Kingdom 203, 217
  Disney's Hollywood Studios 195
  Epcot 127
  Magic Kingdom 83
Parasailing (H) 237
Parasol Parade (H) 233
ParkHopper® ticket option 28
Park hours 39–40
Parking 40
Passport program for kids (E) 137
Pedal boat rentals (FW, H) 230, 235
Peter Pan's Flight (MK) 75, *112*
Pets, bringing 40
Petting zoo (Affection Section) (AK) 207
Phone numbers for WDW 41–43
Photo exhibits, interactive (MK) 68
PhotoPass system, Disney's 63
Photo quiz 241–243
Photos, taking
  tips for 61–63
Pin trading 239
Pirates of the Caribbean (MK) 70
Planning your vacation 13–63
  "Orlando Visitors Guide" 23
  budgeting 35–36
  what to bring 45–46
  when to go 16–17
  where to stay 17–23
Playgrounds. See also Water playground
  Disney's Animal Kingdom 209
  Disney's Hollywood Studios 184

Playgrounds cont'd.
  Epcot 131
  Magic Kingdom 72, 77–78
Playhouse Disney - Live on Stage! (DH) 186
Pleasure Island (DD) 221
Pluto's Palate (DH) 248
Polynesian (H) 20
Pontoon boat rentals (DD, H) **224**, 226–
    227, 230
  decorated for special occasions 226
  pirates-themed 226
Pony ride (FW) 235
Pooh's Playful Spot (MK) 77–78
Pop Century (H) 22
Port Orleans–French Quarter (H) 21
Port Orleans–Riverside (H) 21
Pressed pennies, collecting 239
Primeval Whirl (AK) 210, **217**
Princess Tea Party (H) 232
Privileges, special, for WDW Resort hotel
    guests 17–19
Project Tomorrow (E) 130

R

Race to Space, The (MK) 90–91
Rafiki's Planet Watch (AK) 206–207
Raglan Road Irish Pub (DD) 221
Rainforest Café (AK) **213**
Reflections of China (E) 139
Researching your vacation
  WDW phone numbers 41–43
  web sites 38–39
Resorts, WDW. See Where to stay: WDW
    lodgings
Restaurant ratings 51–53
Restaurants, WDW. See Where to eat
    See also Restaurant ratings
Resting places
  Disney's Animal Kingdom 212
  Disney's Hollywood Studios 190
  Epcot 144
  Magic Kingdom 85
Richard F. Irvine (ferry) **247**
Richard Petty Driving Experience 236
Rock 'n' Roller Coaster Starring Aerosmith
    (DH) 187–188

Roller coasters
 Disney's Animal Kingdom 208, 210
 Disney's Hollywood Studios 187
 Epcot 131–132
 Magic Kingdom 72, 79–80, 82, 82–83
Rose & Crown pub (E) *177*

S

Scavenger hunt (MK) 225
Scuba diving (E) 227–228
Seas with Nemo & Friends, The (E) 135, *243*
Sergio (E) 139
Seven Seas Lagoon cruise 226
Shades of Green (H) 20
Shrunken Ned's Junior Jungle Boats (MK) 70
Sid Cahuenga's (DH) *242*
Simply Segway (E) 227
Simulator rides
 Disney's Animal Kingdom 210
 Disney's Hollywood Studios 182
 Epcot 131, 134
 motion sickness and 145, 182, 211
Singing, participatory (H) 231–232
Singles lines 38
Snow White's Scary Adventures (MK) 76–77
Soarin' (E) 134
Society Orchestra, Grand Floridian (H) 232
Sorcerer Mickey Hat (DH) *178*
Sounds Dangerous - Starring Drew Carey (DH) 183–184
SoundWorks (DH) 183
Space Mountain (MK) 82–83
 fastest route to 89–91
Spaceship Earth (E) *126*, 130
Spas (H) 231
Special seasonal events 16–17, 227, 228, 239
Speedboating (H) 230, 238
Spirit of Aloha show (H) 50
Splash Mountain (MK) 71–72
 fastest route to 89, 91–92
Sports
 participatory
  Richard Petty Driving Experience 236

Sports, cont'd.
 professional
  Atlanta Braves 237
  Tampa Bay Buccaneers 237
Stage shows, live
 Disney's Animal Kingdom 204, 209
 Disney's Hollywood Studios 185, 186, 187, 188
Star Tours (DH) 182, *195*
Stitch's Great Escape! (MK) 80
Stock car driving 236
Stories about African culture (H) 233
Storytime at Fairytale Garden (MK) 114
Streetmosphere performers (DH) 199
Studio Backlot Tour (DH) 184–185
Stunt shows
 Indiana Jones (DH) 183
 Lights, Motors, Action! (DH) 179
Suite 1501 (H) 230
Summit Plummet (WP) 222
Sunrise Safari (H) 233
Surfing lessons (WP) 236–237
Surrey rentals (H) *224*, 231
Swimming (FW, H) 230, 235
Swiss Family Treehouse (MK) 68–69
Switching off, program explained 41

T

Tables in Wonderland membership 29
Talking drinking fountains (E) 152, 159, 167, 173
Talking trash can (MK) 225
Tampa Bay Buccaneers, summer training (SC) 237
Tea, afternoon (H) 232
Tennis (FW, H) 230
 play the professional 230
Test Track (E) 131–132
Tetherball (FW) 22
Theater in the Wild (AK) 209
The Oasis (AK) 201, 203
Tickets. See Admission tickets
Tinker Bell, wake up (MK) 223
Tinker Bell's Flight (MK) 74
Tomorrowland (MK) 80–83
Tomorrowland Indy Speedway (MK) 80
Tomorrowland Transit Authority (MK) 82

Tom Sawyer Island (MK) 72
Toontown Fair, Mickey's (MK) 78–80
Toontown Hall of Fame (MK) 78–79
Touring the theme parks
    basic rules for 57–59
    Disney's Animal Kingdom 213–217
        getting to 213
    Disney's Hollywood Studios 191–199
        getting to 191
    Epcot 145–177
        entrances to 145
        getting to 145–146
    Magic Kingdom 86–124
        getting to 86–89
        getting to the 'Mountains' 89–92
Touring plans
    adult and teen
        one-day Epcot 149–152
        one-day MK 93–97
        two-day Epcot 157–163
        two-day MK 105–111
    all visitors
        one-day AK 214–217
        one-day DH 192–197
        two-day DH 192–199
    families with young children
        one-day Epcot 153–157
        one-day MK 97–101
        two-day Epcot 164–171
        two-day MK 111–118
    senior
        one-day Epcot 149–152
        one-day MK 102–104
        two-day Epcot 171–177
        two-day MK 119–124
    using 60
Tours, guided. See Guided tours
Tower of Terror (DH) 188, *199*
    fun tip for riding 193, 194
Town Square (MK) 65
Toy Story Midway Mania (DH) 185, *194*
Train to Rafiki's Planet Watch (AK) 206
Transportation
    around WDW 26–27
    between WDW theme parks 88, 146,
        191
    Disney, hours of operation 27

Transportation, cont'd.
    to/from Disney's Animal Kingdom 213
    to/from Disney's Hollywood Studios 191
    to/from Epcot 145–146
    to/from Magic Kingdom 86–87
    to/from the Orlando area 24–26
    to/from WDW water parks 221
Transportation and Ticket Center (MK) 86,
    88
Tree of Life, The (AK) **200**, 203
TriceraTop Spin (AK) 209–210
TTC. See Transportation and Ticket Center
    (MK)
Tubing (H) 236
Tunnels under the Magic Kingdom.
    See Guided tours: in Magic King-
    dom: Backstage Magic, Keys to the
    Kingdom
Turtle Talk with Crush (E) 135
Twilight Zone Tower of Terror, The (DH)
    188, *199*
    fun tip for riding 193, 194
Typhoon Lagoon (WP) 18, 221, 222
Tyrannosaurus rex skeleton (replica) (AK)
    211

U

Undiscovered Future World (E) 227
United Kingdom (UK), charter airlines from
    25
United Kingdom Pavilion (E) 141, *177*
Universe of Energy (E) 130–131
Upside-down waterfall (E) 132

V

Vacation packages, WDW 35
Value WDW resorts 22
Village Beatniks (AK) **246**
VIP Tour of WDW 239
Voices of Liberty (E) 140
Volleyball (H) 236
Voyage of The Little Mermaid (DH) 185

W

Wagon ride (FW) 235
Wakeboarding (H) 236
Wake up Tinker Bell (MK) 223

Walking trails (FW, H) 230, 235
Walt Disney: One Man's Dream (DH) 185
Walt Disney World Railroad (MK) 68, *125*, *244*
Walt Disney's Carousel of Progress (MK) 81–82
Wanyama Safari (H) 233
Water ballet (Fountain of Nations, E) 136
Water Mouse speedboat rental (DD, FW, H) 230–231, 238
Water Park Fun & More ticket option 28
Water parks 18, 221–222, 238. *See also* Blizzard Beach, Typhoon Lagoon
Water playgrounds
   Magic Kingdom 76, 79
Waterskiing (H) 236
WDW Dolphin (H) 21
WDW lodgings 19–22. *See also* by name of resort
   family suites 22
WDW phone numbers 41–43
WDW Resort
   map of 14–15
WDW Speedway 236
WDW Swan (H) 21
WDW vacation packages 35
Web sites, helpful 38–39
West Side (DD) 219–221
What to bring 45–46, 61–62
What to do on arrival day 43
What to do on departure day 43
What to do when it's very crowded 43–44
When to visit WDW 16–17
Where to eat 47–56. *See also* Character meals
   dinner shows 50, 234
   Disney's Animal Kingdom 49–50
   Disney's Hollywood Studios 49
   Epcot 49

Where to eat, cont'd.
   Magic Kingdom 48–49
   outside the theme parks 50
Where to stay 17–23
   Downtown Disney Hotel Plaza 22–23
   off-property near WDW 23
   on property or off? 17–19
   WDW lodgings 19–22
      deluxe resort hotels 20–21
      local phone numbers for 41–43
      moderate resort hotels 21–22
      value resort hotels 22
Whiz Quiz (AK) 207
Wide World of Sports Complex, Disney's 237
Wild by Design (AK) 229
Wilderness Back Trail Adventure Segway Tour (FW, H) 234
Wilderness Lodge and Villas (H) 21
Wilderness Swamp Trail (FW) 235
Wildlife Discovery Excursion (H) 233
Winnie the Pooh, The Many Adventures of (MK) 77
Winter Summerland miniature golf course *236, 248*
Wishes (MK) 83. *See also* Fireworks, special ways to watch
   viewing spots for 96, 101, 104, 115, 118, 122
Wishes cruises (H) 226
Wonderland Tea Party (H) 232
World of Disney, The (DD) 221
World Showcase (E) 137–142
World Showcase Players (E) 137

Y

Yacht Club (H) 20
Yacht rental (H) 226–227, 231
Yuletide Fantasy Tour 239